SPORTS COMPARISONS

SPORTS COMPARISONS

by the Diagram Group

ARTHUR BARKER LIMITED   LONDON
A subsidiary of Weidenfeld (Publishers) Limited

Dedication
To Cornelius Cardew,
1936-1981.

Copyright © 1982 by Diagram Visual Information Ltd

First published 1982 in the United States of America by
St. Martin's Press, New York

Published 1982 in Great Britain by
Arthur Barker Limited
91 Clapham High Street
London SW4 7TA

ISBN 0 213 16844 8

Printed in Hong Kong

The Diagram Group: "Sports Comparisons"

Authors David Heidenstam
Susan Bosanko

Copy editors Maureen Cartwright
Damian Grint
Gail Lawther

Research assistant Moira Gavin

Indexer Mary Ling

Art director Kathleen McDougall

Associate designer Cornelius Cardew

Art editors Richard Hummerstone
Mark Evans

Artists Sheila Galbraith
Sean Gilbert
Brian Hewson
Pavel Kostal
Janos Marffy
Graham Rosewarne
Max Rutherford

Art assistant Neil Copleston

Acknowledgments
The authors and publishers wish to extend their warmest thanks to the many individuals and institutions who have responded with great patience and generosity to numerous research enquiries. Special thanks are due to the following:

Brian Barfoot and David Lawrence, *British Canoe Union;* JH Blake, international aerobatic judge; Michael Blake, *British Olympic Association;* JJ Bray, *Grand National Archery Society* (UK); *British Balloon and Airship Club; British Horse Society; British Show Jumping Association;* LR Brooks, *British Pétanque Association;* Captain EM Brown, *Helicopter Club of Great Britain;* Les Bryant, Frisbee authority; Philip Buttinger, authority on korfball; DB Carr, *The Cricket Council* (UK); Peter Christopherson, *British Landsailing Federation;* MD and S Cooper, Accuracy International Ltd, UK; Tony Duffy and Steve Powell, All-Sport Photographic Ltd; Derek Evans, *British Hang Gliding Association;* Dr EC Frederick, Nike Sport Research Laboratory, USA; Lesley Hackett and Will Sutherland, *UK Boardsailing Association;* W Holland, *British Amateur Weight Lifters' Association;* Tony Gittings, *British Surf Casting Association; Gaelic Athletic Association* (Eire); R Giordano, Athletic Director, RAF Mildenhall, UK; D Gray, *British Mountaineering Council;* Jenny Gray, *Amateur Swimming Association;* H Green, Director of Sports, 3rd US Air Force; Stan Greenberg, honorary statistician to the *British Amateur Athletic Board;* Tim Grimwade and Graham Johnston, *Australasian Express,* UK; David Hamilton, *British Precision Flying Association;* JB Hogg, authority on touchball; R Houle, *National Roller Hockey Puck Committee* (US); HI Jacob, *English Olympic Wrestling Association;* AE Knight, *Bicycle Polo Association of Great Britain;* Linda Lemieux, manager of *British Freestyle Ski Team;* Tim Lewis, *Mountain Magazine* (UK); Mike Lockley, *Boxing News* (UK); Vic Mercer, *International Powerlifting Federation; National Air Rifle and Pistol Association* (UK); *National Rifle Association* (UK); *National Rounders Association* (UK); *National Small-bore Rifle Association* (UK); Dougie Peacock, *British Parachute Association;* Jane Power, *National Ski Federation of Great Britain;* Reg Prytherck, *British Surfing Association;* Godfrey Rock, Bedford College, University of London; *Royal Automobile Club; Royal Yachting Association;* Lisa Rubarth, *National Association for Girls and Women in Sport* (USA); Don Smallwood, *British Amateur Baseball and Softball Federation;* RNC Smith, *International Steel Strandpulling Association; Sports Council Information Centre* (UK); Jon Stevenson, *UK Practical Pistol Association;* Roy Stevenson, Eley Bullets Ltd, UK; Moira Stowe and Beverley Waites, *Guinness Book of Records;* Mike Taylor, *National Affiliated Society of Crossbowmen* (UK); Cliff Underwood, *British Sub-Aqua Club;* A Wakelin, *British Association of Parascending Clubs;* Jenny Warren, *British Amateur Gymnastics Association;* Colonel G Webber, authority on show jumping.

FOREWORD

Comparisons are not always odious! They can be informative, intriguing, and even incredible. "*Sports Comparisons*" looks at the world of sport in a new and exciting way. It compares familiar sports with each other, contrasts them with some that are less well-known, and confronts you with some curiosities you may never have considered.

In the process, "*Sports Comparisons*" ranges from gymnastics to baseball, from figure-skating to greyhound racing, from billiards to free-fall parachuting, from table tennis to the world land speed record. It covers not only football, boxing, motor racing, and track athletics, but also tchouk-ball, broomball, buzkashi, and dwyle flunking!

But always the emphasis is on comparisons, and what they can tell us. Comparisons within a sport – between its various forms of competition. Comparisons between similar sports. Comparisons between sports that are at first sight quite dissimilar! Comparisons, finally, between things you would never have thought of comparing – but which teach you something if you do. Between the length of a par 4 golf hole and the length of a railway train. Between the weight of a discus and the weight of a four-week-old baby. Between the drop on a skiing course and the height of the Eiffel Tower. Between the world water speed record and the velocity of an airgun pellet. Between the size of a jai alai court and the space it takes to park a Volkswagen.

Throughout, the presentation follows the now familiar Diagram Group philosophy: that through the medium of illustrations and diagrams, fully integrated into an explanatory text, far more information can readily be presented and understood than through photographs or prose alone.

Editorial notes

1) Some points about metric measurements. In our formal lists and tables of measurement, we give both metric and familiar non-metric forms. But we do not give metric equivalents in the body of the text, where it would be distracting, unless the sport is one in which metric is universally used – as in track athletics, for example, or Olympic swimming events. Further, for consistency the conversions given between metric and non-metric are always our own. Some international governing bodies quote their own acceptable equivalent measurements for, for example, the size of a pitch. We have always taken the main form of measurement used in a sport (metric in many cases, but not in many of the games peculiar to English-speaking countries) and then applied our own standard conversion. Finally, all conversions, of course, are only to an appropriate level of accuracy: we do not give fractions of an inch when converting kilometers!

2) A warning. Any attempt to break a record of any kind is dangerous without careful preparation, training, and supervision; and even to take part in an unfamiliar sport can be potentially hazardous without expert guidance.

CONTENTS

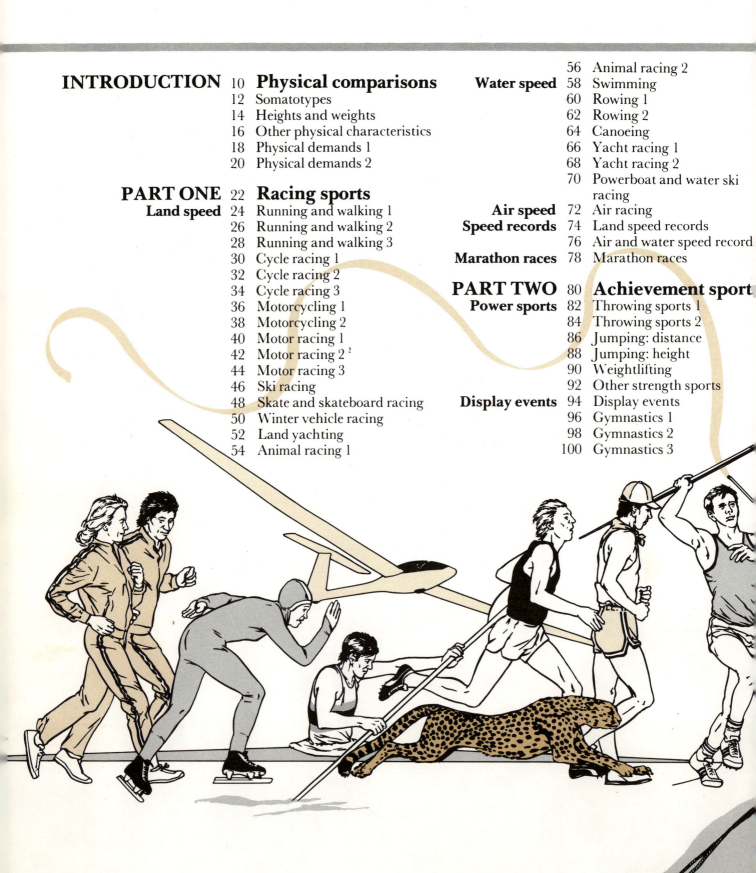

INTRODUCTION 10 **Physical comparisons**
12 Somatotypes
14 Heights and weights
16 Other physical characteristics
18 Physical demands 1
20 Physical demands 2

PART ONE 22 **Racing sports**
Land speed 24 Running and walking 1
26 Running and walking 2
28 Running and walking 3
30 Cycle racing 1
32 Cycle racing 2
34 Cycle racing 3
36 Motorcycling 1
38 Motorcycling 2
40 Motor racing 1
42 Motor racing 2
44 Motor racing 3
46 Ski racing
48 Skate and skateboard racing
50 Winter vehicle racing
52 Land yachting
54 Animal racing 1

56 Animal racing 2
Water speed 58 Swimming
60 Rowing 1
62 Rowing 2
64 Canoeing
66 Yacht racing 1
68 Yacht racing 2
70 Powerboat and water ski racing
Air speed 72 Air racing
Speed records 74 Land speed records
76 Air and water speed record
Marathon races 78 Marathon races

PART TWO 80 **Achievement sport**
Power sports 82 Throwing sports 1
84 Throwing sports 2
86 Jumping: distance
88 Jumping: height
90 Weightlifting
92 Other strength sports
Display events 94 Display events
96 Gymnastics 1
98 Gymnastics 2
100 Gymnastics 3

102 Skating
104 Skiing 1
106 Skiing 2
Target ball games 108 Synchronized swimming
110 Diving
112 Board control 1
114 Board control 2
116 Aerial skills 1
118 Aerial skills 2
120 Slalom skills
122 Equestrian skills 1
124 Equestrian skills 2
Endeavor sports 126 Endurance records
128 Mountaineering and
     spelunking
130 Depth and altitude records
Combined sports 132 Combined sports

PART THREE 134 **Opponent and
                    tournament sports**
Combat sports 136 Combat sports 1
138 Combat sports 2
140 Combat sports 3
Target sports 142 Target sports 1

144 Target sports 2
146 Target sports 3
Target ball games 148 Golf
150 Croquet
152 Terrain games
154 Alley games
156 Billiard games
Court games 158 Net games
160 Wall games
162 Balls, rackets, paddles
Team games 164 Handball games
166 Football games
168 Stick-and-ball games
170 Run-scoring games
172 Playing areas
174 Goals, baskets, bases
176 Team sizes
178 Dress and safety equipment
180 Sticks and bats
182 Balls, pucks, Frisbees
184 Duration, starting, and scoring

INDEX 186

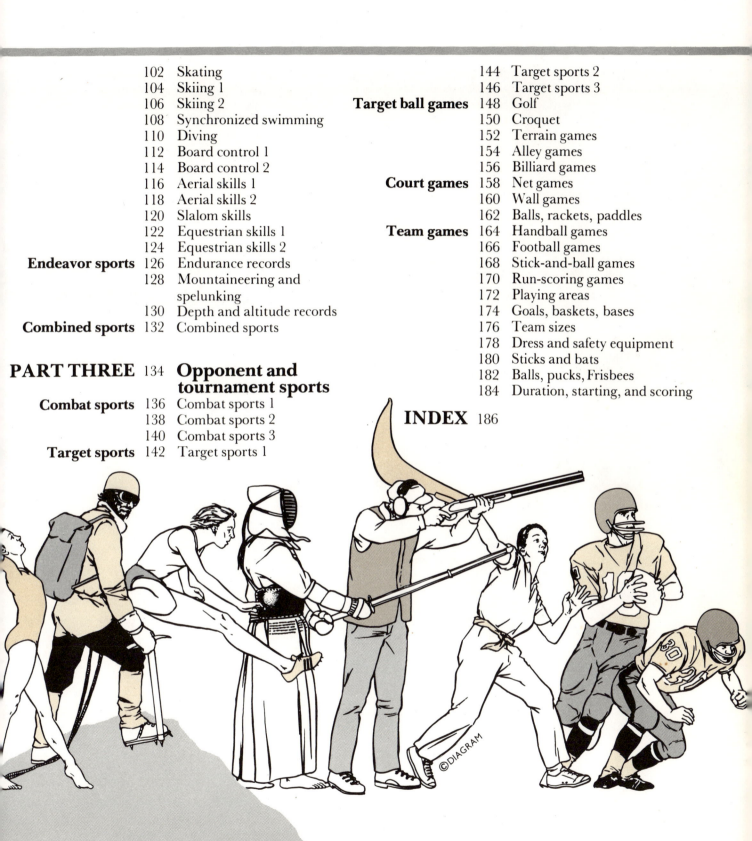

©DIAGRAM

INTRODUCTION

PHYSICAL COMPARISONS

SOMATOTYPES

The many studies made of Olympic and
other athletes allow us to compare the
physical characteristics of competitors in
different sports. Here we look at the
somatotypes (body shapes) typical of various
athletes. On subsequent pages we go on to
compare their heights, weights, and ages.

Endomorphy *below*
A very endomorphic
person (**a**), with a
somatotype of 711, would
be stocky, with a large
round body, a short thick
neck, short arms and legs,
and a tendency to
considerable body fat.

Mesomorphy *below*
A very mesomorphic
person (**b**), with a
somatotype of 171, would
be strongly built, with
broad muscular chest and
shoulders, very muscular
arms and legs, and little
body fat.

Somatotyping
This is a system for
classifying body types in
terms of three tendencies:
endomorphy, a tendency to
soft roundness in the body;
mesomorphy, a tendency
to muscularity; and
ectomorphy, a tendency to
linearity. A person's body
can score from 1 to 7 on
each tendency, but if it
scores highly on one, it
cannot score highly on the
others also. The three
scores together give the
"somatotype number": the
endomorphy score is listed
first, followed by the
mesomorphy and finally
the ectomorphy.
Somatotype numbers

may also be plotted on a
shield diagram, each
corner of which represents
one of the variables: the
bottom left-hand corner for
endomorphy, the top
corner for mesomorphy,
and the bottom right-hand
corner for ectomorphy. In
practice, somatotypes are
assessed from three
photographs of the subject
in carefully standardized
postures. Scoring is a
matter of judgment, but
experienced assessors
rate the same body very
similarly. Extreme and
"average" somatotypes
are shown *right,* and those
typical of various sports
are compared *below.*

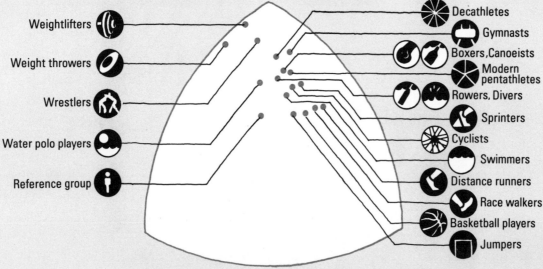

Weightlifters
Weight throwers
Wrestlers
Water polo players
Reference group

Decathletes
Gymnasts
Boxers, Canoeists
Modern
pentathletes
Rowers, Divers
Sprinters
Cyclists
Swimmers
Distance runners
Race walkers
Basketball players
Jumpers

Athletes' somatotypes
Plotted on the shield *left*
are somatotypes typical of
various male athletes;
those typical of female
athletes are plotted on the
shield *right.* The average
somatotypes of the male
and female reference
groups are also shown. The
most endomorphic male
athletes are the water polo
players; the most
mesomorphic are the
weightlifters and the
weight throwers; the most
ectomorphic the long-
distance runners and the
basketball players. The
most endomorphic female
athletes are the weight

Silhouettes
Shown *right* are the body
shapes typical of various
athletes, as described by
the somatotypes on the
shields *above.*

Men
A Weightlifter
B Water polo player
C Canoeist
D Gymnast
E Cyclist
F Basketball player

G Jumper
H Sprinter
Women
I Canoeist
J Weight thrower
K Gymnast
L Jumper

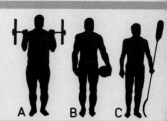

A   B   C

Michaelangelo's David, a typical mesomorph, would probably have succeeded as an athlete. But the Venus de Milo, a typical endomorph, would have fared badly – with or without her arms!

Ectomorphy *below*
A very ectomorphic person (**c**), with a somatotype of 117, would be tall and thin, with a narrow body, thin arms and legs, little body fat, and wiry muscles.

Average somatotypes
A theoretically average person would have a somatotype of 444, displaying endomorphy, mesomorphy, and ectomorphy in equal amounts. In reality, a survey of US college students showed a wide distribution over the whole of the shield (**1**), with some concentration around the center. In contrast, a sample of Olympic track and field athletes showed a great bias toward both mesomorphy and ectomorphy (**2**). The reference groups from the general population used for comparison in studies of athletes had average somatotypes (to one decimal place) of 3.3 4.6 2.9 for the men (**d**), and 5.1 3.9 2.3 for the women (**e**).

throwers. But apart from the canoeists and the weight throwers, female athletes are far more closely grouped on the somatotype shield than male athletes. As we saw above, all the athletes display a marked tendency toward mesomorphy and ectomorphy. In general, mesomorphs rank high on strength, endurance, power, and agility; ectomorphs on endurance, agility, and flexibility. Endomorphs perform poorly in all of these categories, and so make poor athletes.

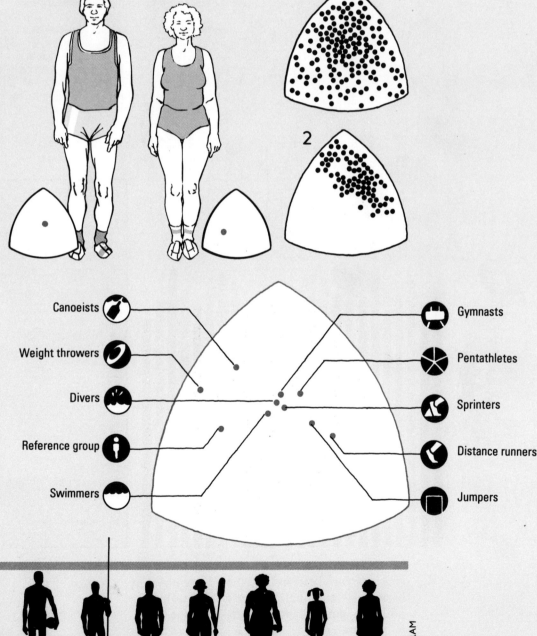

Canoeists
Weight throwers
Divers
Reference group
Swimmers

Gymnasts
Pentathletes
Sprinters
Distance runners
Jumpers

© DIAGRAM

HEIGHTS AND WEIGHTS

Here we compare typical heights and weights for athletes from various disciplines. They tend to be taller and lighter than reference groups drawn at random from the general population. But we should always remember that any individual athlete may vary considerably from the average and still be successful.

Heights

Shown in the table *below* and as a scale beside it are average heights for various male and female Olympic athletes. The tallest and shortest of these groups are also illustrated *left*. The average heights of male and female reference groups drawn from the general population are also included in the table and illustrated *bottom left*. The tallest male athletes are the basketball players (**16**), followed by the rowers (**13**); the tallest women athletes are the weight throwers (**6**), followed by the jumpers and by the

pentathletes (**8**). Apart from the gymnasts (**17**), who form the shortest groups in both cases, the shortest men are the long distance runners (**3**), and the shortest women are the divers (**11**). An average basketball player is over 12in taller than an average woman gymnast. Heights for those sports that have weight classes – boxing, judo, etc – are not included They range from just over 5ft in the lightest divisions to over 6ft in the heaviest.

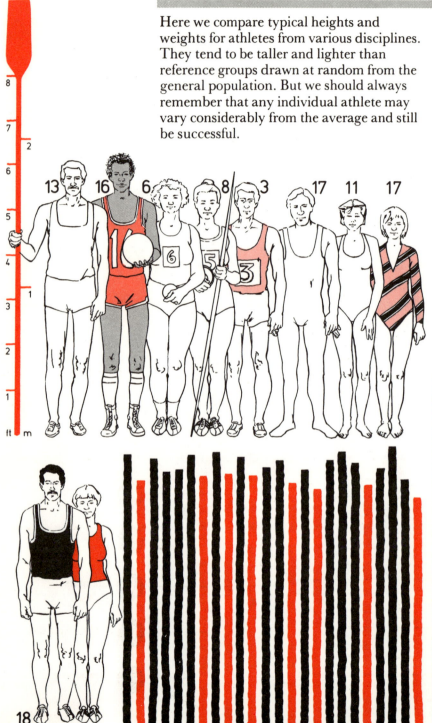

Event	Average height
1 Sprinting	m 182.9cm (6ft 0in)
	w 165.9cm (5ft 5¼ in)
2 Middle-distance running	m 180.3cm (5ft 11in)
3 Long-distance running	m 171.5cm (5ft 7½ in)
4 Race walking	m 173.2cm (5ft 8¼ in)
5 Jumping	m 182.8cm (5ft 11¾ in)
	w 169.5cm (5ft 6¾ in)
6 Weight throwing	m 185.4cm (6ft 1in)
	w 170.9cm (5ft 7¼ in)
7 Decathlon	m 181.3cm (5ft 11½ in)
8 Pentathlon	w 169.5cm (5ft 6¾ in)
9 Modern pentathlon	m 174.8cm (5ft 8¾ in)
10 Swimming	m 179.3cm (5ft 10½ in)
	w 164.4cm (5ft 4¾ in)
11 Diving	m 172.1cm (5ft 7¾ in)
	w 160.4cm (5ft 3¼ in)
12 Water polo	m 179.9cm (5ft 10¾ in)
13 Rowing	m 186.1cm (6ft 1¼ in)
14 Canoeing	m 178.5cm (5ft 10¼ in)
	w 163.1cm (5ft 4¼ in)
15 Cycling	m 174.8cm (5ft 8¾ in)
16 Basketball	m 189.1cm (6ft 2½ in)
17 Gymnastics	m 167.4cm (5ft 6in)
	w 156.9cm (5ft 1¾ in)
18 Reference group	m 175.3cm (5ft 9in)
	w 161.9cm (5ft 3¾ in)

One over the eight? In 1962 the Libyan men's basketball team included the world's tallest athlete to date. At 8ft 0.4in tall he is one of only 11 men ever to reach a reliably recorded height of over 8ft.

The largest boxer to win a world championship title to date was the heavyweight Primo Carnera. At 6ft 5½in tall, and weighing 267lb, he was 18in taller and 2½ times as heavy as the smallest world title winner to date, the flyweight Pascual Perez. Perez was 4ft 11½in tall, and weighed in at 107lb.

Heights of runners *below*
The longer the race over 400m, the shorter the runner. Shown to scale are various male athletes:
a 400m sprinters, average height 185.4cm (6ft 1in)
b 800m/1500m runners, average height 180.3cm (5ft 11in)
c 5000m/10,000m runners, average height 172.7cm (5ft 8in)
d Marathon runners, average height 170.2 cm (5ft 7in)
At the Rome Olympics, the shortest 400m sprinter was the same height as the tallest marathon runner.

Weights
Shown in the table *below* and as a scale at the bottom of the page are average weights for various male and female Olympic athletes. We compare them with the average weights of male and female reference groups drawn from the general population. The heaviest male athletes, the weight throwers, are on average over 97lb heavier than the lightest, the long-distance runners. Similarly the heaviest women, the weight throwers again, are on average over 52lb heavier than the lightest, the gymnasts. Among the male runners, the longer the race, the lighter the runner: in the Rome Olympics the heaviest marathon runner was 10lb lighter than the lightest 400m sprinter.

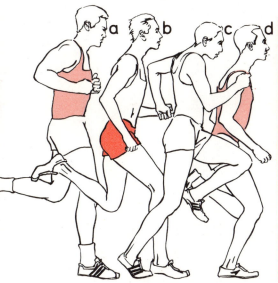

	Event	Average weight	
A	Sprinting	m 68.2kg (150¼ lb)	w 55.6kg (122½ lb)
B	Middle-distance running	m 65.0kg (143¼ lb)	—
C	Long-distance running	m 58.2kg (128¼ lb)	—
D	Race walking	m 62.9kg (138¾ lb)	—
E	Jumping	m 73.1kg (161¼ lb)	w 56.4kg (124¼ lb)
F	Weight throwing	m 102.3kg (225½ lb)	w 73.5kg (162lb)
G	Decathlon	m 77.5kg (170¾ lb)	—
H	Pentathlon	—	w 60.0kg (132¼ lb)
I	Modern pentathlon	m 69.6kg (153½ lb)	—
J	Swimming	m 72.1kg (159lb)	w 56.9kg (125½ lb)
K	Diving	m 65.5kg (144½ lb)	w 52.3kg (115¼ lb)
L	Water polo	m 77.8kg (171½ lb)	—
M	Rowing	m 82.6kg (182lb)	—
N	Canoeing	m 74.4kg (164lb)	w 61.0kg (134½ lb)
O	Cycling	m 68.9kg (152lb)	—
P	Basketball	m 79.7kg (175¾ lb)	—
Q	Gymnastics	m 61.5kg (135½ lb)	w 49.8kg (109¾ lb)
R	Reference group	m 72.9kg (160¾ lb)	w 61.2kg (135lb)

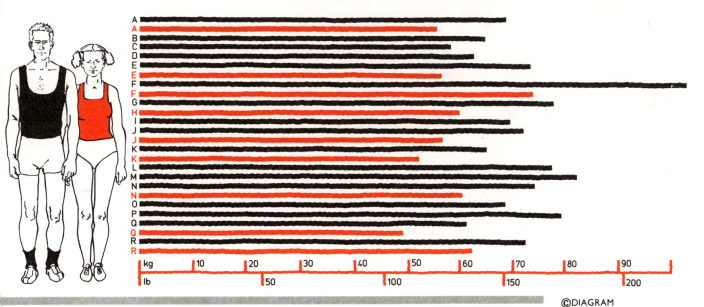

©DIAGRAM

At 49lb the lightest jockey on record weighed about one twentieth as much as an average 1000lb racehorse.

OTHER PHYSICAL CHARACTERISTICS

Although the average age of Olympic athletes is 24 for men and 20 for women, Olympic medal winners have ranged in age from seven to 72! Here we compare the average ages of competitors in different sports. But first we consider some other physical characteristics that have not been dealt with on the preceding pages.

Body fat *below*
About 15% of an average man's bodyweight (**a**) is fat; for an average woman (**b**) the proportion is 25%. Athletes have lower body fat levels, averaging 7.5% for men (**c**), and 12% for women (**d**). Endurance athletes such as distance runners, cyclists, and Nordic skiers (**e**) may have a body fat level as low as 2-5%. But long-distance open-water swimmers (**f**) are both fit and fat: their 20+% body fat helps to maintain their body temperature in very cold water.

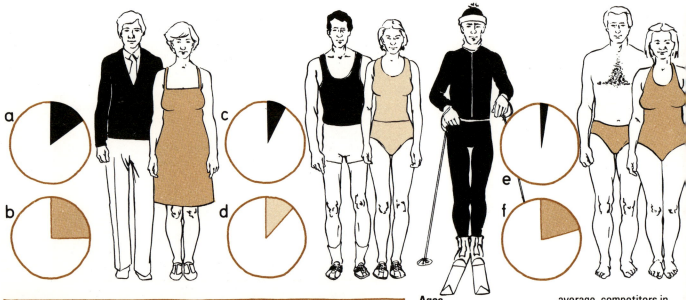

Event	Average age in years	Event	Average age in years
1 Sprinting	m 23.6	13 Swimming	m 19.2
	w 20.4		w 16.3
2 Middle-distance running	m 24.9	14 Diving	m 21.3
3 Long-distance running	m 25.9		w 21.1
4 Race walking	m 27.1	15 Water polo	m 22.9
5 Jumping	m 23.5	16 Rowing	m 24.3
	w 21.5	17 Canoeing	m 24.2
6 Weight throwing	m 27.3		w 22.0
	w 21.5	18 Cycling	m 23.6
7 Decathlon	m 25.1	19 Gymnastics	m 23.6
8 Pentathlon	w 22.5		w 17.8
9 Modern pentathlon	m 24.9	20 Wrestling	m 25.8
10 Shooting	m 37.8	21 Boxing	m 22.9
11 Fencing	m 31.6	22 Weightlifting	m 26.7
12 Equestrian events	m 35.6		

Ages
Listed in the table *left* are average ages for athletes competing in various sports. The youngest male athletes are the swimmers (**13**) and divers (**14**); the youngest women, the swimmers (**13**) and gymnasts (**19**). Usually, the longer a race, the older the athlete: distance runners are older than sprinters. But in pool swimming the reverse is true: distance swimmers are younger than sprint swimmers. The oldest athletes are found in the shooting (**10**) and equestrian events (**12**). On average, competitors in sports where accuracy is the major factor (e.g. shooting) or those where the human body is not the main means of propulsion (e.g. riding) are older than those competing in sports that make heavy physical demands. Research in fact suggests that after age 25 an athlete's physical capacity diminishes by about 1% per year. So a 50-year-old athlete is approximately 75% as efficient as he was at 25; his normal performance at 25 becomes his maximum effort at 50.

Sir Gordon Richards first won the Derby in 1953, when he was 49 years old. Scobie Breasley had to wait until he was 50 for his first Derby win, in 1964. Oscar G. Swahn of Sweden won a gold medal for shooting in the 1912 Olympics when he was 65, and took a silver medal eight years later in the 1920 Olympics. He also qualified for the 1924 Olympics but withdrew without competing.

The boy who coxed the winning pair in the rowing events at the 1900 Olympics is believed to have been only seven years old. The 1958 Jamaican table tennis champion was just one year older. Sonja Henie was 11 when she first skated in the Olympics in 1924, and 15 when she first won a gold medal.

Long and short *below*
Of male athletes, rowers (**A**) and basketball players (**B**) have the longest arms and legs, gymnasts (**C**) the shortest arms, and divers (**D**) the shortest legs. Freestyle swimmers have rather longer limbs than breaststroke swimmers, sprinters than distance runners. Weightlifters have a similar physique to weight throwers, but have shorter limbs proportional to their height. Among boxers and wrestlers, all body dimensions increase in direct relation to their weight.

Wide and narrow *below*
Among male athletes, rowers (**A**), basketball players (**B**), and water polo players (**E**) have the broadest shoulders. Rowers, basketball players, and canoeists (**F**) have the widest hips – with canoeists racing in kayaks having wider hips than those racing in Canadian canoes. Gymnasts (**C**), sprinters, and distance runners (**G**) have the narrowest hips; race walkers have wider hips than sprinters. Women canoeists, swimmers (**H**), and weight throwers (**I**) all have wider hips than male gymnasts, as do the women pentathletes. In fact, pentathletes and weight throwers have the widest shoulders and hips of all the women athletes; the gymnasts (**J**) have the narrowest.

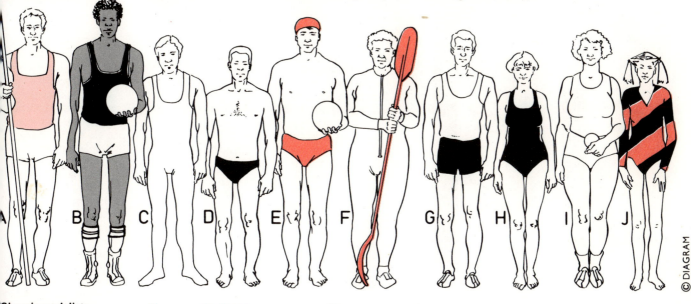

© DIAGRAM

Olympic medalists
In the diagram *right* we show the percentage distribution by age of all the Olympic medals awarded to date. Of the male medalists, 81% were under 30 years old (**I**); 15% between 30 and 42 years old (**II**); 3% between 43 and 55 years old (**III**); and 1% were 56 years old or older (**IV**). Among the women medalists, 95% were under 30 years old (**V**), and 5% were 30 years old or older (**VI**).

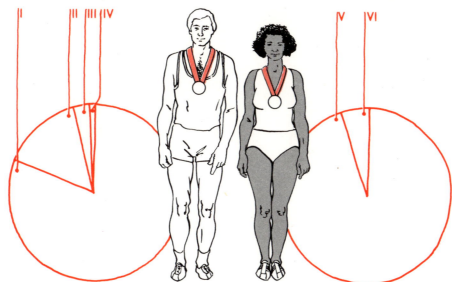

Ralph Craig of the USA was 23 when he won gold medals in the 100m and 200m sprints at the 1912 Olympics, and 59 when he competed in the yachting events at the 1948 Olympics. Jean Borota of France won his first Wimbledon singles tennis championship in 1924, was still competing in the main tournament 40 years later, and in 1977 played in the Wimbledon veterans' doubles – at the age of 78.

PHYSICAL DEMANDS 1

To compare the physical demands made on the body by different sports we must consider several factors. Here we look at the various demands made on the heart-lung system and on other parts of the body. Overleaf we compare calorie consumption and, from all these details, arrive at an overall rating for each sport.

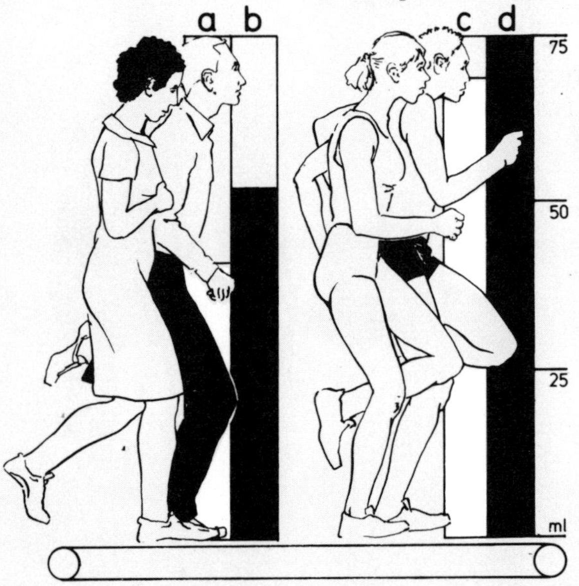

Save your breath *left*
An athlete uses more of the oxygen he breathes in than an average person does. By measuring the pulse and respiration of an individual running on a treadmill, a measure of the oxygen taken up by the system can be reached. The figure is expressed as milliliters of oxygen per kilogram of bodyweight per minute. On our scale we show the maximum oxygen uptake of an average woman (**a**), 40ml/kg/min; an average man (**b**), 52ml/kg/min; a female athlete (**c**), 68ml/kg/min; and a male athlete (**d**), 75ml/kg/min.

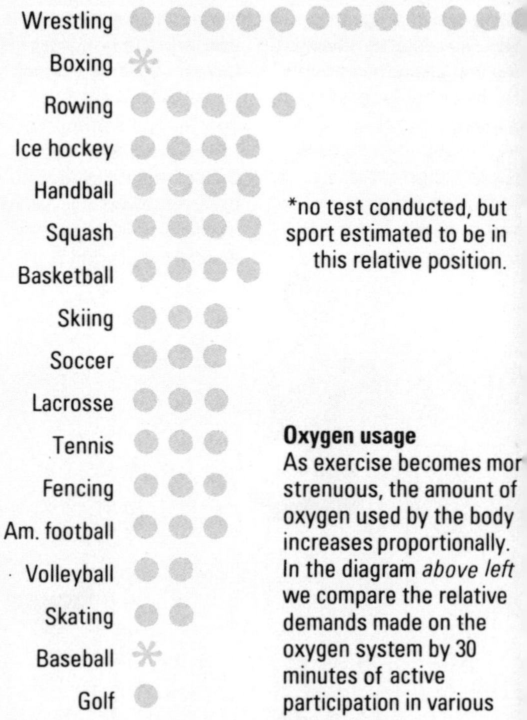

Wrestling
Boxing *
Rowing
Ice hockey
Handball
Squash
Basketball
Skiing
Soccer
Lacrosse
Tennis
Fencing
Am. football
Volleyball
Skating
Baseball *
Golf

*no test conducted, but sport estimated to be in this relative position.

Oxygen usage
As exercise becomes more strenuous, the amount of oxygen used by the body increases proportionally. In the diagram *above left* we compare the relative demands made on the oxygen system by 30 minutes of active participation in various sports.

Heart size
Another indication of the physical demands made by various sports is given by an index of heart size, based on measurements of the actual heart sizes of athletes. The higher the figure, the more constantly strenuous the activity. Shown in the diagram are
A Tour de France cyclists, 24.8
B Marathon runners, 21.5
C Long-distance runners, 20.5
D Rowers, 19.3
E Boxers, 18.9
F Sprint cyclists, 18.1
G Middle-distance runners, 18.1
H Weightlifters, 17.6
I Swimmers, 16.4
J Sprinters, 16.0
K Decathletes, 15.7

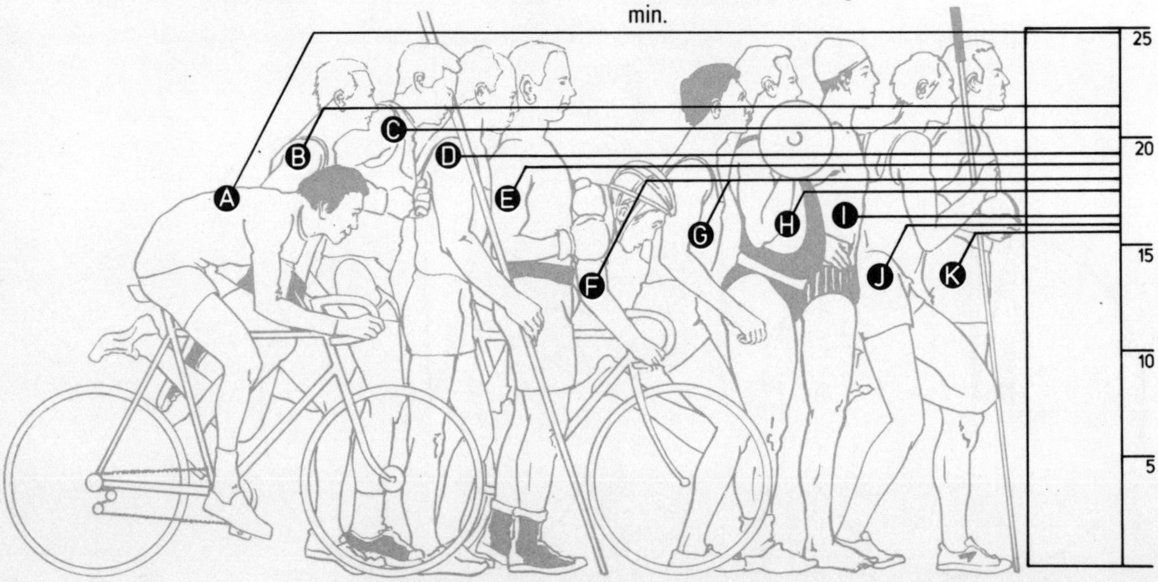

Mile runners breathe in about half of the oxygen they need to run a race during the race itself; for 5000m runners, the proportion is about 90%. But sprinters have to take in nearly all their oxygen needs before they leave the starting blocks – many 100m sprinters do not breathe at all during a race.

Heart-lung system
Having looked at oxygen usage and heart size separately, we now consider the efficiency of the heart-lung system as a whole. In the Harvard step test, athletes step up and down a 20in step 30 times a minute for five minutes. Measurements of their pulse rates are taken before, during, and after the test. The results are entered into a complex formula, giving the index shown *below*. The higher the score, the greater the demand to which the heart-lung system is accustomed. It is interesting to note that although decathletes do not rank high in the survey of relative heart size quoted *opposite*, they have achieved exceptional results in the Harvard step test.

Bodywork
Different sports make demands on different parts of the body. In the chart *below* we show the demands made by various sports on the muscle strength, muscular endurance, and mobility and flexibility of various body areas.

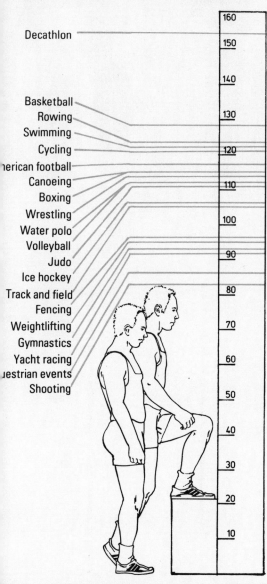

Decathlon
Basketball
Rowing
Swimming
Cycling
American football
Canoeing
Boxing
Wrestling
Water polo
Volleyball
Judo
Ice hockey
Track and field
Fencing
Weightlifting
Gymnastics
Yacht racing
Equestrian events
Shooting

160 150 140 130 120 110 100 90 80 70 60 50 40 30 20 10

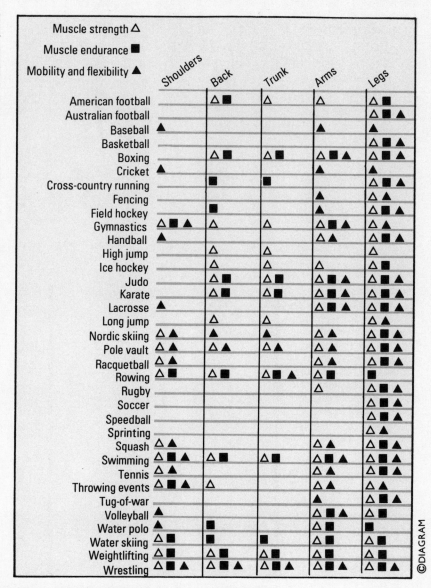

Muscle strength △
Muscle endurance ■
Mobility and flexibility ▲

Shoulders · Back · Trunk · Arms · Legs

American football, Australian football, Baseball, Basketball, Boxing, Cricket, Cross-country running, Fencing, Field hockey, Gymnastics, Handball, High jump, Ice hockey, Judo, Karate, Lacrosse, Long jump, Nordic skiing, Pole vault, Racquetball, Rowing, Rugby, Soccer, Speedball, Sprinting, Squash, Swimming, Tennis, Throwing events, Tug-of-war, Volleyball, Water polo, Water skiing, Weightlifting, Wrestling

©DIAGRAM

Men can make more effective use of the oxygen they breathe in than women can – their blood is richer in the red corpuscles that carry the hemoglobin needed to absorb oxygen. A man's blood contains 4.6-6.2 million red corpuscles per cubic milliliter; a woman's, only 4.2-5.4 million.

PHYSICAL DEMANDS 2

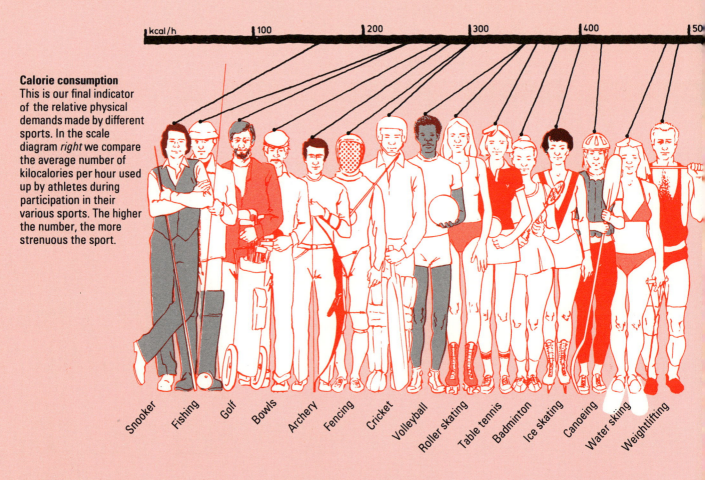

Calorie consumption
This is our final indicator of the relative physical demands made by different sports. In the scale diagram *right* we compare the average number of kilocalories per hour used up by athletes during participation in their various sports. The higher the number, the more strenuous the sport.

kcal/h   100   200   300   400   500

Snooker · Fishing · Golf · Bowls · Archery · Fencing · Cricket · Volleyball · Roller skating · Table tennis · Badminton · Ice skating · Canoeing · Water skiing · Weightlifting

Overall ratings
By combining the types of data shown on these and the previous two pages, various researchers have arrived at overall ratings for the demands made on the body by different sports. One such rating is shown *right,* on a scale from one to 10: the higher the figure, the more demanding the sport. It must be remembered though that ratings of this kind are always approximate, and that the relative positions of different sports can vary considerably in individual cases.

1	2	3	4	5
Archery	Bobsleigh racing	Baseball	Ice skating	Alpine skiing
Billiards	Cricket	Canoeing	Long jump	Badminton
Boules	Diving	Equestrian three-day event	Paddleball	Fencing
Bowls	Frisbee games	Motor racing	Sprint cycling	Hammer
Casting	Javelin	Motorcycle racing	Surfing	Horse racing (flat)
Croquet	Polo	Roller derby	Tug-of-war	Karate
Fishing	Roller skating	Scuba diving	Weightlifting	Pole vault
Golf	Shot put			Touchball
Harness horse racing	Softball			Volleyball
Horseshoe pitching	Table tennis			
Pool	Tenpin bowling			
Powerboat racing	Yacht racing			
Snooker				
Water skiing				

A typical day's diet for track and field athletes would provide them with 3750-4350 kilocalories, made up of 40% carbohydrate, 20% protein, 19% saturated fats, and 21% unsaturated fats.

It takes about 1½ hours of continuous hard exercise
to use up all the carbohydrate stored in the body.

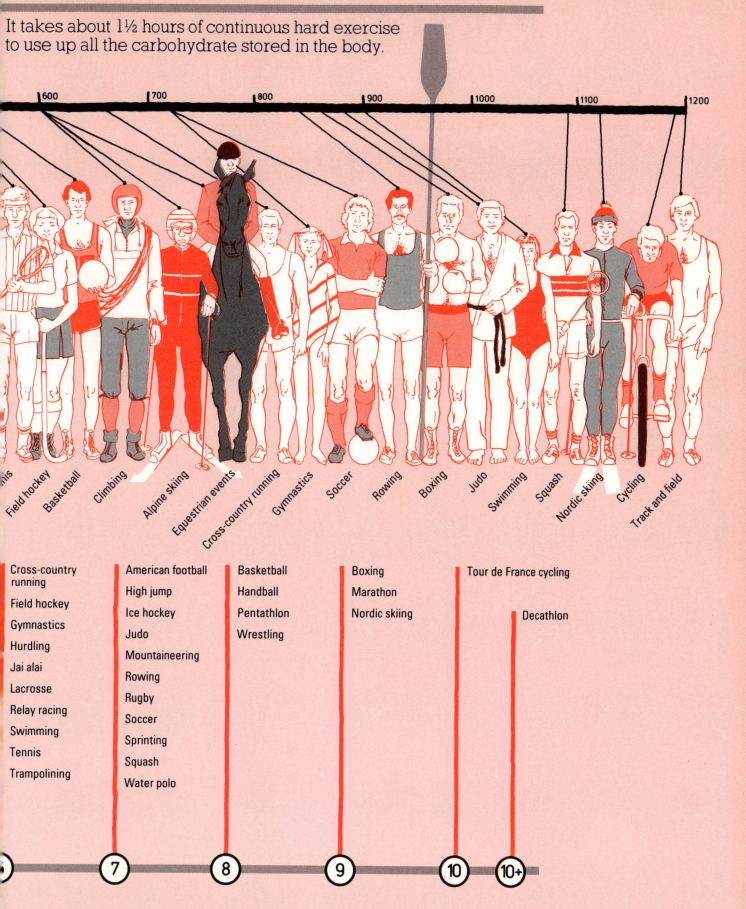

600   700   800   900   1000   1100   1200

Field hockey   Basketball   Climbing   Alpine skiing   Equestrian events   Cross-country running   Gymnastics   Soccer   Rowing   Boxing   Judo   Swimming   Squash   Nordic skiing   Cycling   Track and field

Cross-country running	American football	Basketball	Boxing	Tour de France cycling
Field hockey	High jump	Handball	Marathon	
Gymnastics	Ice hockey	Pentathlon	Nordic skiing	Decathlon
Hurdling	Judo	Wrestling		
Jai alai	Mountaineering			
Lacrosse	Rowing			
Relay racing	Rugby			
Swimming	Soccer			
Tennis	Sprinting			
Trampolining	Squash			
	Water polo			

7   8   9   10   10+

**Someone running at average speed uses up about 0.8
kilocalories per pound of bodyweight per mile. Walking
requires about half as much energy – 0.4 kilocalories per
pound of bodyweight per mile.**

PART ONE

RACING SPORTS

RUNNING AND WALKING 1

Running and walking seem familiar to us all. But in fact race walking requires a highly specialized technique, while the running styles used in track competition vary with the length of the race. Hurdlers and steeplechasers have to introduce further modifications to enable them to clear the obstacles in their events.

Starting positions *right*
Sprinters and hurdlers start from a crouched position, with their hands at shoulders' width apart on the start line (**A**). Most use adjustable starting blocks, nailed to the track, to provide a stable base against which they can brace their feet. The front block is usually 15-20in behind the start line, the rear block 16-20in behind the front one. Middle-distance and long-distance runners usually start without blocks from a crouched standing position (**B**).

Sprinting *right*
On each stride a sprinter's bodyweight falls on the balls of his feet, and his heels do not quite touch the ground. Sprinters pump their arms vigorously and have a high knee action.

Hurdling *right*
The hurdler sprints over obstacles without breaking stride. The leading leg is lifted over the hurdle along the line of running: the bent trailing leg crosses in a horizontal position, at right angles to the leading leg.

Middle-distance and long-distance running *right*
The runner's stance is more upright than the sprinter's, and his knee and arm action is less pronounced. His stride is shorter, with his heels assisting in supporting his bodyweight.

Steeplechasing *right*
This is a middle-distance obstacle race, in which the obstacles used are hurdles and water jumps. But steeplechasers, unlike hurdlers, are allowed to place their hands or feet on the obstacles when jumping over them.

Race walking *right*
Competitors must maintain unbroken contact with the ground: the rear foot must not leave the ground until the advancing foot has made contact. The walker must also momentarily straighten his leg while the foot is on the ground.

An average-height sprinter will take about 50 strides in a 100m race. An average-height hurdler will take seven or eight strides to reach the first hurdle in the 110m hurdles, and three strides between subsequent hurdles. In the 400m hurdles, the first hurdle is 22-24 strides from the start, and there are about 15 strides between hurdles.

©DIAGRAM

RUNNING AND WALKING 2

Here we compare distances and surfaces for the various events. Most take place on a purpose-built running track: we compare the starting and lane arrangements. But some (the marathon, and top-level race walking events) are held on roads, while others (cross-country, and peak and fell races) are set over rough terrain.

Race lengths
Listed in the table *right* and illustrated to scale *below* are the lengths of running and walking races. We indicate whether the races are track events, and whether they have Olympic status.

Key
1 Men's events
2 Men's Olympic events
3 Women's events
4 Women's Olympic events

Track events:
● Sprints
△ Middle-distance races
■ Long-distance races
○ Hurdles and steeplechases

▲ Non- track events

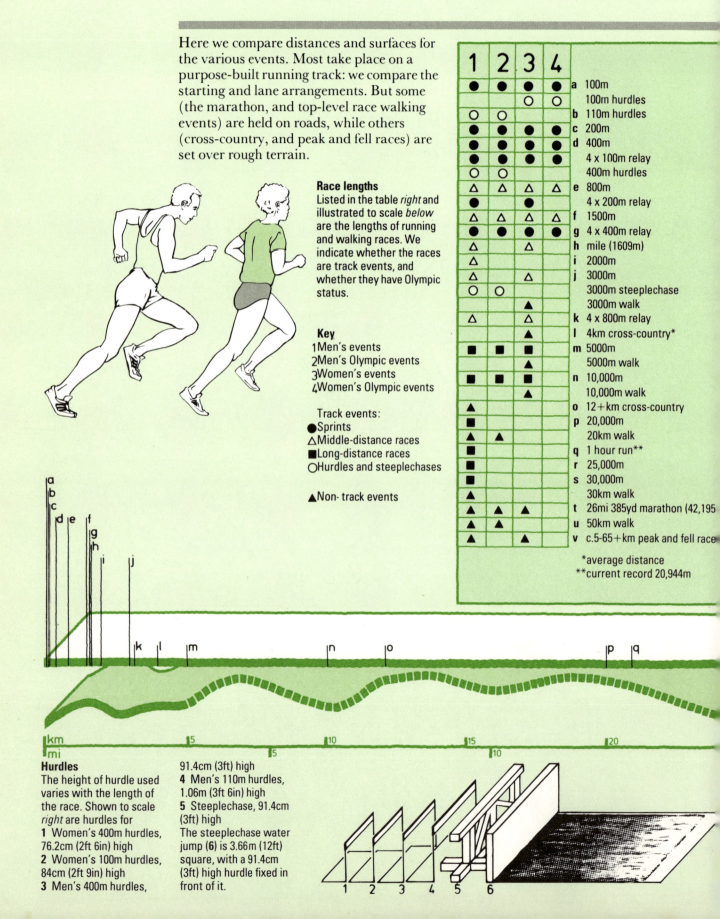

1	2	3	4		
●	●	●	●	a	100m
		○	○		100m hurdles
○	○			b	110m hurdles
●	●	●	●	c	200m
●	●	●	●	d	400m
●	●	●	●		4 x 100m relay
○	○				400m hurdles
△	△	△	△	e	800m
●		●			4 x 200m relay
△	△	△	△	f	1500m
●	●	●	●	g	4 x 400m relay
△			△	h	mile (1609m)
△				i	2000m
△			△	j	3000m
○	○				3000m steeplechase
			▲		3000m walk
△			△	k	4 x 800m relay
			▲	l	4km cross-country*
■	■	■		m	5000m
			▲		5000m walk
■	■	■		n	10,000m
			▲		10,000m walk
▲				o	12+km cross-country
■				p	20,000m
▲	▲				20km walk
■				q	1 hour run**
■				r	25,000m
■				s	30,000m
▲					30km walk
▲	▲	▲		t	26mi 385yd marathon (42,195
▲	▲			u	50km walk
▲			▲	v	c.5-65+km peak and fell race

*average distance
**current record 20,944m

a
b
c
d e f
g
h
i j
k l m n o p q
km 5 10 15 20
mi 5 10

Hurdles
The height of hurdle used varies with the length of the race. Shown to scale *right* are hurdles for
1 Women's 400m hurdles, 76.2cm (2ft 6in) high
2 Women's 100m hurdles, 84cm (2ft 9in) high
3 Men's 400m hurdles, 91.4cm (3ft) high
4 Men's 110m hurdles, 1.06m (3ft 6in) high
5 Steeplechase, 91.4cm (3ft) high
The steeplechase water jump (6) is 3.66m (12ft) square, with a 91.4cm (3ft) high hurdle fixed in front of it.

1 2 3 4 5 6

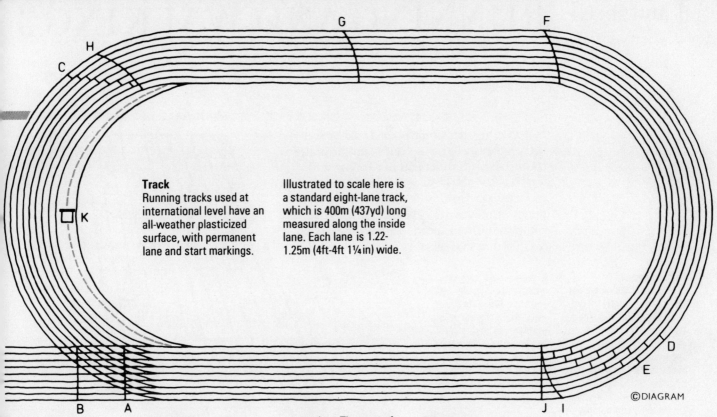

Track
Running tracks used at international level have an all-weather plasticized surface, with permanent lane and start markings.

Illustrated to scale here is a standard eight-lane track, which is 400m (437yd) long measured along the inside lane. Each lane is 1.22-1.25m (4ft-4ft 1¼in) wide.

©DIAGRAM

On your marks
The start positions for various track running events are shown on the diagram *above*:

A 100m, 100m hurdles
B 110m hurdles
C 200m
D 400m, 400m hurdles
E 800m
F 1500m
G 3000m steeplechase
H 5000m
I 10,000m

All races use the same finish line (**J**). The water jump is placed as shown (**K**): steeplechasers follow the dotted line.

Track races
Sprinters and hurdlers must normally keep in their own lanes for the whole of the race. (The exceptions are the 4 x 200m relay, where they may break lane from the third leg, and the 4 x 400m relay, where they may break from the second.) Because 100m and 110m races are run on the straight part of the track, the competitors start in line abreast. But as the 200m and 400m races and the relays are run around the curve, the starts are staggered so the distance from start to finish is the same for each competitor. The start of the 800m is also staggered: competitors must run in their own lanes as far as the end of the first bend. Runners in other middle-distance races, in long-distance races, and in the steeplechase do not race in lanes. The start lines for these races are curved, again ensuring that all runners start at the same distance from the finish line.

Other races
At international level, the marathon and the race walking events are held on public roads closed to traffic. In cross-country running, the courses are marked by flags, and are set across open country, avoiding roads. Some plowed land and woodland may be included. Peak and fell races are endurance events held on hilly or mountainous courses. Runners take their own line between start and finish points: there are no set routes. Maps and compasses may be used in poor weather conditions.

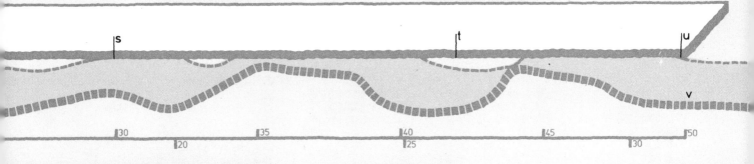

In the first steeplechase on record (held in 1850) the obstacles were 3ft 6in high sheep hurdles – the same height as the obstacles used today in the men's 110m hurdles.

RUNNING AND WALKING 3

In 1981 the men's mile record was broken three times in 10 days – one example of the continuing improvement in running and walking speeds. Here we look at current records over various distances, and at how they compare with 25 years ago. We also compare human speeds with animal speeds over similar distances.

Record speeds

In the table *below* we list the current (1981) record speeds achieved by men and women in various races. Also listed are the record speeds for the same races in 1956 or, in the case of some of the women's events, in the earliest year for which a comparable record is available. (There are no earlier comparable records for women's race walking events.) Each of the speeds listed and shown to scale in the diagram *right* is an average over the whole length of the race. The speeds over similar distances of some of the world's fastest animals are also illustrated and included in the table. Because of the inevitable problems in assessing the maximum speeds of wild animals, those quoted are the best possible approximations from the data available.

1956 (or as indicated)

1981

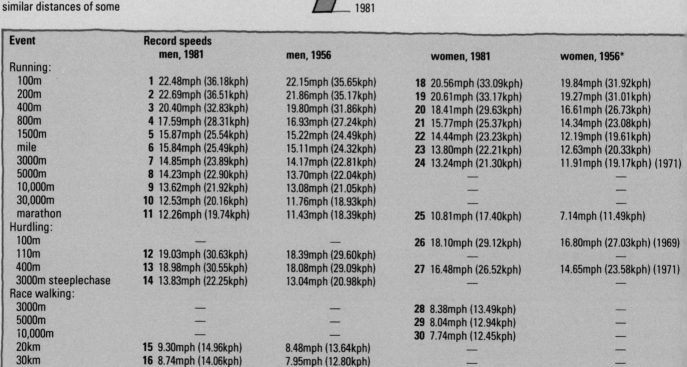

Event	Record speeds men, 1981	men, 1956	women, 1981	women, 1956*
Running:				
100m	**1** 22.48mph (36.18kph)	22.15mph (35.65kph)	**18** 20.56mph (33.09kph)	19.84mph (31.92kph)
200m	**2** 22.69mph (36.51kph)	21.86mph (35.17kph)	**19** 20.61mph (33.17kph)	19.27mph (31.01kph)
400m	**3** 20.40mph (32.83kph)	19.80mph (31.86kph)	**20** 18.41mph (29.63kph)	16.61mph (26.73kph)
800m	**4** 17.59mph (28.31kph)	16.93mph (27.24kph)	**21** 15.77mph (25.37kph)	14.34mph (23.08kph)
1500m	**5** 15.87mph (25.54kph)	15.22mph (24.49kph)	**22** 14.44mph (23.23kph)	12.19mph (19.61kph)
mile	**6** 15.84mph (25.49kph)	15.11mph (24.32kph)	**23** 13.80mph (22.21kph)	12.63mph (20.33kph)
3000m	**7** 14.85mph (23.89kph)	14.17mph (22.81kph)	**24** 13.24mph (21.30kph)	11.91mph (19.17kph) (1971)
5000m	**8** 14.23mph (22.90kph)	13.70mph (22.04kph)	—	—
10,000m	**9** 13.62mph (21.92kph)	13.08mph (21.05kph)	—	—
30,000m	**10** 12.53mph (20.16kph)	11.76mph (18.93kph)	—	—
marathon	**11** 12.26mph (19.74kph)	11.43mph (18.39kph)	**25** 10.81mph (17.40kph)	7.14mph (11.49kph)
Hurdling:				
100m	—	—	**26** 18.10mph (29.12kph)	16.80mph (27.03kph) (1969)
110m	**12** 19.03mph (30.63kph)	18.39mph (29.60kph)	—	—
400m	**13** 18.98mph (30.55kph)	18.08mph (29.09kph)	**27** 16.48mph (26.52kph)	14.65mph (23.58kph) (1971)
3000m steeplechase	**14** 13.83mph (22.25kph)	13.04mph (20.98kph)	—	—
Race walking:				
3000m	—	—	**28** 8.38mph (13.49kph)	—
5000m	—	—	**29** 8.04mph (12.94kph)	—
10,000m	—	—	**30** 7.74mph (12.45kph)	—
20km	**15** 9.30mph (14.96kph)	8.48mph (13.64kph)	—	—
30km	**16** 8.74mph (14.06kph)	7.95mph (12.80kph)	—	—
50km	**17** 8.41mph (13.54kph)	7.14mph (11.49kph)	—	—

*or as indicated

In 1936 – the year in which he won four Olympic gold medals – the sprinter Jesse Owens beat a racehorse over a 100yd course.

Record breaking

Two traditional running "barriers" are the four-minute mile, and running 100m in under 10 seconds. Men have broken both these barriers (in 1954 and 1968 respectively); women have yet to do so. To run a three-minute mile, an athlete would need an average speed of over 20mph – about the speed of the current 400m record holder. For 100m in under nine seconds, he would need an average of almost 25mph. The top speed touched by a sprinter to date is over 27mph (in a 100yd race in 1963); sustaining this speed over 100m would set a record of 8.29 seconds.

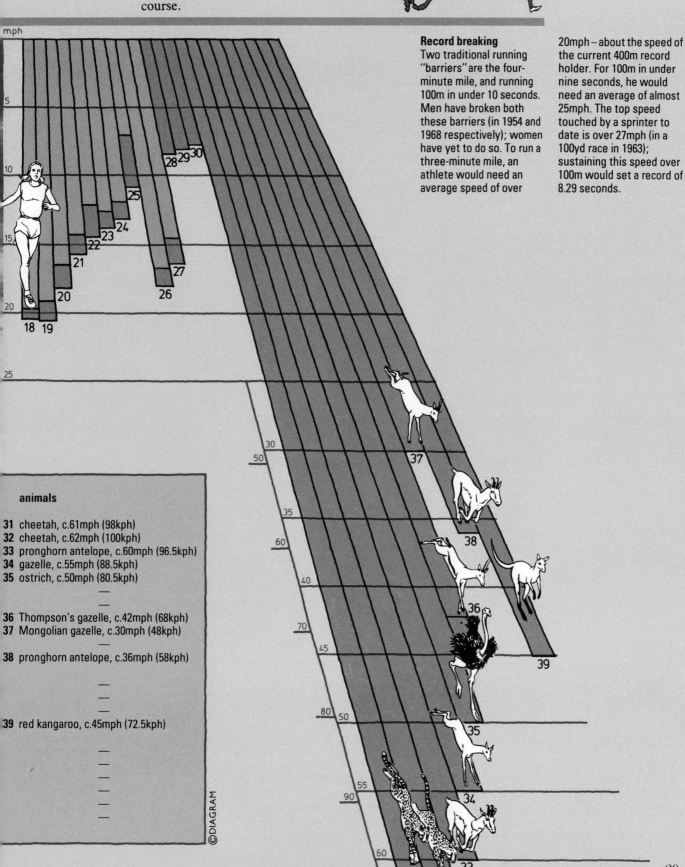

animals

31 cheetah, c.61mph (98kph)
32 cheetah, c.62mph (100kph)
33 pronghorn antelope, c.60mph (96.5kph)
34 gazelle, c.55mph (88.5kph)
35 ostrich, c.50mph (80.5kph)
—
36 Thompson's gazelle, c.42mph (68kph)
37 Mongolian gazelle, c.30mph (48kph)
—
38 pronghorn antelope, c.36mph (58kph)
—
—
—
39 red kangaroo, c.45mph (72.5kph)
—
—
—
—

©DIAGRAM

CYCLE RACING 1

The first organized cycle race took place in Paris in 1868: since then, a wide range of events has been developed. Cyclists race against each other, or against the clock; on purpose-built tracks, on roads, or across country. Here we compare different circuits and surfaces, and look at some of the events held on them.

Road races *left*
In cycling, a road is any surface that is suitable for vehicles but that is not a purpose-built cycle track. It may be a public highway (either open or closed to other traffic), or a course may be marked out on an airfield or on a motor-racing circuit. In road time trials (**a**), the cyclists are racing against the clock. Each individual or team aims to be the fastest over a set distance: as they start at timed intervals, they must be able to judge their own pace as they cannot know how fast their competitors are traveling. The hill climb (**b**) is a specialized form of road time trial. The cyclist is still racing against the clock, but the course is always uphill. In a massed start road race (**c**), the cyclists race each other: the first rider past the finishing post wins. Probably the best-known road races are the stage races (**d**) – the most famous of all is the Tour de France. Each of these events is a series of massed start road races, but may also include time trials, hill climbs, special mountain stages, and *criterium* and *kermesse* races (described *right*).

1) Criterium
This is a circuit road race, or series of races, held in a town or along the roads connecting a group of villages. The roads are closed to other traffic, and the cyclists race each other over a set number of laps.

2) Cyclocross
This is cross-country cycle racing. Only one third of the course may be road: the rest will include plowed land, woods, streams, gates, hedges, and similar obstacles. Competitors ride whenever possible, or run carrying their cycles.

3) Kermesse
Like the *criterium* event, this is a massed start road race held on an urban circuit. The difference is in the size of the circuit: the *criterium* circuit is at least four times as long as the one used in the *kermesse*.

4) BMX (bicycle motocross)
Here the cyclist is again racing over difficult terrain but, unlike the cyclocross circuit, the BMX track is purpose-built with a surface of smooth, sandy soil. After a steep, downhill start, the circuit includes banked curves ("berms"), tabletop jumps several feet high, and double jumps over raised mounds in the track ("whoop-de-doos").

In 1967 Britain's Beryl Burton became the only woman athlete ever to break a man's record competing on equal terms. In a 12-hour road time trial she covered 277¼ mi: the U.K. men's record at the time was 271½ mi.

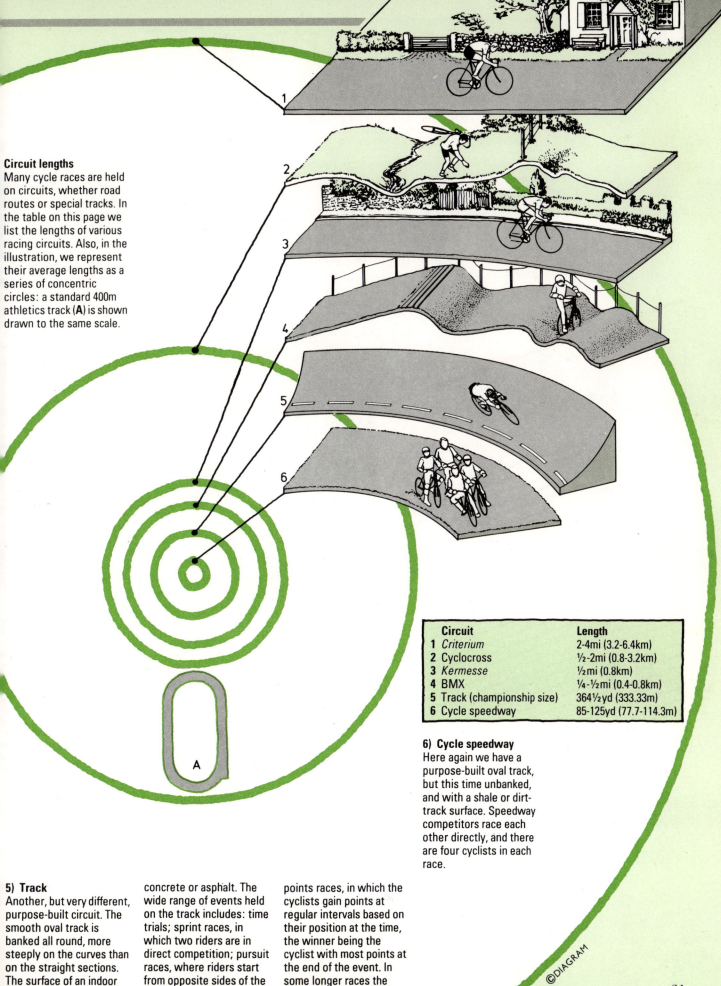

Circuit lengths

Many cycle races are held on circuits, whether road routes or special tracks. In the table on this page we list the lengths of various racing circuits. Also, in the illustration, we represent their average lengths as a series of concentric circles: a standard 400m athletics track (**A**) is shown drawn to the same scale.

Circuit	Length
1 *Criterium*	2-4mi (3.2-6.4km)
2 Cyclocross	½-2mi (0.8-3.2km)
3 *Kermesse*	½mi (0.8km)
4 BMX	¼-½mi (0.4-0.8km)
5 Track (championship size)	364½yd (333.33m)
6 Cycle speedway	85-125yd (77.7-114.3m)

6) Cycle speedway
Here again we have a purpose-built oval track, but this time unbanked, and with a shale or dirt-track surface. Speedway competitors race each other directly, and there are four cyclists in each race.

5) Track
Another, but very different, purpose-built circuit. The smooth oval track is banked all round, more steeply on the curves than on the straight sections. The surface of an indoor track is usually wood: outdoor tracks may be concrete or asphalt. The wide range of events held on the track includes: time trials; sprint races, in which two riders are in direct competition; pursuit races, where riders start from opposite sides of the track and attempt to overtake each other; and points races, in which the cyclists gain points at regular intervals based on their position at the time, the winner being the cyclist with most points at the end of the event. In some longer races the cyclist is paced by an especially built motorcycle.

CYCLE RACING 2

Here we look at the lengths of cycle races – ranging from 100 yards to several hundred miles. Scale diagrams help in visualizing the distances involved. To illustrate the shorter races, distances in and around New York can be used. But we need a scale from New York to the Pacific to represent the most famous stage races.

Counting the miles
Lengths of races are given in the table *opposite.* Each of the illustrations *below* shows a distance 10 times greater than the one before. (The small rectangle on each map marks the area of the previous one.) So our 500m scale (**a**) shows the Metropolitan Museum, New York, while the 5km scale (**b**) shows all of Central Park. Scale **c** (50km) covers all central New York, and scale **d** shows 500km around the city. On our last scale (**e**), (5000km) we see much of North and Central America.

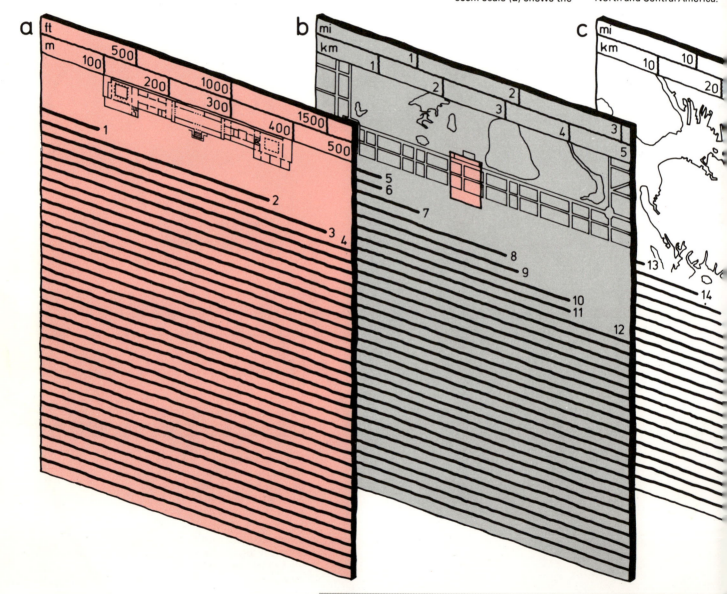

Hit the high spots? The winner of the mountain stages in the Tour de France (the "King of the Mountains") wears a white jersey covered in large red polka dots! The overall race leader wears a yellow jersey; in the Giro d'Italia he would wear a pink one. A world champion is always entitled to a rainbow jersey – white, with a broad horizontal band made up of red, black, blue, yellow and green stripes.

	Event	Distance		Event	Distance
1	Unicycle race, minimum distance	100yd (91.44m)	19	Individual time trial	50mi (80.5km)
2	Hill climb, minimum distance	400yd (365.76m)	20	Team time trial	62.14mi (100km)
3	Cycle speedway, 4-lap race	c.500yd (457.2m)	21	Motor-paced race	62.14mi (100km)
4	Women's sprint	547yd (500m)	22	Team time trial	62.14mi (100km)
5	Olympic individual time trial	1091yd (1km)	23	Individual time trial	100mi (161km)
6	Men's Olympic sprint	1091yd (1km)	24	Olympic individual race	108.7-124.3mi (175-200km)
7	Unicycle race, maximum distance	1mi (1.6km)	25	Tour of Flanders (race)	c.150mi (241km)
8	Women's individual pursuit	1.86mi (3km)	26	Paris-Tours race	c.155mi (249km)
9	Hill climb, maximum distance	2mi (3.22km)	27	Tour of Lombardy (race)	c.165mi (265km)
10	Olympic team pursuit	2.49mi (4km)	28	Milan-San Remo race	c.179mi (288km)
11	Olympic individual pursuit	2.49m (4km)	29	Tour of Britain Milk Race (stage race)	c.1500mi (2410km)
12	Men's individual professional pursuit	3.1mi (5km)	30	Vuelta a Espagna (Tour of Spain – stage race)	c.1900mi (3060km)
13	Women's points race	4.97mi (8km)	31	Giro d'Italia (Tour of Italy – stage race)	c.2480mi (4000km)
14	Individual time trial	10mi (16.1km)	32	Tour de France (stage race)	c.2480mi (4000km)
15	Cyclocross race	c.12.43mi (20km)			
16	Men's points race	12.43mi (20km)			
17	Individual time trial	25mi (40km)			
18	Grand Prix des Nations (individual time trial)	49.7mi (80km)			

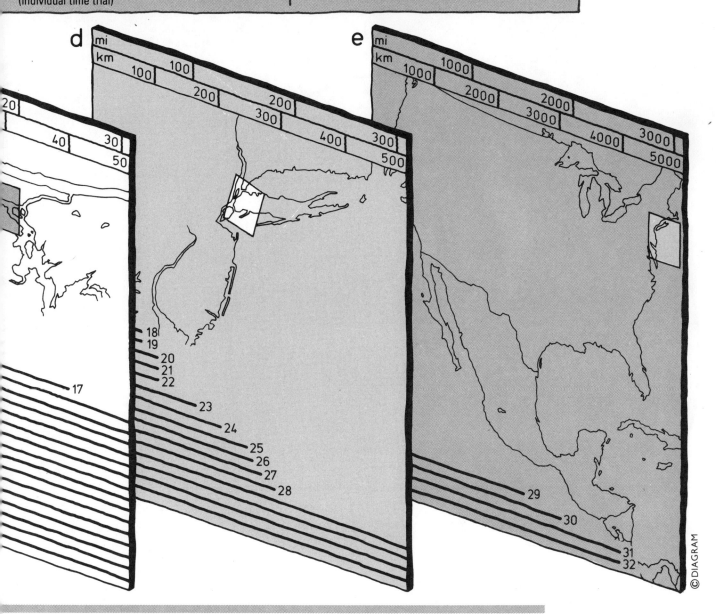

Paradoxically, cyclists travel further when they're getting nowhere fast. The 24-hour roller-cycling record is 792.7mi – 1½ times the 24-hour road time trial record of 507mi.

(Roller-cyclists ride normal, but stationary, bicycles mounted on rollers. The rollers turn to record the "distance" the cyclist has traveled.)

© DIAGRAM

CYCLE RACING 3

We have already seen that there is a wide variety of cycling races, held over a wide range of distances. Here we look at some speeds achieved by cyclists, and at the weights of the bicycles used in different events. We also compare our present-day bicycles with some of their predecessors.

Speed
In the list *right* and the illustration *below* we can see the effect on a cyclist's speed of bicycle design, streamlining, and pacing (i.e. traveling in the slipstream of a faster vehicle). We also compare cyclists with the world's fastest animals, and with the current skateboard standing speed record.

1 Unicycle, unpaced flying start over 100m, record speed 15.03mph (24.19kph)
2 Racing ordinary (penny-farthing) bicycle, 1882, average speed 20mph (32kph)
3 Pronghorn antelope, average cruising speed 35mph (56kph)
4 Unpaced flying start over 200m, record speed 41.42mph (66.6kph)
5 Streamlined bicycle, unpaced over 200m, record speed 50.84mph (81.81kph)
6 Cheetah, average cruising speed 51mph (82kph)
7 Skateboard, record speed in standing position 53.45mph (86kph)
8 Motor-paced, standing start in 1hr race, record speed 58.38mph (94kph)
9 Paced by locomotive, 1889 world bicycle speed record 62.28mph (100.23kph)
10 Paced by 1955 Chevrolet, current world bicycle speed record (set 1973) 138.67mph (223.17kph)

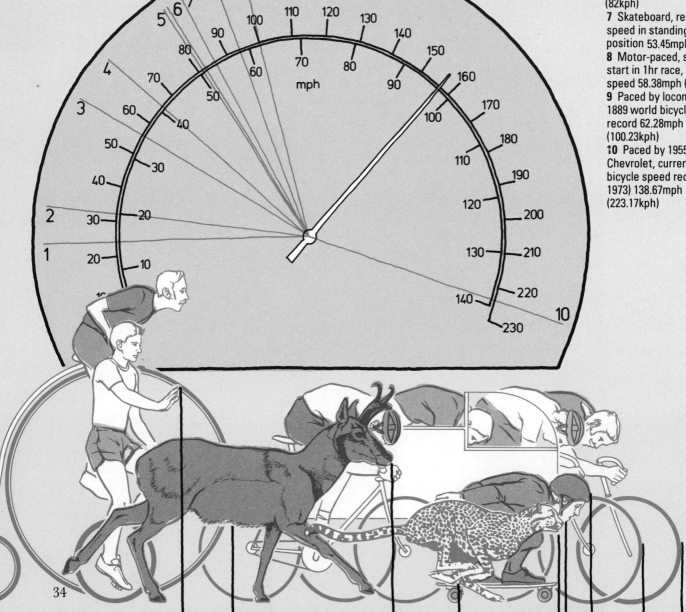

Weight

Right we list the average weights of modern racing bicycles, and of two from the 19th century. In the illustration *above* we use tenpin bowling balls and pins as a comparative scale. Each ball weighs 16lb, each pin 3lb 10oz.

Bicycle	Average weight
1 Macmillan, 1839	57lb (25.85kg)
2 BMX	25lb (11.34kg)
3 Road	23lb (10.43kg)
4 Racing ordinary (penny-farthing) 1882	20lb (9.07kg)
5 Cyclocross	20lb (9.07kg)
6 Track	18lb (8.16kg)

Olympic speeds

Listed *below* and shown by the colored needles on the speedometers *right* are the speeds reached by cyclists in the different events included in the 1980 Olympics. The white needles show the speeds achieved in the earliest Olympic Games for which comparable records are available.

Event	Year	Speed
A 4000m team pursuit	1920	27.96mph (45kph)
	1980	35mph (56.33kph)
B 1000m sprint (speed over last 200m)	1924	34.95mph (56.25kph)
	1980	42.73mph (68.77kph)
C 1000m time trial	1928	30.07mph (48.39kph)
	1980	35.54mph (57.2kph)
D 1000km road team time trial	1960	27.71mph (44.59kph)
	1980	30.72mph (49.43kph)
E 4000m individual pursuit	1964	29.36mph (47.25kph)
	1980	32.55mph (52.38kph)

kph/mph

MOTORCYCLING 1

Motorcycle racing includes a wide variety of events. Apart from road racing, there are races on many other types of track surface, as well as courses set over rough ground. We look at these events and the surfaces involved, before going on (over the page) to compare track and circuit sizes, speeds, and engine capacities.

Trials and rallies
Competitors in observation trials (1) must negotiate cross-country courses filled with obstacles (rocks, streams, tree stumps, etc.). They are penalized if they stop or put a foot to the ground, and each section must be completed in a set time. Observed sections are included in time trials (2), but the rider must also travel at speed between control points or be further penalized. A rally (3) is similar to a time trial, but the course is set on roads, and the observed sections are replaced with special speed sections. Mass-start races across country are called enduros (4), although in some parts of the world an enduro is the same as a time trial.

Road racing
The circuits used for road races (5) are usually purpose-built. Most races have a massed start, and the winner is the first to complete a set number of laps. (There are some famous exceptions – the Isle of Man TT is held on closed-off public roads, and, because of the large number of entries, riders are started in pairs at timed intervals.) Events are held for solo motorcycles and also for sidecar combinations. The sidecar passenger can move freely, using his weight to best advantage. Many of the machines used are especially designed for racing, but there are also classes for slightly modified production motorcycles (e.g. Formula TT).

Motocross
Also known as scrambling, motocross (6) is mass-start racing over a number of laps of a rough cross-country track. There are events for solo motor-cycles, and (in "sidecar-cross") for sidecar combinations.

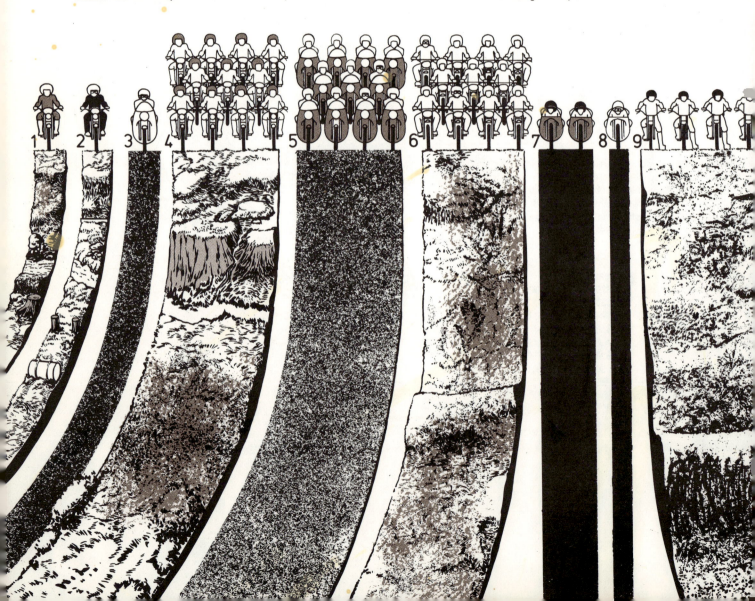

Motorcycles also put in an appearance in cycle races! In motor-paced cycle events the motorcycle acts as a moving windbreak for the cyclist riding behind it. The large, heavy pacing machines are deliberately unstreamlined – very different from racing motorcycles, with their emphasis on aerodynamic efficiency.

Drag racing and sprinting
Riders in these events aim to cover a short straight road track as quickly as possible. Drag races (7) are run on a knock-out basis: competitors set off in pairs, and the winner goes on to the next round. All events are for solo motorcycles, which may be fitted with more than one engine. In sprints (8) riders set off singly and race against the clock. Events are for solo motorcycles or sidecar combinations, but in the latter ballast may be carried instead of a passenger.

Speedway events
The characteristic feature of these events is the riding style: the rider uses one leg as a pivot to allow him to corner in a deliberate broadside known as a "power slide." Most of the races are held on oval tracks: the exception is the TT steeplechase (9), where the dirt track includes left- and right-hand bends, and at least one 30-40ft jump. In long track racing (10), eight riders compete over three laps on a sand track. Grass track circuits (11) are laid out in suitable fields: six to

10 riders race over four laps. The event most commonly referred to as speedway is classical speedway (12): four competitors (six in Australia) race over four laps of a dirt or shale track. Events are usually for solo motorcycles, but sidecar combinations are also sometimes raced. None of the machines is fitted with brakes. Brakes are also forbidden on the machines used in ice racing (13), but the tires are fitted with sharp spikes, 1½in long, to enable them to grip the ice. Again, riders race in fours

over four laps: the ice on the track must be at least 1ft 6in thick to stand the wear and tear. Not illustrated are flat track and short track racing: these are mass-start races held on unpaved oval tracks.

©DIAGRAM

MOTORCYCLING 2

Road racing features a wider range of engine capacity classes than the other types of motorcycle racing, and road racing circuits are usually longer than other types of track. Here we compare these factors, which – with the type of surface involved – affect the speeds that can be achieved in races.

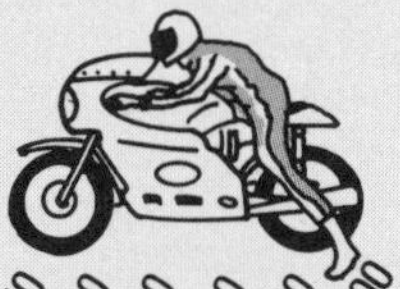

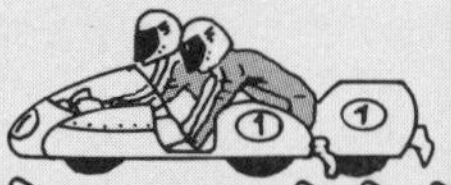

◖ 2-stroke engine
⊕ 4-stroke engine
● all engines

Engine capacities *right*
Motorcycles compete in classes determined by engine capacity. Class divisions for different events are shown in the diagram; solo motorcycle classes on the immediate right, and sidecar combination classes on the far right.

Engine capacities (cc)

	50	80	125	175	200	250	350	400	500	600	750	1000	1200	1300	2000	3500		500	750	1000	1200	1300
Ice racing									●													
Short track						●																
Speedway									●													
Grass track						●	●		●													
Long track									●													
TT steeplechase											●											
Flat track											●											
Motocross			●			●			●									●		●		
Drag racing							●		●		●	●	●		●	●						
Sprinting			●			●	●		●		●	●		●	●			●				●
Dirt track									●													
Enduro	●	●	●		●				⊕	⊕	⊕	⊕	⊕	⊕								
Road racing	●		●			●	●		●		●	●			●			●	●			
Formula TT		◖		⊕	⊕	⊕	⊕	⊕	◖	⊕		⊕										

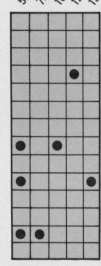

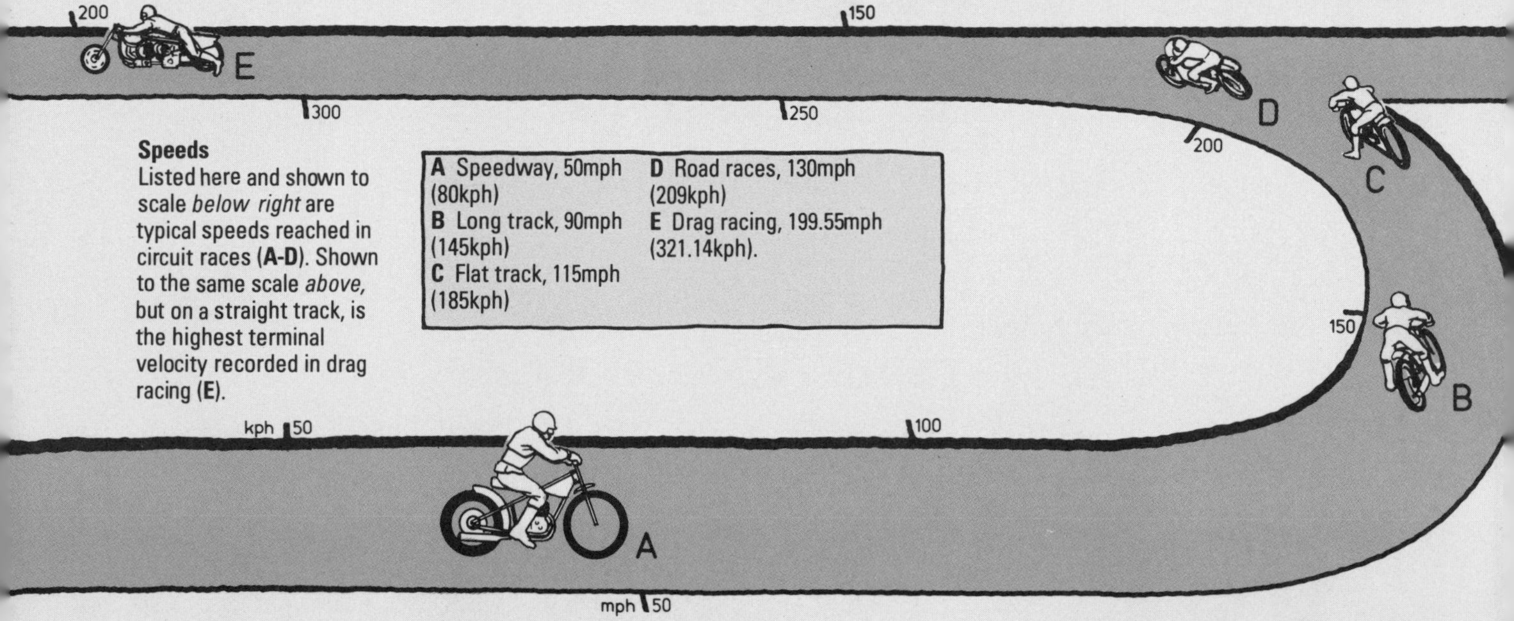

Speeds
Listed here and shown to scale *below right* are typical speeds reached in circuit races (**A-D**). Shown to the same scale *above*, but on a straight track, is the highest terminal velocity recorded in drag racing (**E**).

A Speedway, 50mph (80kph)	**D** Road races, 130mph (209kph)
B Long track, 90mph (145kph)	**E** Drag racing, 199.55mph (321.14kph).
C Flat track, 115mph (185kph)	

Capacities and capacities? 50cc of wine would fill about one third of an average wine glass: 3500cc would fill five standard (70cl) bottles.

The Isle of Man not only boasts the longest road race circuit in the world, but also is home to the oldest motorcycle race – the first Isle of Man Tourist Trophy race was held in 1907.

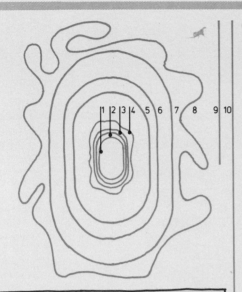

Event	Length of track
1 Ice racing	219-328yd (200-300m)
2 Short track	440yd (402m)
3 Speedway	300-470yd (275-430m)
4 Grass track	up to 656yd (600m)
5 Long track	1093yd (1000m)
6 TT steeplechase	660-1320yd (604-1207m)
7 Flat track	½mi or 1mi (805 or 1609m)
8 Motocross	1-3mi (1609-4827m)
9 Drag racing	440yd (402m)
10 Sprint racing	¼-1mi (402-1609m)

Tracks and circuits
In the illustration and table *above* we compare the lengths of tracks used in different forms of track racing. These are also shown to smaller scale in one corner of the illustration *right,* which compares the plans of some of the world's most famous road race circuits. Their lengths are listed in the table *below.* Each side of a grid square represents one mile; around three sides of the grid we show the length of an athletics marathon (26mi 385yd).

Circuit	Length
a Daytona (USA)	2.5mi (4.02km)
b Brands Hatch (UK)	2.61mi (4.21km)
c Monza (Italy)	3.60mi (5.8km)
d Van Drenthe Assen (Netherlands)	4.78mi (7.68km)
e Dundrod (N. Ireland)	7.5mi (12km)
f Francorchamps (Belgium)	8.74mi (14.12km)
g Nürburgring (W. Germany)	14.19mi (22.84km)
h Isle of Man TT (UK)	37.73mi (60.71km)

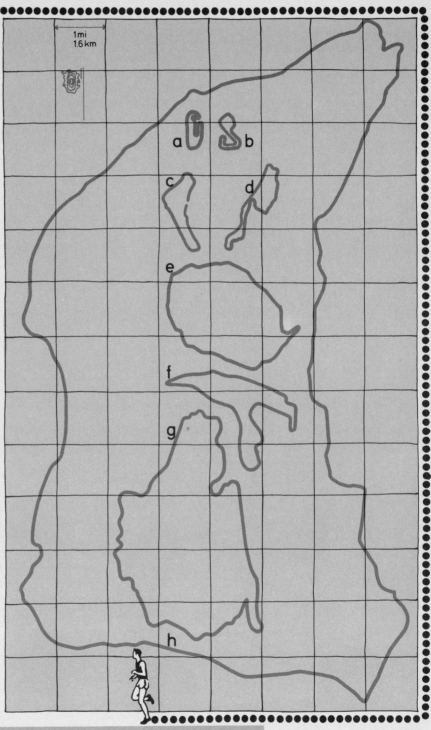

©DIAGRAM

The highest speed ever achieved on a motorcycle is 307.692mph, timed over a flying quarter-mile. If the rider could maintain this speed throughout the world's longest road race, the Liège 24 hour, he would cover 7384.608 miles – over 2½ times the current race record of 2761.9 miles.

MOTOR RACING 1

As a potentially dangerous sport, motor racing is tightly controlled. The world governing body for the best-known forms of the sport – road racing and rallying – is the Fédération Internationale de l'Automobile (FIA). Here we look at the FIA car classifications, and the lengths of some typical races.

km   1000
mi   100

A
B
C
D
1
2
3
4
5
6
7

Road races

These mass-start races are usually held on purpose-built circuits. Positions on the staggered starting grid are determined by the times set by drivers in officially timed practice sessions. The winner is the first car to complete a set number of laps – or in some cases (as in the Le Mans 24-hour race), the car covering the greatest number of laps in a set time. Each year the FIA recognizes up to 16 Grands Prix for Formula 1 cars: together these make up the World Championship.

Rallies

Competitors follow a set route between check-points, and must arrive within a specified time or incur penalty points. The car with fewest penalty points is the winner. Some parts of the course will be on public roads; other sections, called "special stages," are held on private land or closed-off roads. The special stages usually involve high-speed driving over demanding terrain, e.g. very rough ground or ice-covered roads.

Classification of cars

The classes of competition cars recognized by the FIA are summarized *right*, and some typical examples are shown *below*. Regulations for individual races or rallies will indicate which groups are allowed to compete.

Category 1

Cars derived from those on normal sale to the public. *Group N* Large-scale series production touring cars, with four or more seats. At least 5000 identical examples must have been manufactured in 12 consecutive months. Cars used in races may not be more than slightly modified from the versions available to the public.

Group A Large-scale series production cars. In this group the manufacturing requirements are identical with Group N, but the modifications allowed are much greater.

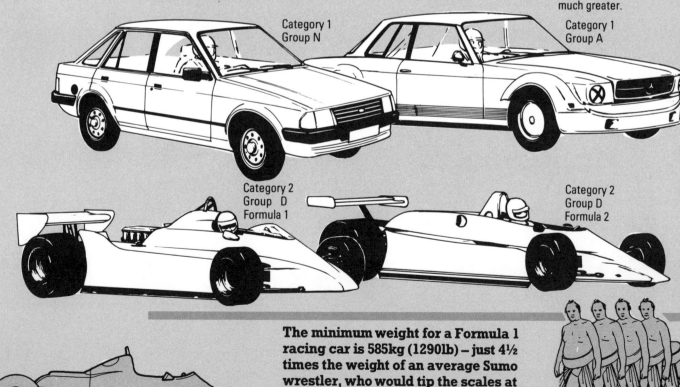

Category 1
Group N

Category 1
Group A

Category 2
Group D
Formula 1

Category 2
Group D
Formula 2

The minimum weight for a Formula 1 racing car is 585kg (1290lb) – just 4½ times the weight of an average Sumo wrestler, who would tip the scales at 287lb.

Peking to Paris was the route of the world's first long-distance rally. It was held in 1907, and won by Prince Scipione Borghese – and his chauffeur!

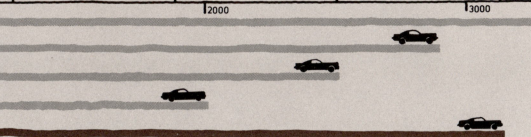

Group B Series production grand touring cars, with two or more seats. Here at least 200 identical examples must have been manufactured in 12 consecutive months. The modifications allowed are similar to Group A.

Category 2
Cars constructed as single examples solely for competition.
Group C Sports cars.
Group D International formula racing cars. This group is divided into:
Formula 1 – Grand Prix cars with a maximum engine capacity of 3000cc (or 1500cc supercharged), and up to 12 cylinders
Formula 2 – maximum engine capacity 2000cc, and up to six cylinders
Formula 3 – the engine has a maximum capacity of 2000cc and up to four cylinders, and must be derived from a series production block of which at least 5000 have been manufactured in 12 consecutive months.
Group E Formula Libre racing cars. These conform to specific manufacturers' or national association formulas, and include Formulas Ford, Indy, 5000, Atlanta/Pacific, etc.

Rally and race lengths
Illustrated to scale *above* and listed in the tables *right* are the lengths of some of the world's most famous rallies and road races. Rally distances are given in the upper table, road race distances in the lower. There are six races in the Trans-Am series, eight in the Can-Am, eight to 10 in the Formula 5000 series, and up to 16 in the Formula 1 World Championship. The various races in a series are held on different circuits. Each Can-Am race is in two parts, a preliminary race followed by a feature race.

Rally	Distance
A East African Safari Rally*	3874mi (6234km)
B Monte Carlo Rally	c.2880mi (4635km)
C RAC Rally (UK)	c.2500mi (4023km)
D Acropolis Rally (Greece)	c.2000mi (3219km)
*longest held to date	

Event	Distance
1 Le Mans 24-hour (France)*	3134.52mi (5044.38km)
2 Indianapolis 500 (USA)	500mi (805km)
3 Trans-Am series (USA & Canada)	c.200-310mi (322-499km)
4 Formula 1 Grands Prix (World Championship)	c.150-200mi (241-322km)
5 Can-Am series: feature races (USA & Canada)	125mi (201km)
6 Formula 5000 series (USA)	c.75-100mi (121-161km)
7 Can-Am series: preliminary races (USA & Canada)	75mi (121km)
*greatest distance achieved on present circuit	

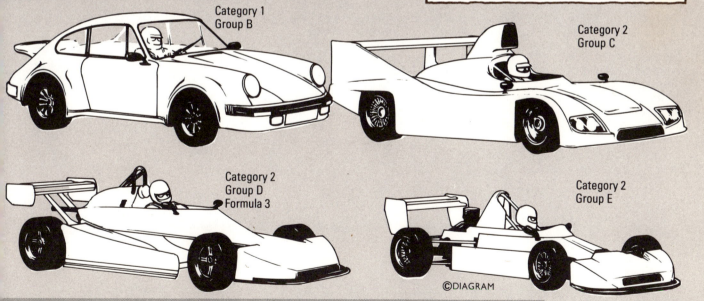

Category 1
Group B

Category 2
Group C

Category 2
Group D
Formula 3

Category 2
Group E

©DIAGRAM

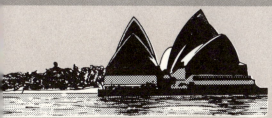

Carmen for car men? The longest rally held to date (19,329 miles) started from the Royal Opera House, Covent Garden in London, England and finished at the Sydney Opera House in Australia.

The Grands Prix that make up the FIA Formula I World Championship are held in many parts of the world: here we look at the circuits used for these races, and at their geographical distribution. We also compare some Grand Prix record speeds with similar records in races for other FIA classes of car.

	Circuit	Circuit length	Group of car	Length of race		Race lap record speed		Race average record speed
1	Monte Carlo (Monaco)	2.058mi (3.312km)	D (F.1)	156.4mi (251.7km)	**1a**	84.729mph (136.36kph)	**1b**	81.338mph (130.90kph)
2	Le Mans (France)	8.467mi (13.627km)	B,C	24 hours	**2a**	142.44mph (229.24kph)	**2b**	130.60mph (210.18kph)
3	Silverstone (UK)	2.932mi (4.719km)	D (F.1)	199.37mi (320.85km)	**3a**	141.87mph (228.31kph)	**3b**	138.80mph (223.37kph)
4	Indianapolis (USA)	2.5mi (4.023km)	E	500mi (804km)	**4a**	193.924mph (312.09kph)	**4b**	162.96mph (262.26kph)

Speeds
In the table *above* we list race lap record speeds and race average record speeds for four road racing circuits. (The races in which these records were set were, respectively, the Monaco Grand Prix, the Le Mans 24-hour race, the British Grand Prix, and the Indianapolis 500.) The speeds are shown by the racing cars on the scale *right,* and scale plans of the circuits are illustrated *above right.* Classification groups of the types of car competing in these four races are also given in the table: we can see that

(given the variations in races and circuits) cars in Groups B, C, and E can record higher lap speeds than Formula 1 cars. But obviously race lengths do affect race records: the difference between the race lap record speed and the race average record speed is greater for the longer distance races (Le Mans and Indianapolis) than for the two Grands Prix. Another factor affecting speed is circuit layout. Formula 1 record speeds at Silverstone (**3**), the fastest Grand Prix circuit, are over 57mph faster than at Monte Carlo

(**1**). The Monte Carlo circuit includes a tunnel and many sharp bends and changes of gradient: it is the slowest Grand Prix circuit. (It is also one of the few road race circuits to use closed-off public roads.) The very long straight at Le Mans (**2**) contributes to high lap speeds, and so does the design of the Indianapolis circuit (**4**) – four straights and four identical banked curves.

The Porsche 917/30 Can-Am car (the fastest racing car built to date) could accelerate from 0-200mph in 12.6sec, and had a recorded top speed of 257mph.

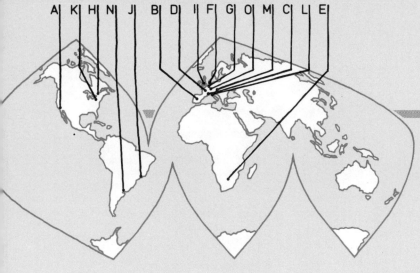

A K H N J B D I F G O M C L E

Grand Prix circuits

Listed in the table *below* are the lengths of the circuits regularly used for Formula 1 Grand Prix racing. The plans of these circuits are shown to scale *below left.* Each Grand Prix is named after the country in which it is held: these are also listed in the table, and are indicated on the map of the world *left.* As the USA is home to two Grands Prix, they are known as USA-East (held at Watkins Glen) and USA-West (at Long Beach).

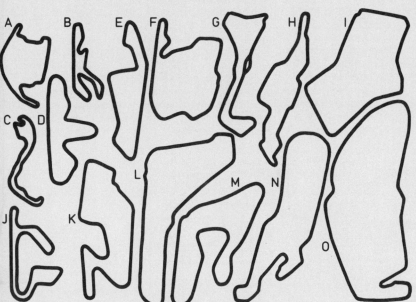

	Circuit	Country	Length
A	Long Beach	USA	2.02mi (3.25km)
B	Járama	Spain	2.058mi (3.312km)
C	Monte Carlo	Monaco	2.058mi (3.312km)
D	Dijon-Prenois	France	2.36mi (3.8km)
E	Kyalami	South Africa	2.55mi (4.104km)
F	Zandvoort	Netherlands	2.642mi (4.252km)
G	Zolder	Belgium	2.648mi (4.262km)
H	Montreal	Canada	2.74mi (4.41km)
I	Silverstone	UK	2.932mi (4.719km)
J	Rio de Janeiro	Brazil	3.125mi (5.03km)
K	Watkins Glen	USA	3.377mi (5.435km)
L	Monza	Italy	3.604mi (5.8km)
M	Österreichring	Austria	3.692mi (5.942km)
N	Buenos Aires	Argentina	3.708mi (5.968km)
O	Hockenheim	W. Germany	4.219mi (6.789km)

© DIAGRAM

If he could only sustain his pace, the holder of the world speed record for a motor-paced bicycle would do quite well at Silverstone, as his record of 138.674mph is almost equal to the race average record speed for the circuit.

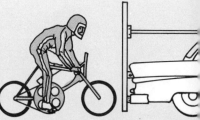

MOTOR RACING 3

Leaving road racing, we now compare some of the many other forms of competition. We look at short-track racing (races held on rough or surfaced circuits up to 2½ miles long) and then at four other events – hill climbs, slaloms, off-road racing, and drag racing. In all these, of course, strict safety regulations remain vital.

Stocks and rods

In the USA, stock cars (1) are steel-bodied sedans especially prepared for racing. In the Grand National division, cars must have a minimum wheelbase of 9ft 7in, and weigh at least 3900lb. Cars in the Grand American division are smaller, with a minimum wheelbase of 8ft 4in and minimum weight of 3200lb. Cars reach 200mph in the 250-600mi races, which are held on banked asphalt tracks, ½-2½mi long. European stock cars (2) are purpose-built from cut-down sedans. Formula 1 stock cars are powered by Jaguar or V8 engines, Formula 2 by 1300cc engines, and Superstox by 1800cc. European tracks are 300-600yd long, and may or may not be banked. Some contact between the cars is allowed, although deliberate ramming is forbidden. (American stock car racing is strictly no-contact.) The European no-contact events are those for stock rods (3), with unmodified 1300cc engines, and hot rods (4), which are sedans with highly modified engines.

Bangers and jalopies

The only restrictions in banger and jalopy racing (5) are for safety, and all glass and trim must be removed from the cars. As this is full-contact racing, strength is more important than speed, but any car can be raced on any track. The final race is usually a "Destruction Derby": the winner is the last car able to move!

Grass and cross

Autocross (6) is racing against the clock on a grass circuit, 600-2000m (656-2187yd) long: the minimum race length is 2km (1¼mi). Up to eight cars compete in each heat, with the fastest qualifying for the finals. Classes are for FIA groups N, A, and B, and for especially built grass-racing cars. Autograss (7) has similar circuits and classes, but is direct racing: up to 25 cars compete at one time.

The current lap speed record in the British Lawn Mower Grand Prix is 37mph.

Rallycross (8) uses circuits combining asphalt with sections of grass, gravel, loose earth, etc. Up to six cars from groups N, A, and B race against the clock, as in autocross: races are 3-6km (1⅞-3¾mi).

Midgets and karts
The exact specifications for midgets (9) vary from country to country, but in all cases they are small, fast, open-cockpit cars. The most usual classes are for 1300cc, 1600cc, or 3.5 liter V8 engines. Karts (10) are even smaller, with tubular frames rather than bodies. Powered by single-cylinder two-stroke engines, they can reach over 100mph. Karts in the 250cc class are fitted with a gearbox: those in the 100cc class are not. With both midgets and karts, any asphalt circuit may be used. Races last from a few minutes up to six hours.

Hill climbs
Cars competing in hill climbs (11) start singly and race against the clock. The course is 5-15km (3⅛-9¼mi) long: the average gradient is 5%. Climbs must cover a minimum of 10km (6¼mi) (in two runs on the shorter courses). Events are for all FIA groups, and there are further subdivisions into engine capacity classes.

Slaloms
Any flat asphalted area large enough to hold a 1-3km (⅝-1⅞mi) winding course is suitable for slaloms (12). The course includes: zigzag sections through lines of 45cm (18in) high cones, set 6-25m (20-82ft) apart; gates, 3-4m (10-13ft) wide, arranged in a staggered pattern and marked by 1.5m (5ft) high posts; and straight lanes up to 300m (328yd) long marked by lines of cones 3-4m (10-13ft) apart. Cars start at timed intervals and race against the clock: time penalties are added for any cones or posts touched. Events are held for all types of car.

Off-road racing
A wide range of vehicles enter off-road races (13): the most popular are four-wheel-drive dune buggies, which can reach 150mph. Courses use almost any surfaces other than those intended for cars! Events are often held in remote areas, and so are also a test of ability in keeping a vehicle going and making stopgap repairs. Races last from one to 30 hours.

Drag racing
In drag racing (14), cars race in pairs on straight asphalted tracks, ¼mi long. Competitions are run on a knock-out basis; terminal velocities can reach over 375mph. Vehicles are divided into classes by engine capacity, but cars from different classes can compete together through a handicapping system.

45

SKI RACING

Alpine skiers race down steep prepared snow slopes on courses marked by pairs of flags known as "gates." Here we compare these Alpine courses with the longer, undulating, cross-country courses used in Nordic skiing. We also look at skiing without snow! Grass skiers use short skis fitted with rollers or caterpillar tracks.

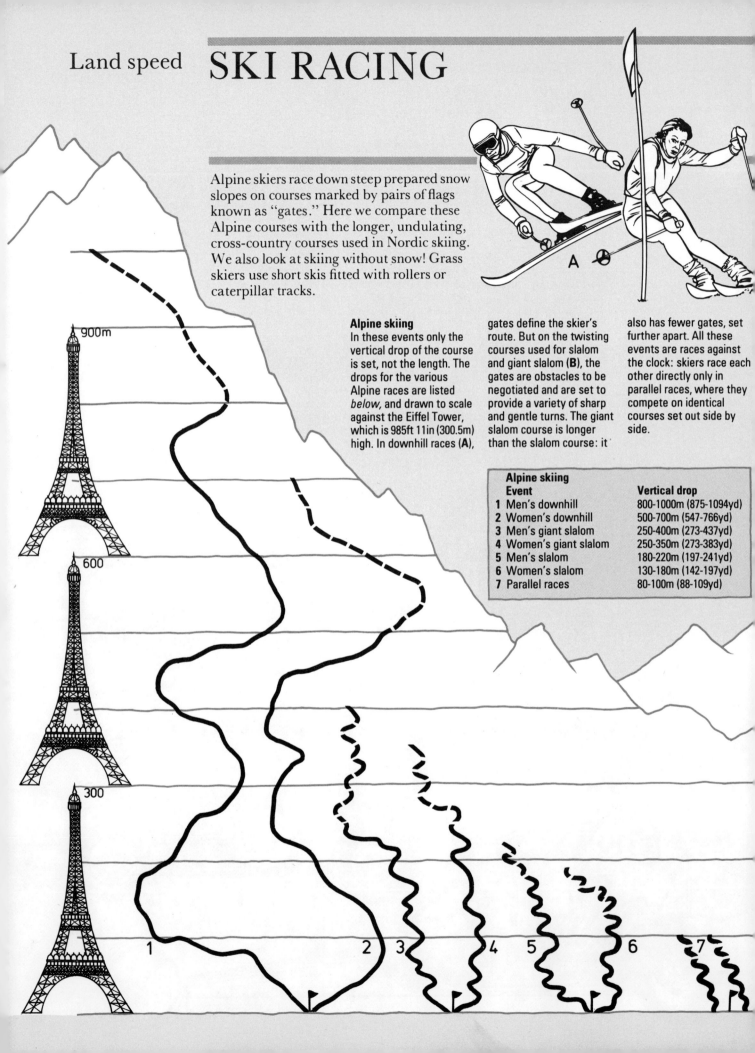

A

Alpine skiing
In these events only the vertical drop of the course is set, not the length. The drops for the various Alpine races are listed *below*, and drawn to scale against the Eiffel Tower, which is 985ft 11in (300.5m) high. In downhill races (**A**), gates define the skier's route. But on the twisting courses used for slalom and giant slalom (**B**), the gates are obstacles to be negotiated and are set to provide a variety of sharp and gentle turns. The giant slalom course is longer than the slalom course: it also has fewer gates, set further apart. All these events are races against the clock: skiers race each other directly only in parallel races, where they compete on identical courses set out side by side.

900m

600

300

Alpine skiing	
Event	**Vertical drop**
1 Men's downhill	800-1000m (875-1094yd)
2 Women's downhill	500-700m (547-766yd)
3 Men's giant slalom	250-400m (273-437yd)
4 Women's giant slalom	250-350m (273-383yd)
5 Men's slalom	180-220m (197-241yd)
6 Women's slalom	130-180m (142-197yd)
7 Parallel races	80-100m (88-109yd)

1   2   3   4   5   6   7

Nordic skiers average 12mph in races: Alpine skiers travel over five times as fast – their race average in the downhill is often over 60mph. Top recorded speed for an Alpine skier is over twice as fast again, at 124.412mph – but water skiers go even faster, with a world speed record of 128.16mph.

Nordic skiing	Max. height difference
Women's events	
a 5km (3.11mi)	100m (109yd)
b 4x5km (3.11mi) relay	100m (109yd)
c 10km (6.2mi)	150m (164yd)
Men's events	
d 4x10km (6.2mi) relay	200m (219yd)
e 15km (9.3mi)	250m (273yd)
f 30km (18.6mi)	250m (273yd)
g 50km (31mi)	250m (273yd)

Nordic skiing
The cross-country courses for Nordic skiing (**C**) are laid out as naturally as possible, preferably in woodland. Approximately one third of the course is flat, one third downhill, and one third uphill; the short-distance and relay courses are the most arduous. Course lengths, listed *left*, are drawn to scale *below*, with the maximum height difference between lowest and highest points scaled against images of St Paul's Cathedral, which is 366ft (111.6m) high. The maximum single climb allowed on the courses is 50m (55yd) in the women's 5km race, 75m (82yd) in the women's 10km, and 100m (109yd) in the men's events. All races are held against the clock except the relay, which is a direct race.

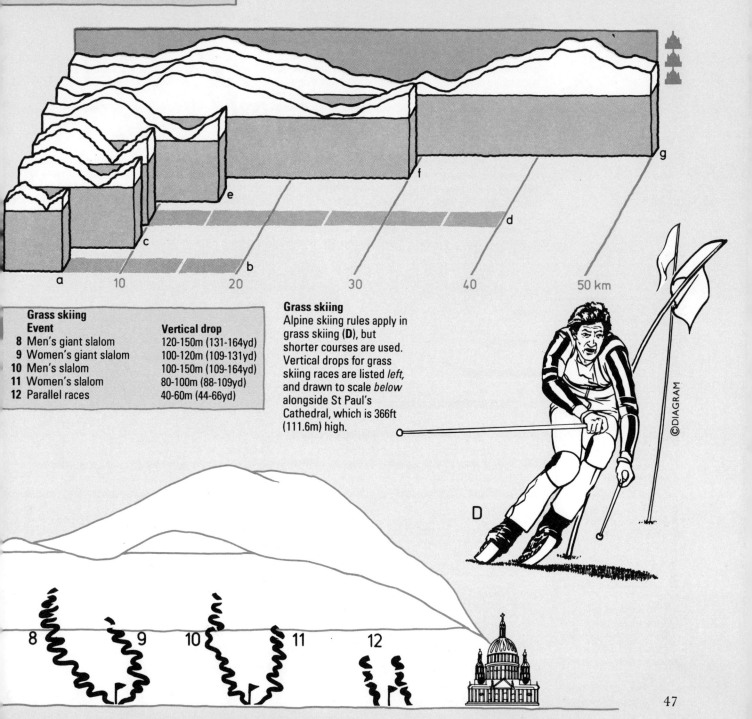

Grass skiing	
Event	**Vertical drop**
8 Men's giant slalom	120-150m (131-164yd)
9 Women's giant slalom	100-120m (109-131yd)
10 Men's slalom	100-150m (109-164yd)
11 Women's slalom	80-100m (88-109yd)
12 Parallel races	40-60m (44-66yd)

Grass skiing
Alpine skiing rules apply in grass skiing (**D**), but shorter courses are used. Vertical drops for grass skiing races are listed *left*, and drawn to scale *below* alongside St Paul's Cathedral, which is 366ft (111.6m) high.

©DIAGRAM

SKATE AND SKATEBOARD RACING

Speed skaters are the fastest self-propelled humans on a level surface. The world speed record for ice speed skating is 30.30mph, for roller skating 25.78mph. Skateboarders, racing downhill, have established records of 53.45mph standing and 71.79mph prone. Here we compare the various forms of skate and skateboard racing.

A) Speed skating
Major international speed skating events are held on outdoor tracks. Four, five, or six races are held, over a wide range of distances. Skaters race in pairs, changing lanes on every lap, and all races are against the clock. Each competitor must enter every race: the final winner is decided on a points basis, depending on the time recorded for each event. (However, Olympic medals are awarded to the winners of individual races.) "Short-track" speed skating events are held on shorter indoor tracks: usually four or six skaters compete in each heat, with the winners going on to the next round. Other short-track events are pursuit races (similar to cycling pursuit races), and relay races for teams of four skaters.

B) Roller skating races
Four or more skaters race each other directly in roller skating races, which may be held either indoors or outdoors, on purpose-built tracks or on suitable roads. There are also relay races, for teams of four skaters.

C) Roller derby
Unlike other speed skating events, a roller derby permits considerable body contact. Each team includes five men and five women: a match consists of eight 12-minute periods, with men and women alternating on the banked oval track. Points are scored for lapping the members of the opposing team.

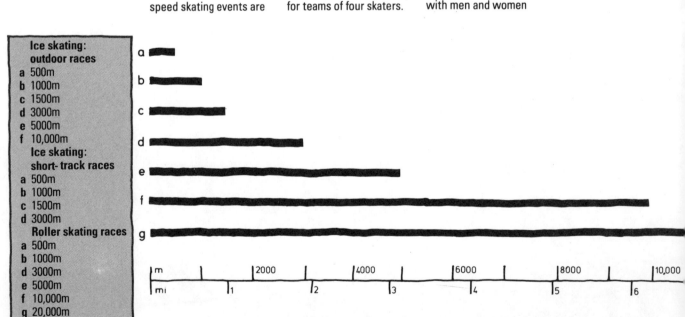

Ice skating: outdoor races	
a	500m
b	1000m
c	1500m
d	3000m
e	5000m
f	10,000m
Ice skating: short-track races	
a	500m
b	1000m
c	1500m
d	3000m
Roller skating races	
a	500m
b	1000m
d	3000m
e	5000m
f	10,000m
g	20,000m

Race lengths
In the table *above* we list the distances raced by men and women in ice and roller skating speed events. These distances are also shown to scale in the illustration *above right*.

A man competing in the ice speed skating world championship covers 21km in his six races — equa[l] to three and a half 18-hole rounds of golf on the Old Course at St Andrews in Scotland.

The current 1500m ice speed skating record holder averaged 29.24mph; the 1500m athletics record holder averaged 15.87mph. So, to ensure a photo finish in a race between them, the skater would need to give the runner a 685m start.

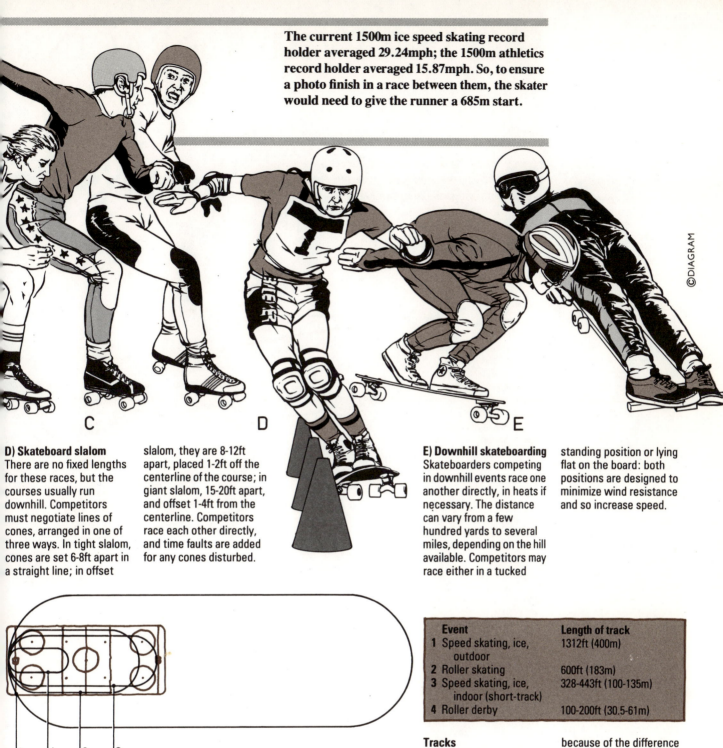

©DIAGRAM

C   D   E

D) Skateboard slalom
There are no fixed lengths for these races, but the courses usually run downhill. Competitors must negotiate lines of cones, arranged in one of three ways. In tight slalom, cones are set 6-8ft apart in a straight line; in offset slalom, they are 8-12ft apart, placed 1-2ft off the centerline of the course; in giant slalom, 15-20ft apart, and offset 1-4ft from the centerline. Competitors race each other directly, and time faults are added for any cones disturbed.

E) Downhill skateboarding
Skateboarders competing in downhill events race one another directly, in heats if necessary. The distance can vary from a few hundred yards to several miles, depending on the hill available. Competitors may race either in a tucked standing position or lying flat on the board: both positions are designed to minimize wind resistance and so increase speed.

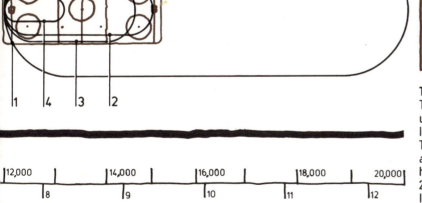

1 4 3 2

	Event	Length of track
1	Speed skating, ice, outdoor	1312ft (400m)
2	Roller skating	600ft (183m)
3	Speed skating, ice, indoor (short-track)	328-443ft (100-135m)
4	Roller derby	100-200ft (30.5-61m)

Tracks
The lengths of the tracks used in skating races are listed in the table *above*. They are shown to scale *above left* against an ice hockey pitch measuring 200 x 100ft (61 x 30.5m). Indoor ice skate racing is known as "short-track" because of the difference in the size of track used compared with outdoor ice skate racing events.

12,000	14,000	16,000	18,000	20,000
8	9	10	11	12

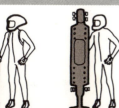

Competition skateboards vary greatly in length. Those used for slalom average 30in; those for downhill in standing position, 42in; and those for downhill lying down, 72in.

WINTER VEHICLE RACING

Here we look at three vehicles raced on ice – the bobsleigh, the luge toboggan, and the skeleton toboggan – and one, the skibob, raced on snow. Bobsleigh and toboggan courses are artificial downhill tracks of solid ice with banked curves. Skibob courses, like ski courses, are marked out with flags on suitable slopes.

Bobsleighs

These have four steel runners and are steered with ropes or a wheel. The crew are seated behind a streamlined cowling. Both four-man bobs (**A**) and two-man bobs (or "boblets") (**B**) are raced on the same courses.

Toboggans

These are long lightweight sleds curved upward at the front. Luge toboggans may be single-seater (**C**) or two-man (**D**); skeleton toboggans (**E**) are always one-man. The luger sits leaning backward on a seat made from closely woven straps, and steers with hand ropes. Skeleton toboggan riders lie face down on a sliding seat, and steer by adjusting their own bodyweight. All tobogganers wear spiked boots to assist in steering and braking.

Skibobs

A skibob (**F**) resembles a bicycle with skis instead of wheels. The rear ski is fixed, but the front ski can be steered using the handlebars. The skibobber wears two short skis to assist his balance.

Lengths and weights

A four-man bobsleigh may be up to 3.8m (12ft 6in) long; the maximum weight including crew is 630kg (1389lb). Two-man bobs may be up to 2.7m (8ft 10in) long and weigh up to 375kg (827lb) including crew. A single-seater luge may be up to 1.5m (4ft 11in) long, and weigh up to 20kg (44lb); the two-seaters may be slightly larger and heavier. There are no restrictions on skeleton toboggans; they average 1.2m (4ft) long, and weigh about 36kg (80lb). Skibobs may be up to 2.3m (7ft 6in) long. Men's skibobs weigh 9.3-11.3kg (20-25lb); the women's weigh 8-10.3kg (18-23lb).

Courses

All races are against the clock: the lengths of the courses used are shown to scale *below*. Bobsleigh courses (**1**) are at least 1500m (1640yd) long, with a minimum of 15 bends. Luge courses (**2**) must be a minimum 1000m (1093yd), with 12 or more bends. The main skeleton toboggan course, the Cresta Run at St Moritz in Switzerland (**3**), is 1212m (1326yd) long. There are no fixed course lengths in skibob racing, but race times should be approximately two minutes. There are 31 or more gates in the skibob giant slalom; 50-60 in the men's special slalom; and 30-40 in the women's special slalom. A skibob downhill course (**4**) averages 3-5km (1.9-3.1mi).

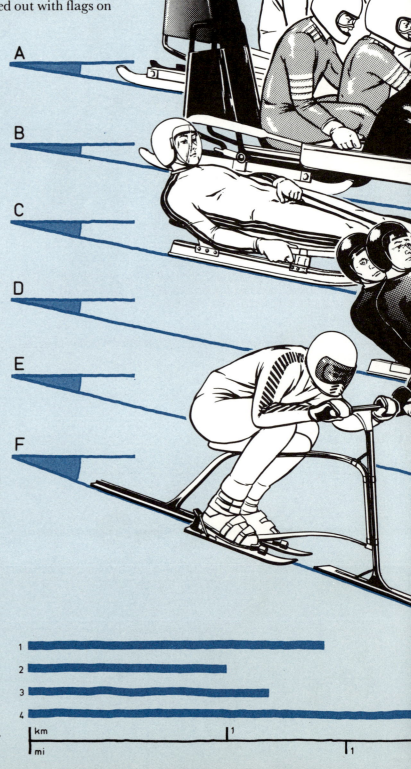

A

B

C

D

E

F

1
2
3
4

km
mi

A bobsleigh traveling at maximum speed could cover the 2451 miles from Los Angeles to New York in 24½ hours – given a suitable ice-covered slope all the way!

	Event	Gradient	Average speed	Top speed
A	Four-man bobsleigh	8-15%	70mph (113kph)	c.100mph (161kph)
B	Two-man bobsleigh	8-15%	65mph (105kph)	c.100mph (161kph)
C	Single-seater luge toboggan	11%	60mph (96kph)	c.80mph (129kph)
D	Two-seater luge toboggan	11%	60mph (96kph)	c.80mph (129kph)
E	Skeleton toboggan	13%	50mph (80kph)	c.90mph (145kph)
F	Skibob	up to 20%	50mph (80kph)	c.100mph (161kph)

Gradients and speeds
The winter vehicles illustrated *left* are listed in the table *above*. The angles of the slopes on which they are shown represent the overall gradients of the courses used in competition, as given in the table. The speeds reached by these vehicles are also listed *above,* and shown on the speedometers *below*. The colored needles show the average race speeds of competitors over an entire course; the white needles, the top speeds reached on the fastest stretches.

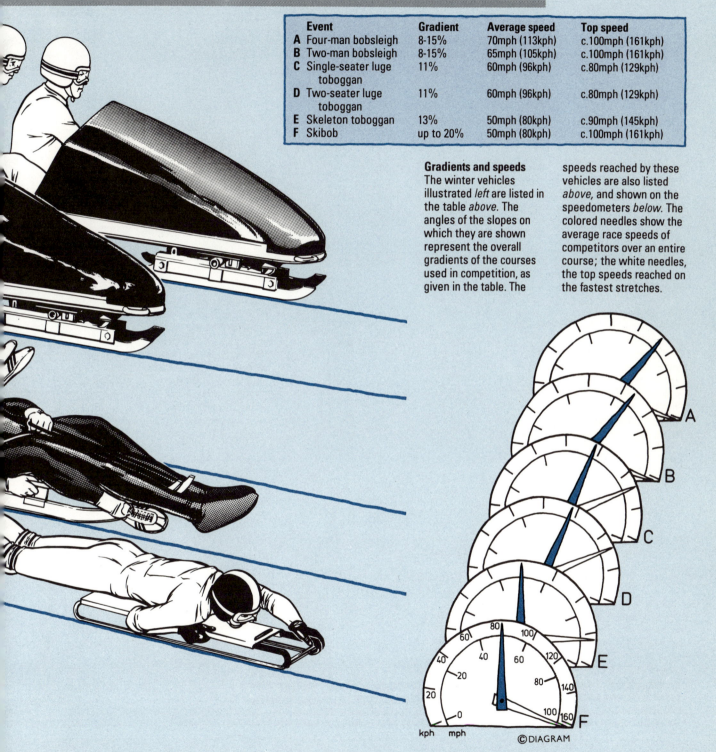

© DIAGRAM

LAND YACHTING

Here we look at sailing, not on water but on hard surfaces. Land yachts are fitted with wheels, similar to those on a car; ice yachts travel on long, sharp, steel runners; sail skaters wear ice skates and carry a sail. We compare the sail areas used in the different yacht classes, and look at the speeds that can be reached.

Land yachting
European land yachts (**A**) carry up to four crew, and are larger and heavier than the American single-seater yachts (**C**). Land-yachting races are held on sandy beaches, on stretches of desert or prairie, or on disused roads or runways.

Ice yachting
This is the world's fastest sailing sport: the average speed of an ice yacht (**D**) is 2-3 times as fast as top speeds recorded for yachts sailing on water. The smaller ice yachts are single-seaters; larger boats carry a crew of two.

Skate sailing
Here again we have sailing on ice – but this time without a boat! The sail skater (**B**) carries the sail on his windward shoulder: its fabric is stretched on a strong, lightweight frame. The skates are the same as for speed skating.

Speed records
Speeds reached by ice and land sailors, listed here, are shown to scale *below*.
A European land yacht, crew of 4, record speed 57.69mph (92.84kph)
B Sail skater, speeds up to 62mph (100kph)
C American land yacht, single-seater, record speed 88.4mph (142.26kph)
D Ice yacht, class A, record speed 143mph (230.1kph)

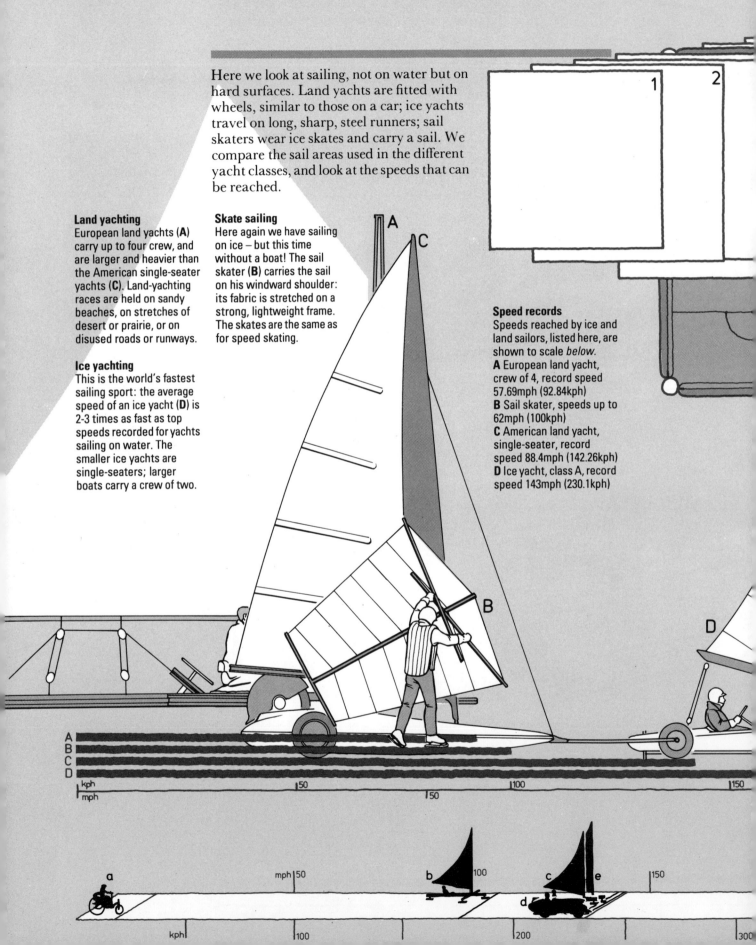

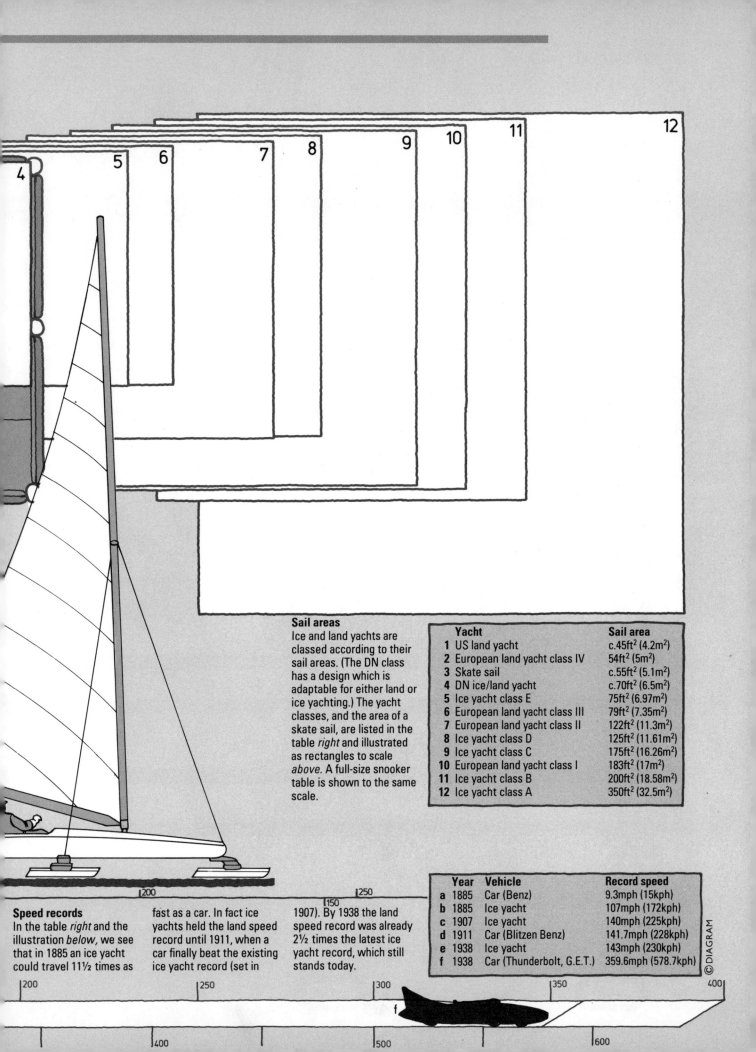

The numbered rectangles (above) are labelled: 4, 5, 6, 7, 8, 9, 10, 11, 12

Sail areas

Ice and land yachts are classed according to their sail areas. (The DN class has a design which is adaptable for either land or ice yachting.) The yacht classes, and the area of a skate sail, are listed in the table *right* and illustrated as rectangles to scale *above*. A full-size snooker table is shown to the same scale.

	Yacht	Sail area
1	US land yacht	c.45ft^2 (4.2m^2)
2	European land yacht class IV	54ft^2 (5m^2)
3	Skate sail	c.55ft^2 (5.1m^2)
4	DN ice/land yacht	c.70ft^2 (6.5m^2)
5	Ice yacht class E	75ft^2 (6.97m^2)
6	European land yacht class III	79ft^2 (7.35m^2)
7	European land yacht class II	122ft^2 (11.3m^2)
8	Ice yacht class D	125ft^2 (11.61m^2)
9	Ice yacht class C	175ft^2 (16.26m^2)
10	European land yacht class I	183ft^2 (17m^2)
11	Ice yacht class B	200ft^2 (18.58m^2)
12	Ice yacht class A	350ft^2 (32.5m^2)

Speed records

In the table *right* and the illustration *below,* we see that in 1885 an ice yacht could travel 11½ times as fast as a car. In fact ice yachts held the land speed record until 1911, when a car finally beat the existing ice yacht record (set in 1907). By 1938 the land speed record was already 2½ times the latest ice yacht record, which still stands today.

	Year	Vehicle	Record speed
a	1885	Car (Benz)	9.3mph (15kph)
b	1885	Ice yacht	107mph (172kph)
c	1907	Ice yacht	140mph (225kph)
d	1911	Car (Blitzen Benz)	141.7mph (228kph)
e	1938	Ice yacht	143mph (230kph)
f	1938	Car (Thunderbolt, G.E.T.)	359.6mph (578.7kph)

ANIMAL RACING 1

Here we look at the many ways in which animals are raced. Some of these events are well known and highly organized, and the animals are purpose-bred: we compare the distances over which they are raced. Other events are held informally, and the lengths of the races will depend on local rules and conditions.

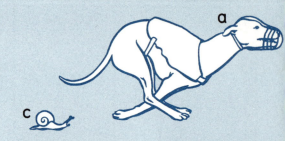

Length of races

Animals are raced over a wide range of distances, from a few hundred yards to over a thousand miles. Shown *below* and listed in the table on the opposite page are the lengths of some of the world's best-known animal races. We compare them with Olympic running distances, and at the foot of the page use circuits of a 400m athletics track as a scale to help show the distances involved. Our longest race, the Alaskan Iditarod Trail Race, would circle the track at least 4023 times.

Animals without riders

above Some animals can be raced without a rider to direct them, by making use of their natural instincts. Greyhounds (**a**) naturally chase after hares: racing greyhounds are trained to chase an electric hare around a prepared circuit.

In pigeon racing (**b**) it is the homing instinct that is exploited. All the birds start from a single point, but each finishes in its own loft, where its flying time is recorded. Patient people have persuaded snails (**c**) to race – but only over short distances.

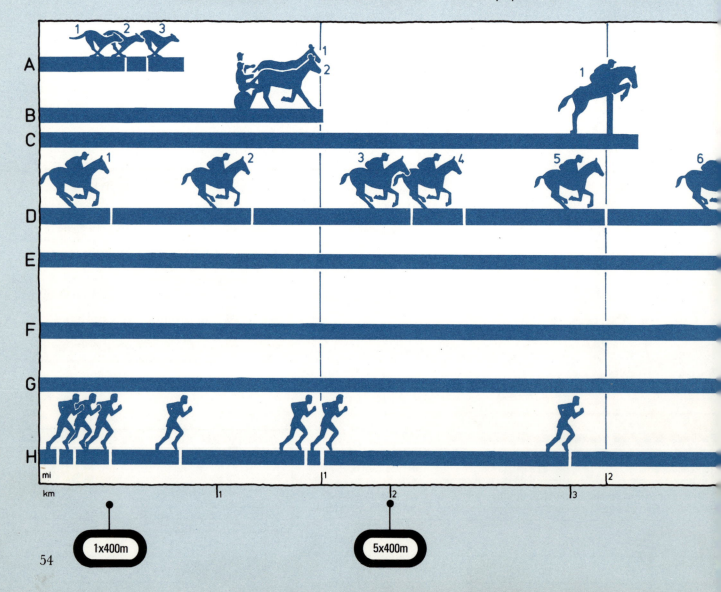

d
e **f**
g **h** **i**

Animals with riders *above*
Horses (**d**) are raced – formally or informally – in most parts of the world. There are three main types of organized races: flat races, where there are no fences or other obstacles; hurdle jumping races; and steeplechases,

another form of jumping race in which the obstacles are a mixture of fences, ditches, and water jumps. But horses are not the only animals ridden in races. Ostriches (**e**) are raced in South Africa, and camels (**f**) in parts of North Africa and the Middle East.

Animals in harness *above*
Probably the earliest races between animals drawing a vehicle were the chariot races (**g**). The chariots were drawn by teams of two to 10 horses. In sled-dog races (**h**), there are classes for three-dog teams, but in the long-distance events

the drivers ("mushers") will have up to 16 dogs pulling the sled over the snow. In harness races (**i**), a single horse pulls his driver along in a small lightweight two-wheeled cart (a "sulky"). The horses in these races are either trotters or pacers: the

difference between them is the stride that they use. A trotter moves diagonally opposite legs in unison; a pacer moves both right legs and both left legs in unison. Trotters race only against other trotters, pacers against other pacers.

© DIAGRAM

Event	Distance	Event	Distance
A Greyhound racing		**D** Flat racing	
1 Greyhound Derby (UK)	525yd (480m)	4 Derby (UK)	1½mi (2.4km)
2 Greyhound Derby (USA)	660yd (603m)	5 Melbourne Cup (Australia)	2mi (3.2km)
3 Greyhound Cesarewitch (UK)	880yd (805m)	6 Ascot Gold Cup (UK)	2½mi (4km)
B Harness horse racing		**E** Steeplechase	
1 Hambletonian (trotting, USA)	1mi (1.6km)	1 Maryland Hunt Cup (USA)	4mi (6.4km)
2 Little Brown Jug (pacing, USA)	1mi (1.6km)	2 Grand National (UK)	4mi 856yd (7.2km)
C Hurdle racing		**F** Sled-dog racing	
1 Champion Hurdle Challenge Cup (UK)	2mi 200yd (3.4km)	1 Three-dog class	3-4mi (4.8-6.4km)
D Flat racing		2 World Championship Derby (USA)	60mi (96km)
1 All American Futurity (USA)	440yd (402m)	3 Alaskan Iditarod Trail Race (USA)	1000-1050mi (1609-1690km)
2 Golden Slipper Stakes (Australia)	1320yd (1207m)	**G** Pigeon racing	60-600mi (96-966km)
3 Kentucky Derby (USA)	1mi 550yd (2.11km)	**H** Olympic running events	109yd-26mi 385yd (100m-42.2km)

1 **2** **2**

1

3 **4** **5**

5 **6** **7** **8**

10x400m **15x400m** **20x400m**

ANIMAL RACING 2

The equivalent of a runner's four-minute mile for racing snails is traveling 24 inches in three minutes – the 5½-day mile.

Animals are raced under many different circumstances: here we compare some average speeds reached in typical races. Also, by looking at flat racing records for horses (the most widespread sport and one of the fastest), we show how even small differences in distances and courses affect the speed achieved.

On the run
In the illustration *below* we compare average racing speeds of different animals (listed *right*). World-class distance runners can keep up with the slowest group, but it needs a top cyclist to match the speed of the faster animals.

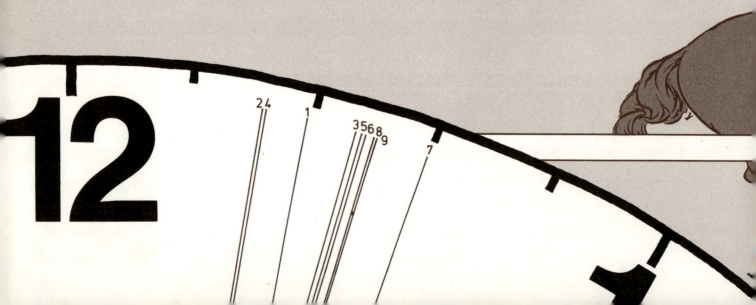

Photo finish
Illustrated and listed *right*, in order of speed, are the race records for some of the world's major horse races held on the flat. The record times for these races, given in the table, are also shown on the clock face *below*.

Race	Distance	Time	Speed
1 Kentucky Derby (USA)	1¼mi (2km)	1min 59.4sec	37.68mph (60.64kph)
2 2000 Guineas (UK)	1mi (1.6km)	1min 35.8sec	37.57mph (60.46kph)
3 Washington, D.C. International (USA)	1½mi (2.4km)	2min 23.8sec	37.55mph (60.43kph)
4 1000 Guineas (UK)	1mi (1.6km)	1min 37sec	37.11mph (59.72kph)
5 King George VI & Queen Elizabeth Stakes (UK)	1½mi (2.4km)	2min 26.98sec	36.64mph (58.96kph)
6 Prix de l'Arc de Triomphe (France)	1½mi (2.4km)	2min 28.3sec	36.20mph (58.26kph)
7 St Leger (UK)	1mi 1447yd (2.9km)	3min 01.6sec	36.12mph (58.13kph)
8 Derby (UK)	1½mi (2.4km)	2min 33.8sec	35.11mph (56.5kph)
9 Oaks (UK)	1½mi (2.4km)	2min 34.33sec	34.99mph (56.31kph)

The world's slowest racing pigeon took 7 years and 2 months to cover a distance of 370 miles – an average speed of 0.00589mph. The world's fastest snail travels at 0.0313mph – over five times as fast.

1 Women's 3000m, world record speed, 13.23mph (21.29kph)
2 Men's 3000m, world record speed, 14.84mph (23.88kph)
3 Camel, average speed, 10-15mph (16.1-24.1kph)
4 12-dog dog-sled team, average speed, 15mph (24.1kph)
5 Steeplechase, average speed, 29mph (46.67kph)
6 Ostrich, average speed, 28-30mph (45.1-48.3kph)
7 Harness horse racing, average speed, trotting, 30mph (48.3kph)
8 Harness horse racing, average speed, pacing, 31mph (49.9kph)
9 Cycling, amateur 1km unpaced standing start, world record speed, 35.84mph (57.68kph)
10 Horse racing, flat, average speed over 1-1½mi distances, 36mph (57.9kph)
11 Greyhound racing, flat, average speed, 37mph (59.5kph)
12 Horse racing, flat, average speed over ¼-½mi distances, 39mph (62.8kph)
13 Pigeon, top speed, no following wind, 60mph (96.6kph)
14 Pigeon, record speed, strong following wind, 110.07mph (177.14kph)

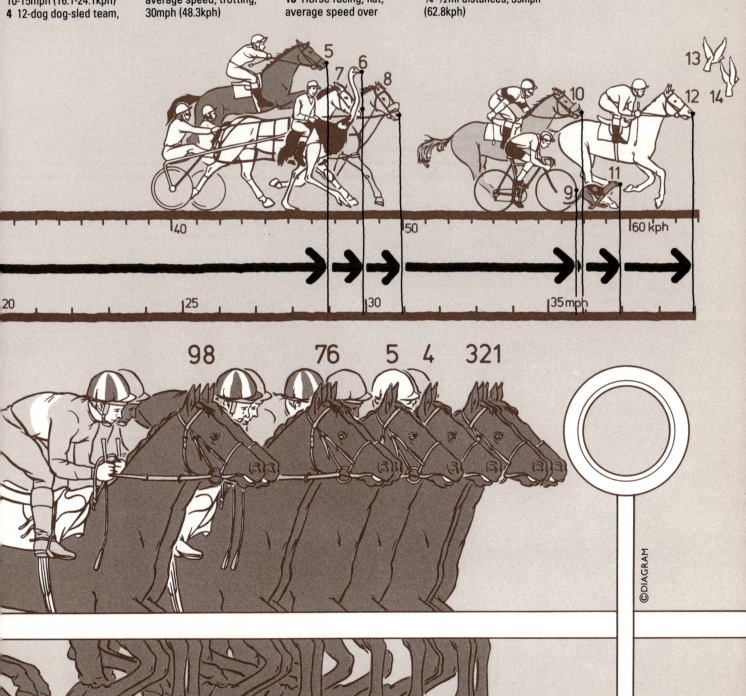

SWIMMING

Four well-known strokes are used in pool swimming races: backstroke, breaststroke, butterfly, and freestyle. (In medley races each of the strokes is used in turn.) Here we compare their speeds, and see how the women swimmers are catching up with the men. But first we look at the lengths of the races and the size of an Olympic pool.

Event	Distance
Backstroke	a 100m
	b 200m
Breaststroke	a 100m
	b 200m
Butterfly	a 100m
	b 200m
Freestyle	a 100m
	b 200m
	c 400m
	d 800m
	e 1500m
Freestyle relay	c 4x100m
	d 4x200m
Individual medley	c 400m
Medley relay	c 4x100m

Pool size *right*
An Olympic-size swimming pool measures 50x21m (164ftx68ft 11in) – large enough to hold the four lawn tennis singles courts that we have shown drawn to the same scale. Each of the eight lanes in the pool is 2.5m (8ft 2½in) wide. A swimmer in fact uses twice as much space as a runner: lanes on an athletics track are 1.22m (4ft) wide.

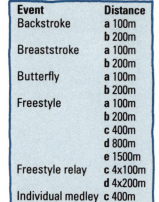

Lengths of races
Listed *right* and shown *below* are the distances swum in international races. The liner *QE2* is shown to the same scale.

a
b
c
d
e

Racing speeds
We compare the speeds of the strokes by showing to scale *below* how far top swimmers in each stroke will travel in two seconds. These distances, and the speeds of the swimmers, are listed in the table *right*.

	Stroke	Speed	Distance traveled in two seconds
A	Breaststroke	3.54mph (5.7kph)	10ft 6in (3.2m)
B	Backstroke	4.03mph (6.49kph)	11ft 9¾in (3.6m)
C	Butterfly	4.11mph (6.63kph)	12ft 1¾in (3.7m)
D	Freestyle	4.47mph (7.2kph)	13ft 1½in (4m)

Mixed bathing
By comparing the current Olympic 100m freestyle records with those set in 1912, we can see that the increase in the women's speed is 1½ times as great as that of the men. At the foot of the page we show to scale how far each swimmer would have traveled in two seconds, and these distances and the swimmer's speeds are listed in the table *right*.

m

ft
3
6

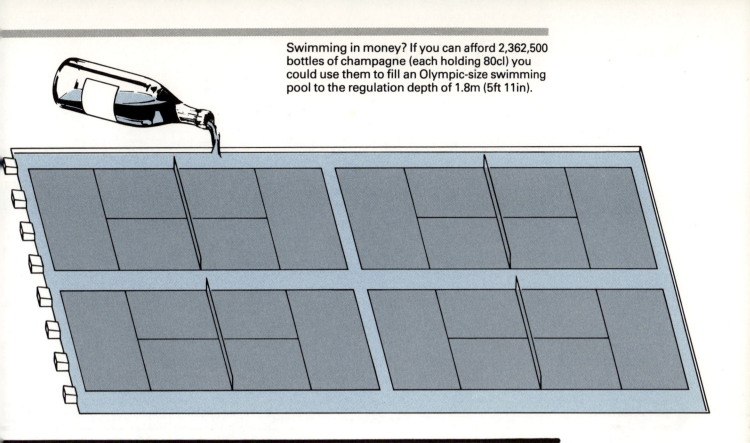

Swimming in money? If you can afford 2,362,500 bottles of champagne (each holding 80cl) you could use them to fill an Olympic-size swimming pool to the regulation depth of 1.8m (5ft 11in).

	Record	Speed	Distance traveled in two seconds
1	Women's 1912 Olympic record	2.72mph (4.38kph)	7ft 10½in (2.4m)
2	Men's 1912 Olympic record	3.59mph (5.77mph)	10ft 6in (3.2m)
3	Women's 1980 Olympic record	4.08mph (6.57mph)	11ft 11¾in (3.65m)
4	Men's 1980 Olympic record (set 1976)	4.47mph (7.2kph)	13ft 1½in (4m)

Swim like a fish? *below* Illustrated to the same scale as the swimmers is a carp (**E**), whose average speed is 7½mph. In two seconds the carp travels 21ft 11¾in – over twice as far as the breaststroke swimmer. On land, man is much faster: the record 100m sprinter (**F**) runs at 22½mph – traveling three times as fast as the carp swims, and five times as fast as the freestyle swimmer. In two seconds the runner travels 65ft 11½in: nearly six pages of this book on our scale.

©DIAGRAM

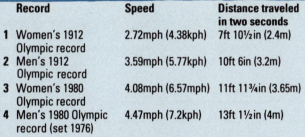

Although "rowing" is the general name for this sport, there are in fact two forms: rowing itself, where each oarsman handles only one oar; and sculling, where each sculler handles two shorter oars called sculls. The crew of a rowing boat may also include a cox, who takes responsibility for the steering and rate of stroke.

Boats and crews
Races are for boats with a specific number of crewmen. The various categories are compared in the table *right* and illustrated *below,* with their appropriate crewmen lined up *opposite.* There are no restrictions on the size or design of boats within each category, but typical lengths are given in the table.

Weighing them up *above*
A single sculls boat weighs approximately 30lb; a golfer's equipment (14 clubs, golf bag, and trolley) weighs the same. An eight boat is eight times as heavy, and weighs about 240lb.

One over the eight *below*
The men's world triple jump record is shown to scale against our longest boat, the eight. The current record holder's jump of 58ft 8½in would not enable him to clear the length of the boat – he would land over 3ft short. However, the men's world long jump record holder, with his jump of 29ft 2½in, would clear our shortest boat, the single sculls, with over 2ft to spare.

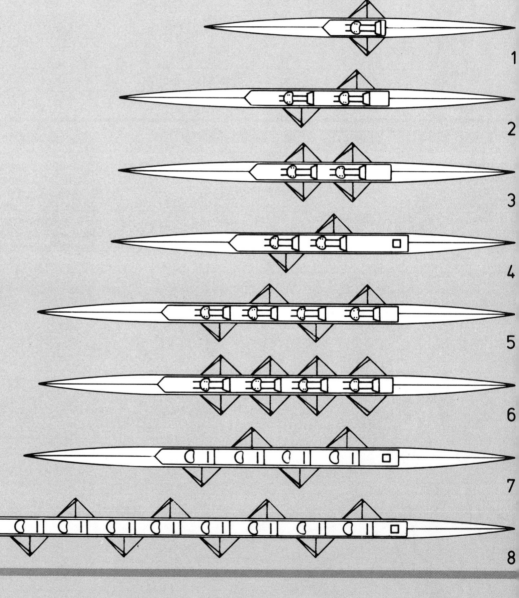

1

2

3

4

5

6

7

8

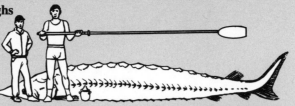

A fully rigged eight, complete with crew, weighs about 2000lb – or much the same as a large Beluga sturgeon! This size of sturgeon would yield about 300lb of caviar – the weight of an average rower (187lb) plus the cox (110lb minimum).

Event	Length of boat	Crew	Oars
1 Single sculls	27ft (8.2m)	1	2
2 Coxless pair	34ft (10.4m)	2	2
3 Double sculls	34ft (10.4m)	2	4
4 Coxed pair	35ft (10.7m)	2+cox	2
5 Coxless four	44ft (13.4m)	4	4
6 Quadruple sculls	44ft (13.4m)	4*	8
7 Coxed four	45ft (13.7m)	4+cox	4
8 Eight	62ft (18.9m)	8+cox	8

*women's quadruple sculls: 4+cox

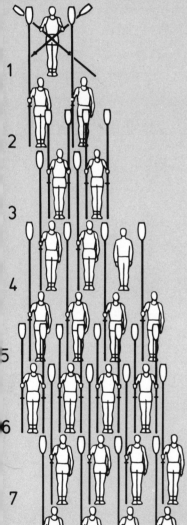

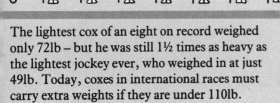

Anyone for tennis?
A rowing crew is very useful if you want to try out some other sports. An "eight" has a crew of nine, including the cox – just enough to make up a baseball team. The crew of a coxed four would be the right number for a basketball team, and the coxless four or quadruple sculls for a polo team. The crew of a coxed pair could switch to an International Soling class yacht, whereas single or double scullers, or the crew of a coxless pair, could try their luck in singles and doubles at Wimbledon!

Eggshell thin
The hull thickness of a racing boat (often called a "shell") is rarely more than 1/8in and it can be as little as 1/16in – the same thickness as the shell of an average ostrich egg.

Oar's length *left*
A typical rowing oar (**a**) is 12ft 6in long; sculls (**b**) are shorter, with an average length of 9ft 8in. The men's javelin, shown to the same scale, measures 8ft 10¼ in.

a   b

©DIAGRAM

The lightest cox of an eight on record weighed only 72lb – but he was still 1½ times as heavy as the lightest jockey ever, who weighed in at just 49lb. Today, coxes in international races must carry extra weights if they are under 110lb.

Rowing races may be regatta races, in which crews compete against each other in knock-out competition, or processional races, in which the boats set out at intervals and the result is decided by their times over the course. After comparing the lengths of these races, we look at the speeds of modern record holders and earlier crews.

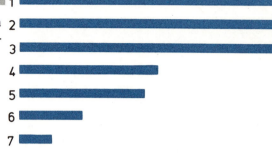

Record speeds

In the modern illustration immediately *below* and the table *right* we compare the speeds of the current world record holders in each event. These speeds were all achieved over a 200m regatta course. A sculling boat is faster than a rowing boat of the same length and crew size, because of the difference in the number of oars and efficiency of propulsion. The additional weight of the cox makes coxed pairs and fours slower than the coxless equivalents.

	Event	
A	Eight	19.75ft/sec (6.02m/sec)
B	Quadruple sculls	18.88ft/sec (5.75m/sec)
C	Coxless four	18.55ft/sec (5.65m/sec)
D	Coxed four	17.77ft/sec (5.42m/sec)
E	Double sculls	17.61ft/sec (5.37m/sec)
F	Coxless pair	16.69ft/sec (5.09m/sec)
G	Single sculls	16.02ft/sec (4.88m/sec)
H	Coxed pair	15.74ft/sec (4.80m/sec)

Race lengths

Illustrated *left* and listed *right* are the distances rowed in regatta (3,4,5,6) and processional (1,2,7) races. (The Ringvaart "Regatta" is, in fact, processional.) Races at international level are always regatta events.

Event	Distance
1 Ringvaart Regatta (Netherlands)	62mi 246yd (100km)
2 Boston Marathon (UK)	31mi (49.8km)
3 Oxford & Cambridge Boat Race (UK)	4mi 440yd (6.8km)
4 Henley Regatta (UK)	1mi 550yd (2.12km)
5 Men's Olympic races	1mi 427yd (2000m)
6 Women's Olympic races	1094yd (1000m)
7 Sprint races	547yd (500m)

Increasing speeds

Improved designs of racing shells have led to faster speeds: in the list *right* and the illustration at the bottom of the page we look at the increases in speed made by racing eights since 1870. We also compare the current world record speed for an eight with similar records for freestyle swimming and for running the mile. Our oldest boat is the ancient Greek trireme, which was approximately 115ft long and powered by 170 oarsmen sitting in three banks. Contemporary descriptions of these boats allow us to calculate their average speed as 8.3ft/sec, but some researchers have estimated that their top speed could have been 19.4ft/sec – only slightly slower than the current world rowing record!

a Eight, current world record speed, 19.75ft/sec (6.02m/sec)
b Eight, 1957 world record, 17.8ft/sec (5.43m/sec)
c Eight, 1897, 16.8ft/sec (5.12m/sec)
d Eight, 1870, 15.8ft/sec (4.82m/sec)

e Greek trireme, 427BC, 8.3ft/sec (2.53m/sec)
f Freestyle swimming, current Olympic record speed, 6.56ft/sec (2m/sec)
g Running, current world record speed for the mile, 23.21ft/sec (7.07m/sec)

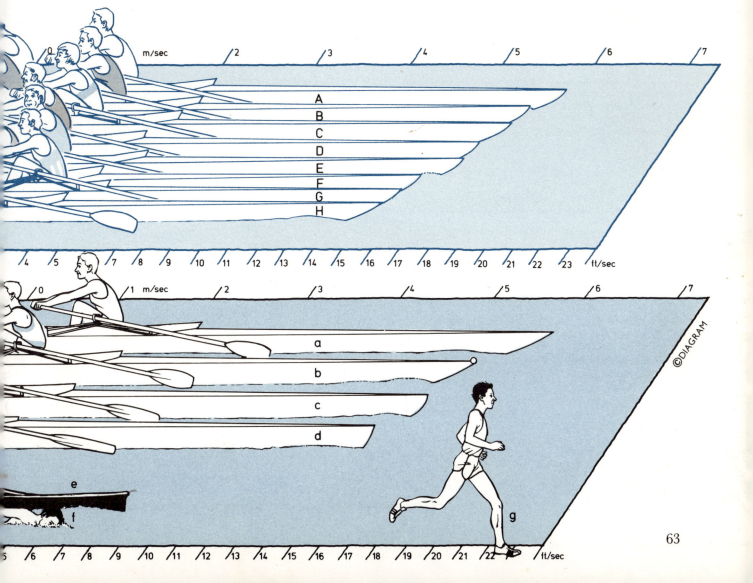

©DIAGRAM

CANOEING

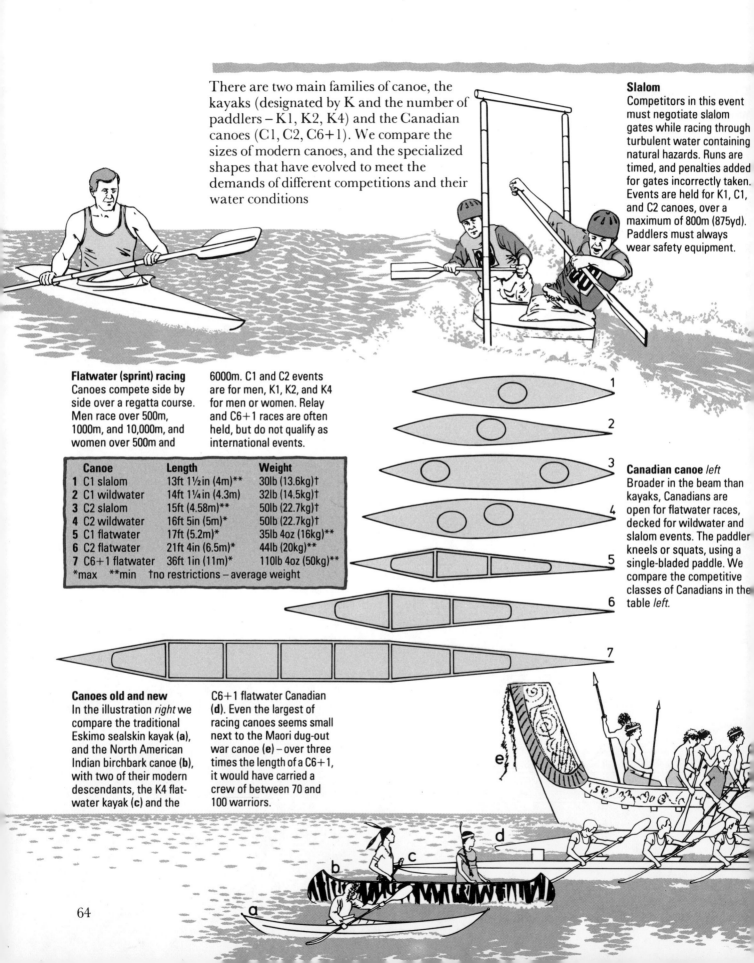

There are two main families of canoe, the kayaks (designated by K and the number of paddlers – K1, K2, K4) and the Canadian canoes (C1, C2, C6+1). We compare the sizes of modern canoes, and the specialized shapes that have evolved to meet the demands of different competitions and their water conditions

Slalom
Competitors in this event must negotiate slalom gates while racing through turbulent water containing natural hazards. Runs are timed, and penalties added for gates incorrectly taken. Events are held for K1, C1, and C2 canoes, over a maximum of 800m (875yd). Paddlers must always wear safety equipment.

Flatwater (sprint) racing
Canoes compete side by side over a regatta course. Men race over 500m, 1000m, and 10,000m, and women over 500m and 6000m. C1 and C2 events are for men, K1, K2, and K4 for men or women. Relay and C6+1 races are often held, but do not qualify as international events.

Canoe	Length	Weight
1 C1 slalom	13ft 1½in (4m)**	30lb (13.6kg)†
2 C1 wildwater	14ft 1¼in (4.3m)	32lb (14.5kg)†
3 C2 slalom	15ft (4.58m)**	50lb (22.7kg)†
4 C2 wildwater	16ft 5in (5m)*	50lb (22.7kg)†
5 C1 flatwater	17ft (5.2m)*	35lb 4oz (16kg)**
6 C2 flatwater	21ft 4in (6.5m)*	44lb (20kg)**
7 C6+1 flatwater	36ft 1in (11m)*	110lb 4oz (50kg)**

*max **min †no restrictions – average weight

Canadian canoe *left*
Broader in the beam than kayaks, Canadians are open for flatwater races, decked for wildwater and slalom events. The paddler kneels or squats, using a single-bladed paddle. We compare the competitive classes of Canadians in the table *left*.

Canoes old and new
In the illustration *right* we compare the traditional Eskimo sealskin kayak (**a**), and the North American Indian birchbark canoe (**b**), with two of their modern descendants, the K4 flat-water kayak (**c**) and the C6+1 flatwater Canadian (**d**). Even the largest of racing canoes seems small next to the Maori dug-out war canoe (**e**) – over three times the length of a C6+1, it would have carried a crew of between 70 and 100 warriors.

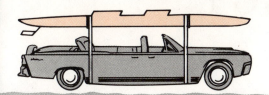

Worried about your K2 flatwater canoe overhanging the ends of your car? Your best buy is the 21ft 6in long 1969 Lincoln Continental Executive – currently belonging to the President of the USA!

A

B

C

D

E

F

Marathons *right*

There are no set distances or conditions for these races. They may include portages, where the canoe must be carried around obstructions. We show the lengths of well-known events, and compare them with an athletics marathon.

Lengths of marathons
A Texas Water Safari, 419mi (674km)
B Devizes-Westminster, 125mi (201km)
C Pietermaritzburg-Durban, 90mi (145km)
D Athletics marathon, 26mi 385yd (42.2km)
E Liffey Descent, 17½mi (28.2km)
F Sella Descent, 10mi (16.1km)

Wildwater racing

Competitors are timed over a fast-flowing course, at least 3km (1.9mi) long, which includes boulders, rapids, weirs, fallen trees, and other similar hazards. There are no slalom gates to be negotiated. K1, C1, and C2 canoes are raced.

Grade Standard of difficulty
— Flat water
I Not difficult: regular stream and waves, small rapids, simple obstructions
II Moderately difficult: irregular stream and waves, medium rapids, small drop
III Difficult: fast-flowing water, larger rapids, high regular waves, boulders
IV Very difficult: very fast water, heavy continuous rapids
V Extremely difficult: extreme rapids, narrow passages, steep gradients
VI Limit of practicability: possibly navigable, high risk

At international level, sprint races are held on flat water, marathons on Grade I, slalom and wildwater races on Grades III-V. Weirs do not affect the grading.

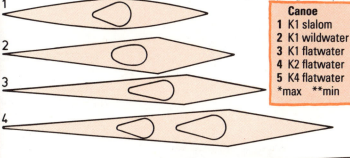

Canoe	Length	Weight
1 K1 slalom	13ft 1½in (4m)**	22lb (10kg)†
2 K1 wildwater	14ft 9in (4.5m)*	25lb (11.4kg)†
3 K1 flatwater	17ft (5.2m)*	26lb 8oz (12kg)**
4 K2 flatwater	21ft 4in (6.5m)*	39lb 11oz (18kg)**
5 K4 flatwater	36ft 1in (11m)*	66lb 2oz (30kg)**

*max **min †no restrictions – average weight

Kayak *left*

The paddler sits low in the narrow, decked canoe, with his knees braced upward, and uses a double-bladed paddle on alternate sides of the kayak. The table *left* compares the lengths and weights of the competitive kayak classes.

©DIAGRAM

YACHT RACING 1

The largest yachts are those used in offshore racing; the smallest are the sailboards, which will be included in the Olympic Games for the first time in 1984. We also look at other Olympic yacht classes, and at sailing canoes. (Canoe sailing is more closely related to yacht racing than to other forms of sport canoeing.)

Class	Rating
I	33-70ft (10.06-21.3m)
II	29-32.9ft (8.84-10.05m)
III	25.5-28.9ft (7.77-8.83m)
IV	23-25.4ft (7.01-7.76m)
V	21-22.9ft (6.4-7.00m)

Offshore yachts
Each yacht has a rating, obtained by inserting its measurements (length, sail area, beam, depth, etc.) into a complex formula, the International Offshore Rule. These ratings are expressed in feet or meters, and are used to divide yachts into offshore racing classes; the five largest are listed *above*. Illustrated to scale *right* are typical hull lengths of yachts in these classes. (These lengths are not necessarily the same as the rating measurements.)

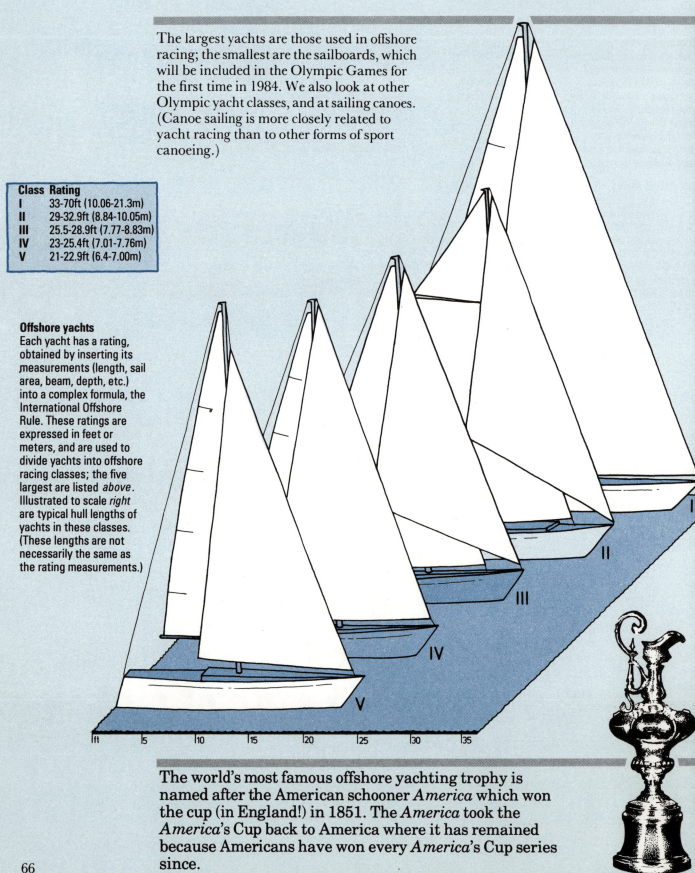

The world's most famous offshore yachting trophy is named after the American schooner *America* which won the cup (in England!) in 1851. The *America* took the *America*'s Cup back to America where it has remained because Americans have won every *America*'s Cup series since.

It's often quite wet during Wimbledon! But you would need the sails from 10 Star class yachts to make the covers for just one of the 2808ft^2 lawn tennis doubles courts.

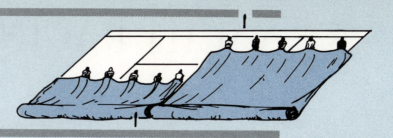

Olympic yachts
Six classes of yacht are currently raced in the Olympic Games: five monohull classes, and one, the Tornado class, for catamarans. The classes are listed in order of hull length in the table *right*, and are shown to scale (with their crews) in the illustration *below*. Also listed *right*, and shown to a second scale as rectangles immediately *below*, are the areas of the sails carried by each class.

	Class	Length	Crew	Sail area
1	Soling	26ft 9in (8.16m)	3	250ft^2 (23.22m^2)*
2	Star	22ft 8in (6.92m)	2	281ft^2 (26.13m^2)
3	Tornado	20ft (6.096m)	2	235ft^2 (21.83m^2)
4	Flying Dutchman	19ft 10in (6.04m)	2	202ft^2 (18.76m^2)*
5	470	15ft 4¾in (4.70m)	2	145ft^2 (13.48m^2)*
6	Finn	14ft 9in (4.50m)	1	107ft^2 (9.94m^2)

*spinnaker carried, but not included in sail area figure

Sailboards (A) *below*
These may be up to 3.9m (12ft 9½in) long, with a maximum sail area of 6.8m^2 (73.19ft^2). Classes are based on the competitor's weight: 75kg (165¼lb) maximum weight in the lightweight class, and 70kg (154¼lb) minimum in the heavyweight class.

Sailing canoes (B) *below*
The International 10m^2 canoe is 5.18m (17ft) long, with a maximum sail area of 10m^2 (107.6ft^2).

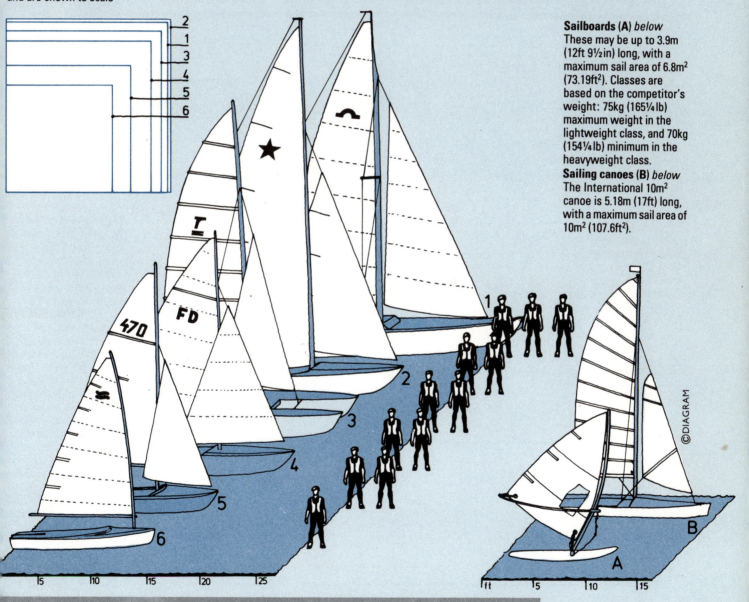

©DIAGRAM

The Ranger *(which won the* America's Cup *in 1937) carried the largest sail ever made. With an area of 18,000ft^2, it could have provided wardrobes of sails for 72 Soling class yachts.*

YACHT RACING 2

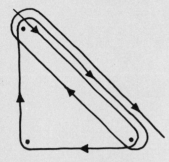

Yacht races take two main forms: ocean races from port to port across open sea, and races held closer to shore over a triangular course marked by buoys. We look at the courses and distances involved, at the speeds yachts achieve, and at the handicapping systems that allow different classes to race together.

Courses and distances
The layout of a triangular course *far left* depends on local conditions and in particular on the prevailing wind. There are no fixed race lengths, but the smaller yachts usually race over shorter courses than the larger, faster boats.

The distances involved in ocean races also vary considerably: some famous examples are listed in the table *right*. Their lengths are shown to scale *below left,* and their routes are indicated on the map of the world.

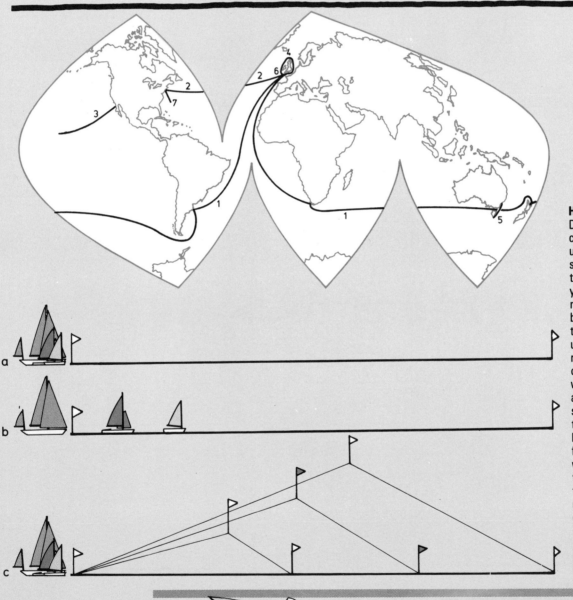

Handicapping *below left*
Different classes of yacht can compete together by using a handicapping system. Handicaps are time allowances given to yachts based on their ratings. If competitors begin the race at the same time (**a**) the handicap is used to adjust each yacht's recorded time for the course, and decide the winner. Handicaps may also be used to calculate staggered start times (**b**): the slower yachts start before the faster, and the first boat home is the winner. An alternative to time handicapping is triangulation (**c**): the buoys marking the turning points on the course are staggered, and the faster boats must round the further marks. Again, the first yacht home wins.

As well as using standard triangular courses set in deep water, sailboarders also race over various types of course set close to shore. Two types feature slalom sections, and in one case the is set if possible in breaking surf, so that surfing and wave hopping skills are needed.

Single-handed transatlantic yacht races have been held regularly since 1960, but the first was held very much earlier, in 1891. The winner took 45 days to complete the crossing – over twice the current race record of 20 days 13¼ hours.

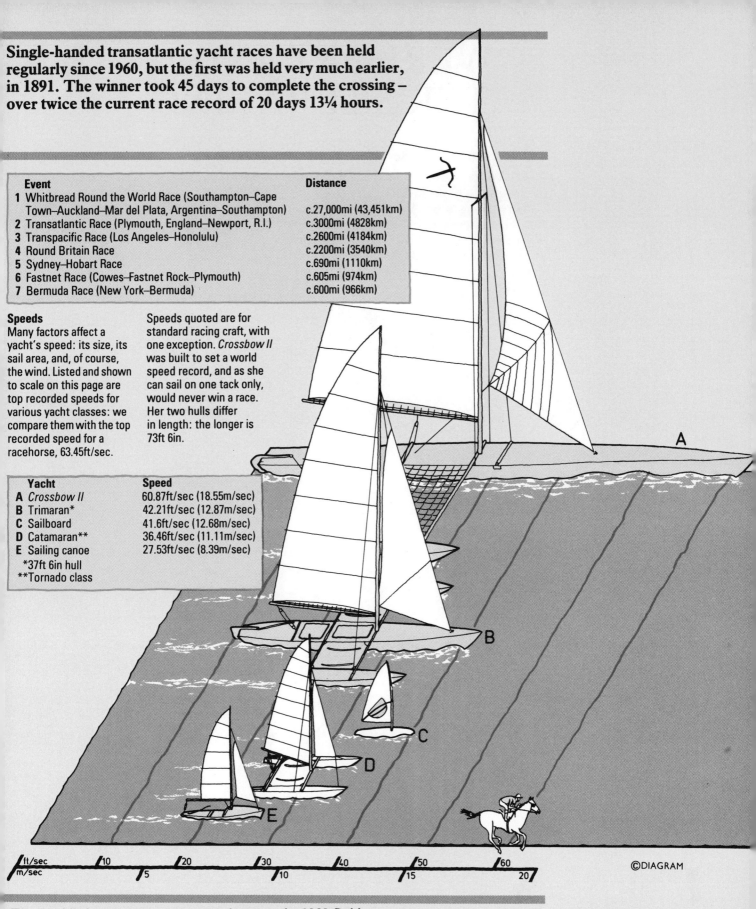

Event		Distance
1	Whitbread Round the World Race (Southampton–Cape Town–Auckland–Mar del Plata, Argentina–Southampton)	c.27,000mi (43,451km)
2	Transatlantic Race (Plymouth, England–Newport, R.I.)	c.3000mi (4828km)
3	Transpacific Race (Los Angeles–Honolulu)	c.2600mi (4184km)
4	Round Britain Race	c.2200mi (3540km)
5	Sydney–Hobart Race	c.690mi (1110km)
6	Fastnet Race (Cowes–Fastnet Rock–Plymouth)	c.605mi (974km)
7	Bermuda Race (New York–Bermuda)	c.600mi (966km)

Speeds
Many factors affect a yacht's speed: its size, its sail area, and, of course, the wind. Listed and shown to scale on this page are top recorded speeds for various yacht classes: we compare them with the top recorded speed for a racehorse, 63.45ft/sec.

Speeds quoted are for standard racing craft, with one exception. *Crossbow II* was built to set a world speed record, and as she can sail on one tack only, would never win a race. Her two hulls differ in length: the longer is 73ft 6in.

	Yacht	Speed
A	*Crossbow II*	60.87ft/sec (18.55m/sec)
B	Trimaran*	42.21ft/sec (12.87m/sec)
C	Sailboard	41.6ft/sec (12.68m/sec)
D	Catamaran**	36.46ft/sec (11.11m/sec)
E	Sailing canoe	27.53ft/sec (8.39m/sec)

*37ft 6in hull
**Tornado class

©DIAGRAM

The world's longest nonstop race to date was the 1968 Golden Globe Race for solo circumnavigation of the world without landfall. Robin Knox Johnston, as the only man to complete the course, became the first person to sail single-handed nonstop around the world.

69

Water speed
POWERBOAT AND WATER SKI RACING

Powerboat racing divides into sportsboat races on stretches of inland water and offshore racing at sea. Water ski races may be held on either type of course. Here we look at the distances covered in the various races, and compare the speeds achieved by water skiers and by the different classes of racing powerboat.

Classes
Powerboats are divided into classes on the basis of a complex series of measurements, including engine capacity, hull length, beam, etc. In some sportsboat classes, the engines are restricted to manufacturers' standard production models; in others, the engine may be built as a single example, intended solely for racing. Hydroplane classes are a subdivision of the sportsboat classes: the boats are designed to rise partially out of the water and skim over the surface.

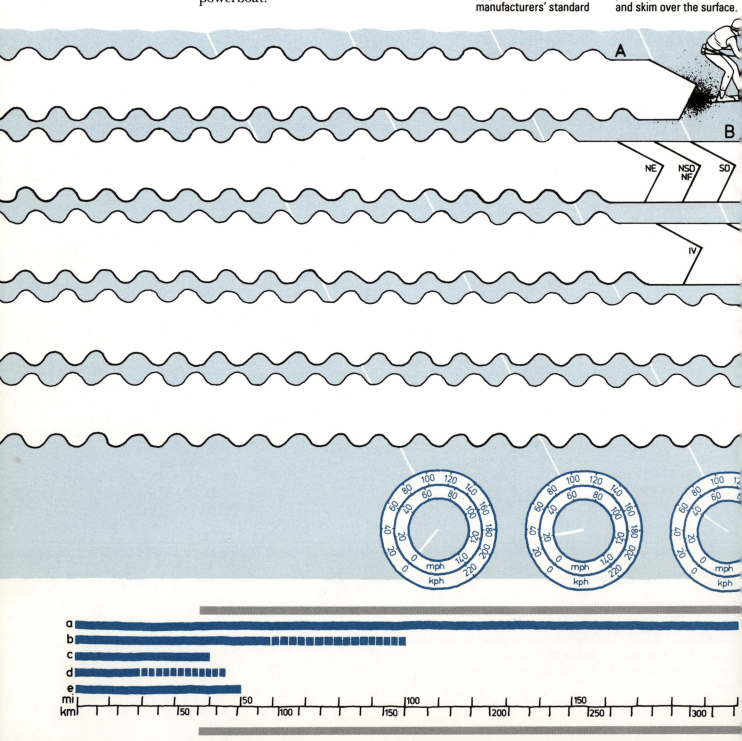

In the newest form of powerboat racing, drag boat racing, the highest terminal velocity recorded to date is 205.19mph – twice the offshore powerboat world speed record of 102.45mph. But a drag racing car can travel nearly twice as fast again, with a top recorded terminal velocity of 377.754mph.

Speeds
Listed *right* and shown to scale *below* are the average speeds achieved in races by water skiers, and by different classes of racing powerboat. For comparison, we show a motorcyclist traveling at 100mph (161kph).

A) Water ski racing
65mph (105kph)

B) Sportsboats with standard stock engines
NE class, 55mph (88kph)
NF class, 60mph (97kph)
NSD class, 60mph (97kph)
SD class, 65mph (105kph)
SE class, 75mph (121kph)

C) Offshore powerboats
Class IV, 55mph (88kph)
Class III, 65mph (105kph)
Class II, 70mph (113kph)
Class I, 85mph (137kph)

D) Hydroplanes
OB stock class, 60mph (97kph)
OA class, 65mph (105kph)
OB class, 75mph (121kph)
R1 class, 90mph (145kph)
OC class, 100mph (161kph)
OD class, 100mph (161kph)
R2 class, 100mph (161kph)

E) Other sportsboats
OE class, 90mph (145kph)
ON class, 120mph (193kph)
OZ class, 130mph (209kph)

©DIAGRAM

Race lengths
The distances covered in powerboat and water ski races are shown to scale *left*. In offshore races, class I and II boats (**a**) usually race 200mi (322km); class III (**b**), 60-100mi (96.5-161km); class IV (**c**), 40mi (64.4km). Sportsboats (**d**) race for 20 minutes on a ¾-2¼mi (1.2-4km) circuit: race lengths therefore range from 20-45mi (32-72km), depending on the class of boat. The average length of water ski races (**e**) is 50mi (80.5km): they may be races from one place to another, or circuit races over 10-15 laps of a 3-5mi (4.8-8.1km) circuit.

AIR RACING

The international governing body for air racing, the Fédération Aeronautique Internationale, was founded in 1905 – only two years after the Wright brothers' first flight. Here we look at the modern forms of air racing: soaring races for sailplanes (gliders), and formula air racing for powered airplanes.

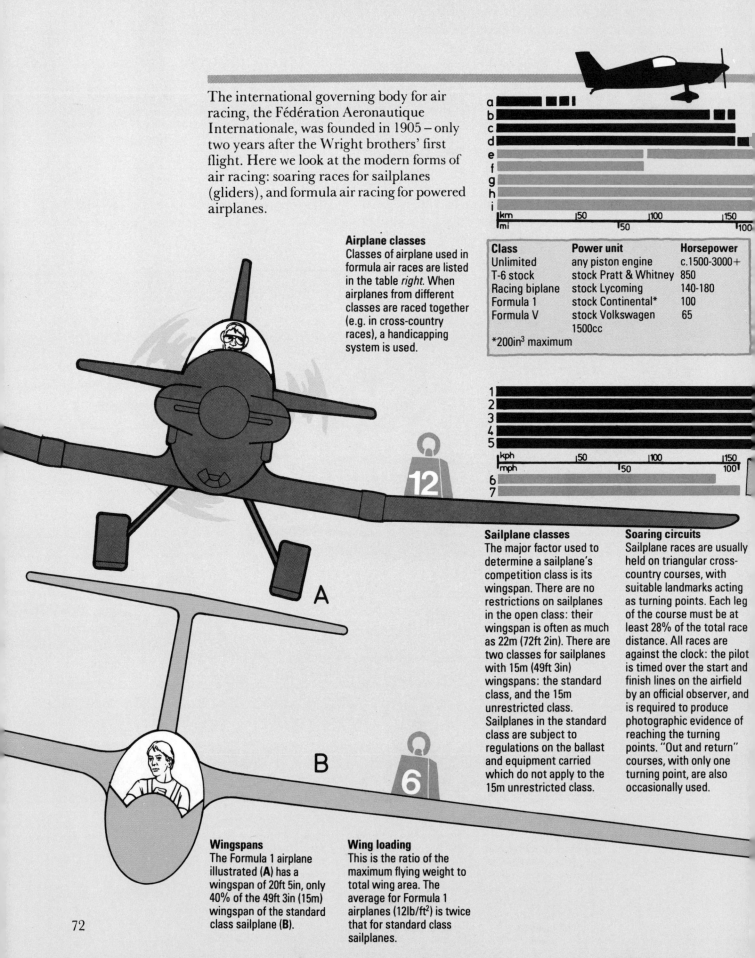

Airplane classes
Classes of airplane used in formula air races are listed in the table *right*. When airplanes from different classes are raced together (e.g. in cross-country races), a handicapping system is used.

Class	Power unit	Horsepower
Unlimited	any piston engine	c.1500-3000+
T-6 stock	stock Pratt & Whitney	850
Racing biplane	stock Lycoming	140-180
Formula 1	stock Continental*	100
Formula V	stock Volkswagen 1500cc	65

*200in³ maximum

A

B

Sailplane classes
The major factor used to determine a sailplane's competition class is its wingspan. There are no restrictions on sailplanes in the open class: their wingspan is often as much as 22m (72ft 2in). There are two classes for sailplanes with 15m (49ft 3in) wingspans: the standard class, and the 15m unrestricted class. Sailplanes in the standard class are subject to regulations on the ballast and equipment carried which do not apply to the 15m unrestricted class.

Soaring circuits
Sailplane races are usually held on triangular cross-country courses, with suitable landmarks acting as turning points. Each leg of the course must be at least 28% of the total race distance. All races are against the clock: the pilot is timed over the start and finish lines on the airfield by an official observer, and is required to produce photographic evidence of reaching the turning points. "Out and return" courses, with only one turning point, are also occasionally used.

Wingspans
The Formula 1 airplane illustrated (**A**) has a wingspan of 20ft 5in, only 40% of the 49ft 3in (15m) wingspan of the standard class sailplane (**B**).

Wing loading
This is the ratio of the maximum flying weight to total wing area. The average for Formula 1 airplanes (12lb/ft²) is twice that for standard class sailplanes.

The average racing speed of Formula 1 airplanes (190-250mph) is approximately twice that of Formula 1 racing cars (80-140mph). The fastest recorded speed for a racing car is in fact slightly higher than this (257mph), but the world record speed for an unlimited-class piston-engined airplane is almost twice as high again, at 499.048mph.

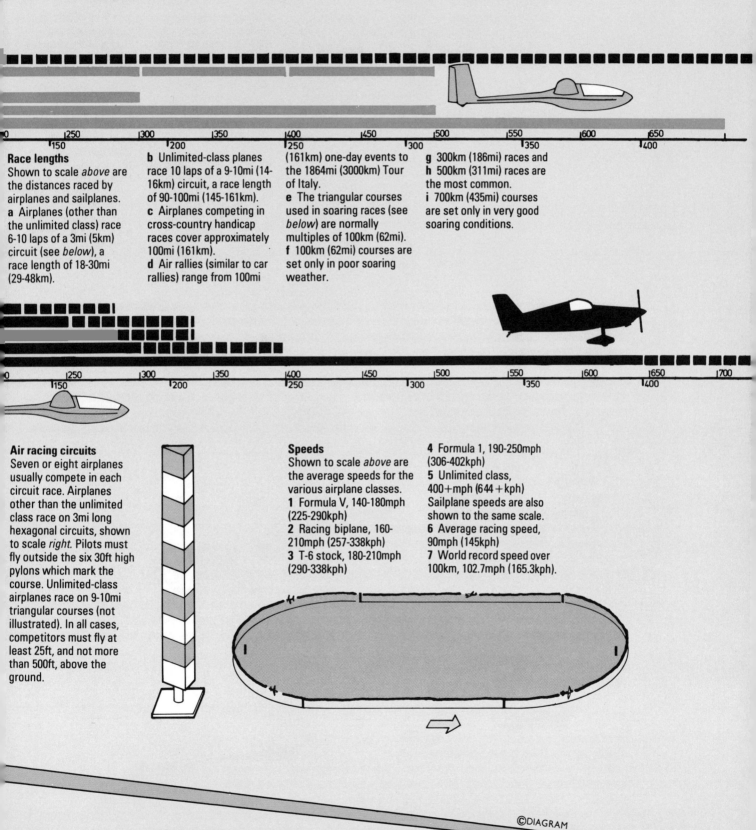

Race lengths
Shown to scale *above* are the distances raced by airplanes and sailplanes.
a Airplanes (other than the unlimited class) race 6-10 laps of a 3mi (5km) circuit (see *below*), a race length of 18-30mi (29-48km).

b Unlimited-class planes race 10 laps of a 9-10mi (14-16km) circuit, a race length of 90-100mi (145-161km).
c Airplanes competing in cross-country handicap races cover approximately 100mi (161km).
d Air rallies (similar to car rallies) range from 100mi

(161km) one-day events to the 1864mi (3000km) Tour of Italy.
e The triangular courses used in soaring races (see *below*) are normally multiples of 100km (62mi).
f 100km (62mi) courses are set only in poor soaring weather.

g 300km (186mi) races and
h 500km (311mi) races are the most common.
i 700km (435mi) courses are set only in very good soaring conditions.

Air racing circuits
Seven or eight airplanes usually compete in each circuit race. Airplanes other than the unlimited class race on 3mi long hexagonal circuits, shown to scale *right*. Pilots must fly outside the six 30ft high pylons which mark the course. Unlimited-class airplanes race on 9-10mi triangular courses (not illustrated). In all cases, competitors must fly at least 25ft, and not more than 500ft, above the ground.

Speeds
Shown to scale *above* are the average speeds for the various airplane classes.
1 Formula V, 140-180mph (225-290kph)
2 Racing biplane, 160-210mph (257-338kph)
3 T-6 stock, 180-210mph (290-338kph)

4 Formula 1, 190-250mph (306-402kph)
5 Unlimited class, 400+mph (644+kph)
Sailplane speeds are also shown to the same scale.
6 Average racing speed, 90mph (145kph)
7 World record speed over 100km, 102.7mph (165.3kph).

©DIAGRAM

LAND SPEED RECORDS

Having surveyed the range of racing sports, we now survey the range of speeds achieved – on land and (on the following pages) on water and in the air. The figures given are either current records or (where no such exist) estimated top speeds. Any date given refers to the year in which a current record was established.

1 Roller skating, official world speed record, set 1963, 25.78mph (41.48kph)
2 Running, peak velocity recorded, achieved in 100yd (91m) sprint, 1963, 27+mph (43.4+kph)
3 Speed skating, record speed over 500m (547yd), set 1981, 30.30mph (48.77kph)
4 Cycling, record speed for unpaced bicycle, set 1977, 49.38mph (79.47kph)

5 Greyhound, top speed recorded, 41.72mph (67.14kph)
6 Racehorse, top speed over ¼mi (402m), set 1945, 43.26mph (69.62kph)
7 Jackrabbit, average top speed, 45mph (72kph)
8 Ostrich, average top speed, 50mph (80kph)

9 Skateboarding, world speed record in standing position, set 1978, 53.45mph (86kph)
10 Land yachting, world speed record for four-crew yacht, set 1956, 57.69mph (92.84kph)
11 Skateboarding, world speed record in prone position, set 1979, 71.79mph (115.5kph)

If he could keep going at peak velocity, the fastest roller skater would travel the length of Manhattan Island (12½ miles) in just over 29 minutes. The fastest rocket car would take just over one minute!

12 Luge toboggan, top speed recorded, 80+mph (128+kph)
13 Land yachting, world speed record for single-seater yacht, set 1976, 88.4mph (142.26kph)
14 Skeleton (Cresta Run) toboggan, estimated top speed, 90mph (145kph)
15 Bobsleigh, estimated top speed, 100mph (161kph)
16 Skibob, top speed recorded, set 1964, 103.4mph (166.4kph)
17 Skiing, top speed recorded, set 1978, 124.412mph (200.222kph)

18 Cycling, official world speed record, cycle paced by car, set 1973, 140.5mph (226.1kph)
19 Ice yachting, world speed record, set 1938, 143mph (230kph)

20 Pronghorn antelope, average top speed, 60mph (97kph)
21 Cheetah, average top speed, 60-63mph (97-101kph)

22 Racing car, top speed recorded, set 1973, 257mph (413.6kph)
23 Motorcycling, official

world speed record, set 1975, 303.81mph (488.935kph)
24 Drag racing, highest terminal velocity recorded, set 1977, 392.54mph (631.732kph)
25 Land speed record, official world record for piston-engined car, set 1965, 418.504mph (673.516kph)
26 Land speed record, official world record for wheel-driven car, set 1964, 429.311mph (690.909kph)
27 Land speed record, official world record for jet-engined car, set 1965,

613.995mph (998.129kph)
28 Land speed record, official world record for rocket-powered vehicle, set 1970, 622.287mph (1001.473kph)
29 Peak velocity achieved on land, set 1979 by rocket-powered car, 739.666mph (1190.377kph)

©DIAGRAM

40 50 60 70 80 kph
30 40 50 mph

200 220 240 260 280 300 320 kph
130 140 150 160 170 180 190 200 mph

800 900 1000 1100 1200 kph
500 600 700 800 mph

75

AIR AND WATER SPEED RECORDS

Here we follow the same procedures as with land speed records on the previous page. But man is a poor swimmer – and an even worse flier! So in water and air, even more than on land, his records reflect the history of his inventiveness. Achievements today, in these alien environments, far exceed those of their natural inhabitants.

1 Gliding, world record speed over 100km (62mi) triangular course, set 1974, 102.74mph (165.35kph)
2 Skydiving, maximum speed reached in free-fall through non-rarefied air, 185mph (298kph)

3 Pigeon, estimated top speed in windless conditions, 60mph (97kph)
4 Peregrine falcon, top speed recorded in dive, 82mph (132kph)
5 Spine-tailed swift, top speed reliably recorded, 106.25mph (171kph)
6 Pigeon, record speed in strong following wind, set 1965, 110.07mph (177.14kph)
7 Helicopter, official world speed record, set 1978, 228.9mph (368.4kph)
8 Air speed record, official world record for piston-engined plane, set 1979, 499.048mph (803.138kph)
9 Skydiving, maximum speed reached in rarefied air during delayed drop from high altitude, set 1960, 625.2mph (1006kph)
10 Air speed record, official world record for jet plane, set 1976, 2193.167mph (3529.56kph)

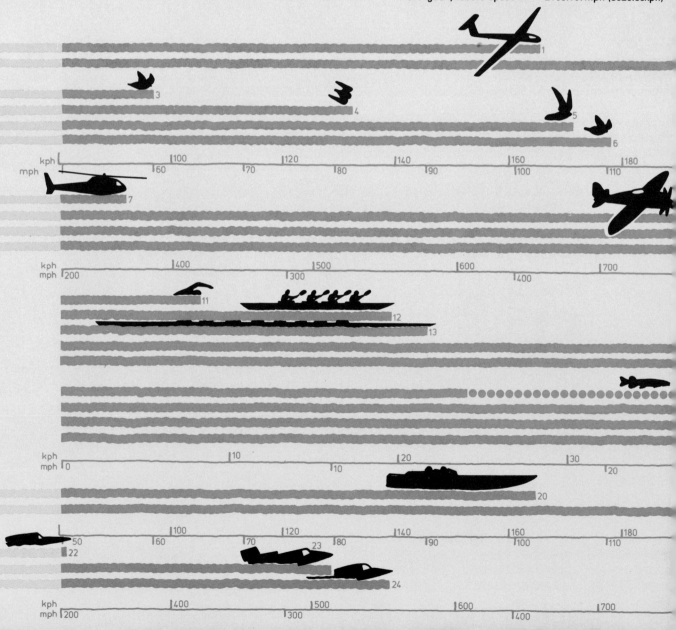

Sailing from London to Australia, the record time for a 19th century clipper was 69 days. Today the world's fastest boat is a jet-powered hydroplane, aptly called *Spirit of Australia*; if it could make that same journey at peak velocity, it would take less than 36 hours!

11 Swimming, highest speed recorded over 50yd (45.7m), set 1977, 5.19mph (8.35kph)

12 Canoeing, record speed for K4 canoe over 1000m (1094yd), set 1980, 12.24mph (19.70kph)

13 Rowing, record speed for eight over 2000m (2187yd), set 1976, 13.46mph (21.67kph)

14 Board sailing, world record speed, set 1980, 28.36mph (45.64kph)

15 Sailing, official world speed record, set 1980, 41.50mph (66.78kph)

16 Pike, estimated top speed, 15-25mph (24-40kph)

17 Dolphin, average reported top speed, 25-28mph (40-45kph)

18 Swordfish, estimated top speed, 35-40mph (56-64kph)

19 Killer whale, estimated top speed, 40mph (64kph)

20 Powerboat, official offshore record, set 1980, 102.45mph (164.87kph)

21 Water skiing, unofficial world speed record, set 1979, 128.16mph (206.25kph)

22 Water speed record, official world record for propellor-driven boat, 202.42mph (325.76kph)

23 Water speed record, official world record for unlimited hydroplane, set 1978, 319.627mph (514.39kph)

24 Water speed record, unofficial world record, set 1977 by unlimited hydroplane, 345mph (556kph)

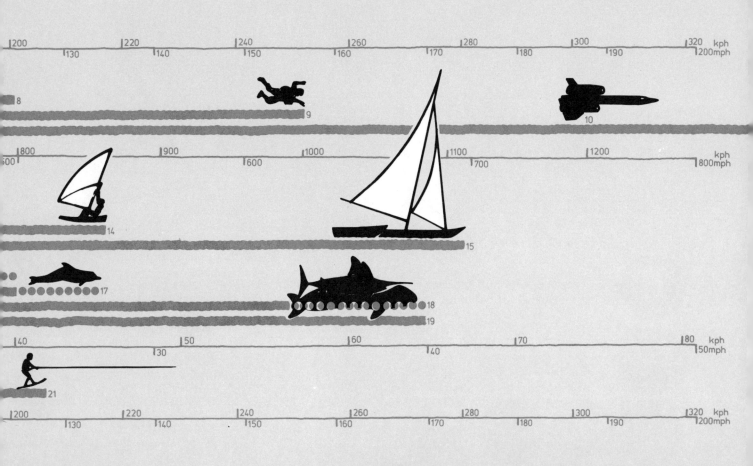

Marathon races

MARATHON RACES

We have seen that there are typical distances for most forms of racing. But unusually long races also occur: some regularly, others only occasionally. Here we survey many such "marathons" from all areas of racing, and use maps to help convey the distances involved, which range from under 10 miles to over 60,000.

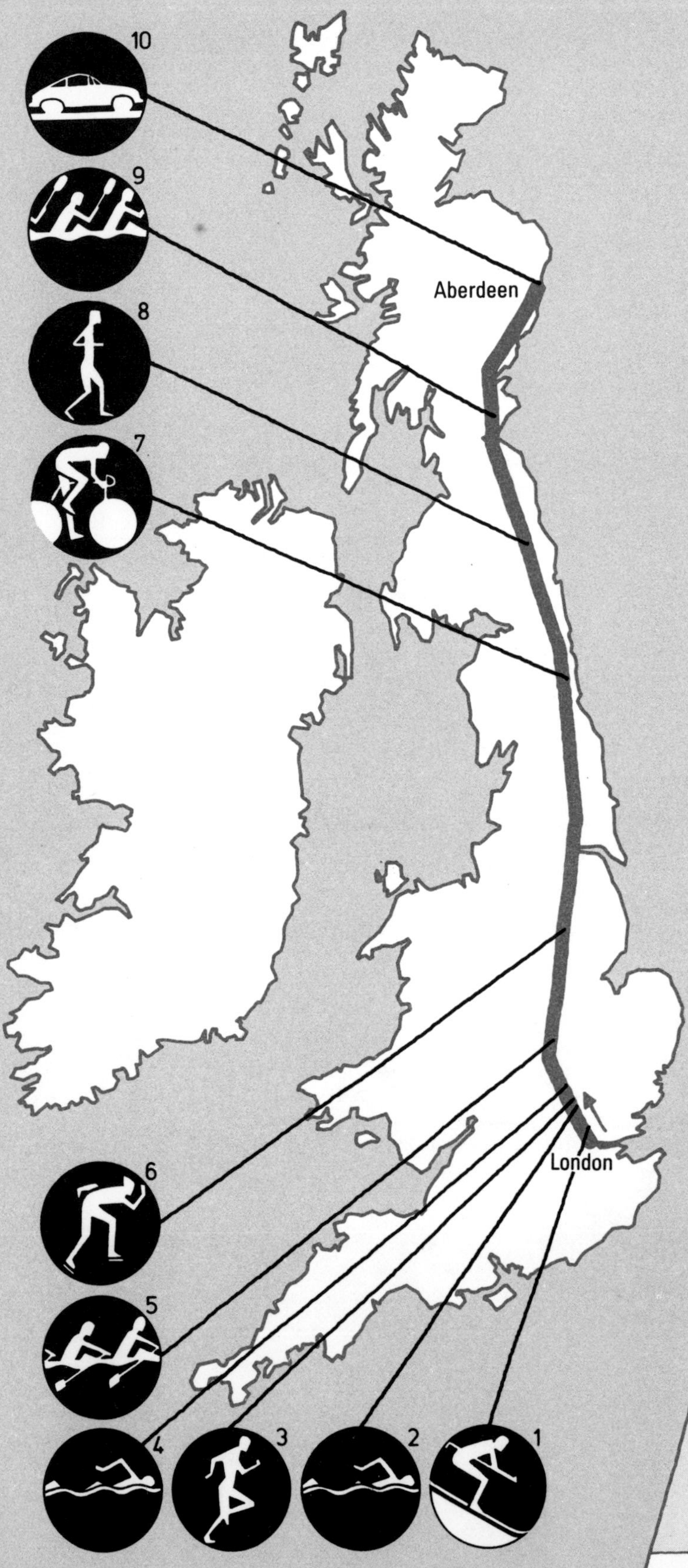

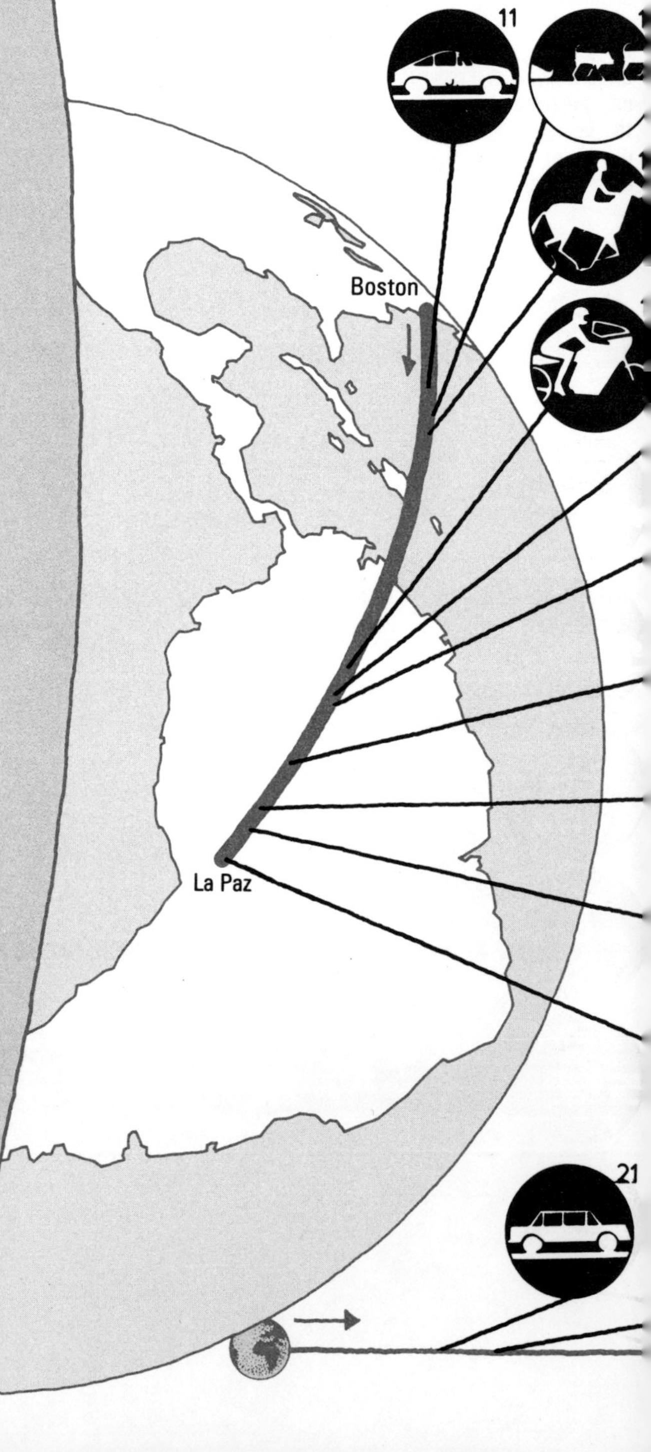

Aberdeen

London

Boston

La Paz

10

9

8

7

6

5

4

3

2

1

11

21

Indian kickball is a kind of running marathon among Mexicans and Hopis. The course is up to 40 miles – and each team has to kick a ball the whole way!

Long suffering?
The marathon races listed on this page are plotted *opposite* and *below,* to illustrate the distances involved. The shorter races are plotted on a map of Great Britain, the longer on a map of the Americas, and the three longest on a scale of the distance from the Earth to the Moon.
In the lists that follow, race distances greater than 125 miles are mostly given to the nearest mile, as such distances are generally approximate.

Long
On our map of Great Britain *opposite,* the lesser marathon race distances are plotted against a road journey from London to Aberdeen (Britain's northernmost city). The longest of these races would cover the whole of the 500 miles involved.
1 Skiing: longest regularly held downhill race (the "Inferno," Switzerland) 8.7mi (14km)
2 Swimming, freshwater: Loch Lomond race, Scotland 22mi (35.4km)
3 Running: the marathon 26mi 385yd (42.2km)
4 Swimming, sea: Dover-Cap Gris Nez (direct distance) 35mi (56.3km)
5 Rowing: longest annual race for eights (Ringvaart Regatta, Netherlands) 62.1mi (100km)
6 Speed skating: longest regularly held race ("Elfstedentocht," Netherlands) 124.3mi (200km)
7 Cycling: longest regularly held one-day massed start road race (London-Holyhead, UK) 265mi (426.5km)
8 Race walking: longest regularly held race (Strasbourg-Paris) 344mi (554km)
9 Canoeing: longest regularly held race (Texas Water Safari) 419mi (674km)
10 Motor racing: longest regularly held road race (Targa Florio, Sicily) (805km)

 15
 16
17
 18
 19
20

Longer!
On our map of the Americas *opposite,* the longer marathon race distances are plotted against an air journey along the shortest (great circle) distance from Boston (USA) to La Paz (Bolivia). The longest of these races would cover the whole of the distance involved – nearly 3900 miles.
11 Motor racing: longest regularly held off-road race (Mexican 1000) 832mi (1339km)
12 Sled-dog racing: longest regularly held race (Alaskan Iditarod Trail Race) 1050mi (1690km)
13 Horse racing: longest race ever held (Portugal) 1200mi (1925km)
14 Motorcycling: longest regularly held race (Liège 24-hour); greatest distance achieved 2761.9mi (4444.8km)
15 Soaring: longest race ever held (Smirnoff Sailplane Derby, USA) 2900mi (4667km)
16 Powerboat racing: longest race ever held (London-Monte Carlo, 1972) 2947mi (4742km)
17 Motor racing: longest regularly held race (Le Mans 24-hour); greatest distance achieved 3315.2mi (5335.3km)
18 Cycling: longest Tour de France ever held (1926; length restrictions were imposed in 1971) 3569mi (5743km)
19 Running: longest race ever held (Trans Continental Race, New York-Los Angeles, 1929) 3665mi (5898km)
20 Car rallying: longest regularly held rally (East African Safari Rally); greatest distance (1971) 3874mi (6234km)

 22 23

Longest!!
Our three lengthiest marathon races are plotted *below* against the mean distance from the Earth to the Moon (238,840 miles). The longest race of all would reach over a quarter of the way to the Moon.
21 Car rallying: longest rally ever held (London-Sydney, 1977) 19,329mi (31,107km)
22 Sailing: longest regularly held race (Whitbread Round the World Yacht Race) c.27,000mi (43,451km)
23 Race walking: longest race ever organized (Touring Club de France, 1910) 62,137mi (100,000km) (never completed)

PART TWO

ACHIEVEMENT SPORTS

THROWING SPORTS 1

The four Olympic throwing events are the javelin, discus, shot put, and hammer. The first three events are for men and women, the last for men only. In all of them, the instrument used must be thrown from within a set throwing area, and land within an arc marked out on the ground. Here we compare basic rules and throwing weights.

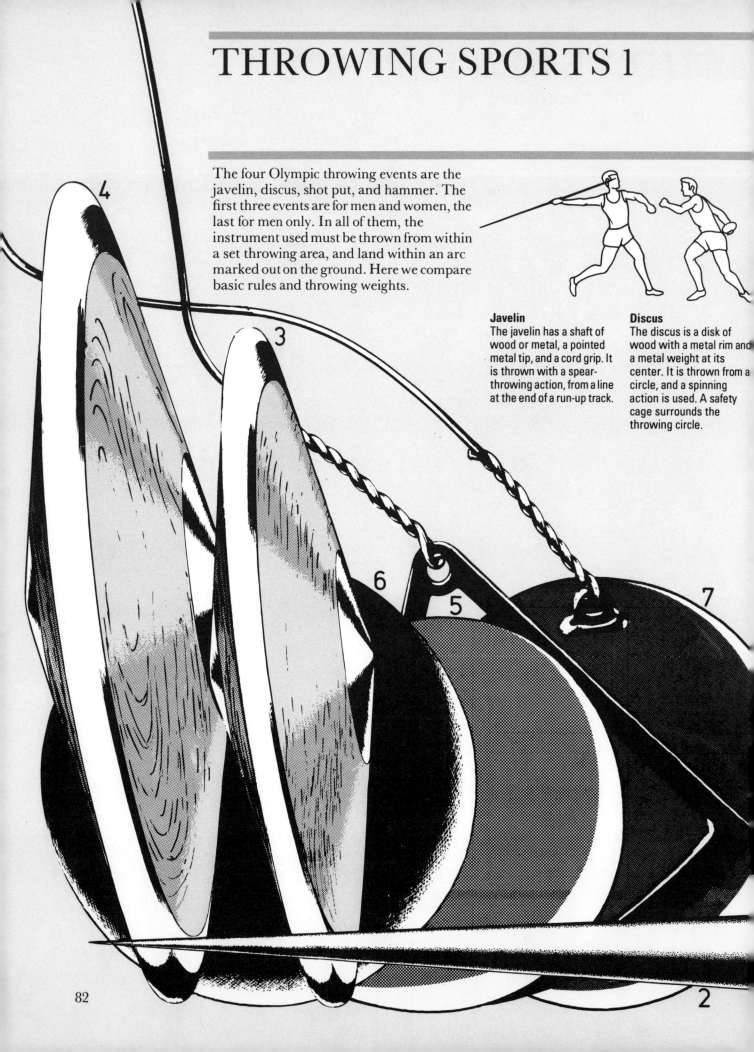

Javelin
The javelin has a shaft of wood or metal, a pointed metal tip, and a cord grip. It is thrown with a spear-throwing action, from a line at the end of a run-up track.

Discus
The discus is a disk of wood with a metal rim and a metal weight at its center. It is thrown from a circle, and a spinning action is used. A safety cage surrounds the throwing circle.

To show the full lengths of the javelins at the bottom of the page, we would need nine more pages for the women's javelin, and 11 more for the men's.

The discus used in the ancient Greek Olympics was very like a modern one in shape and size. But it was made as a solid ingot of bronze – which was then kept by the winner!

Shot put
The shot is a ball of metal (typically either solid iron or brass, or a metal shell filled with lead). It is thrown from a circle, using a pushing and half-turning action.

Hammer
The "hammer" has in fact a round head of metal and a wire handle and grip. It is thrown from a circle, using a spinning action, and again a safety cage is needed.

Implement	Minimum weight
1 Women's javelin	0.6kg (1lb 5¼oz)
2 Men's javelin	0.8kg (1lb 12¼oz)
3 Women's discus	1kg (2lb 3¼oz)
4 Men's discus	2kg (4lb 6½oz)
5 Women's shot	4kg (8lb 13oz)
6 Men's shot	7.26kg (16lb)
7 Hammer (men only)	7.26kg (16lb)

Size and weight
Left and *below* we show full size the implements used in Olympic throwing events. (There is room for only the ends of the javelins, of course!) *Above* we list their regulation minimum weights, and then *right* show the sizes and weights to scale, with some familiar objects as reference points.

A Basketball, minimum weight, 21.2oz (600g)
B Cricket bat, typical weight, 36oz (1.02kg)
C Four- to five-week-old baby, typical weight, 8.6lb (3.9kg)
D Ten-pin bowling ball, maximum weight, 16lb (7.26kg)

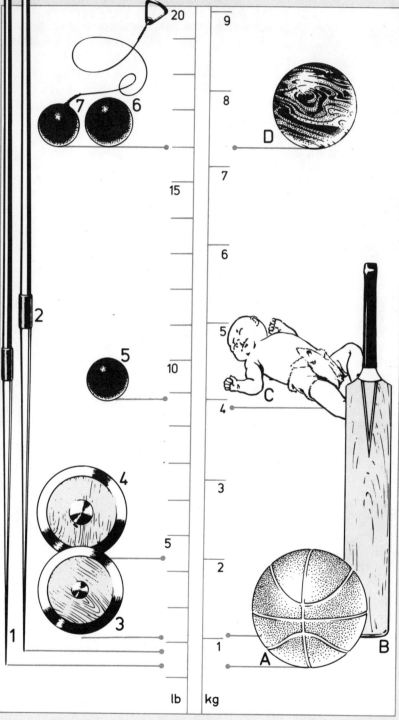

©DIAGRAM

1

THROWING SPORTS 2

Trying to throw rocks and pebbles as far as possible must have been one of the earliest human games. Today a wide range of objects is thrown in sport and play. The distances achieved vary greatly; and they depend not only on the weight of each object, but also on aerodynamic factors and the type of throw that is possible.

At full pitch?
To make the distances involved in different throwing events easier to visualize, we have set them out over the lengths of two

adjacent soccer pitches (each one 110 yards long). Throws are shown as being made from the near goal line of the nearer pitch.

Olympic throwing records
Here we are looking at two lightweight projectiles (javelin and discus) and two heavy ones (shot and hammer). The shapes of the first two also give them a lift from the air, while those of the heavier two do not. Both these factors

affect the distances achieved. Nevertheless the hammer's long handle allows a very effective spinning throw; so it not only far outdistances the equally heavy shot, but also the more aerodynamic and much lighter discus. For the women's events,

the equipment is lighter. In fact, as a result, the women's shot record overtakes that for men. Also, while their javelin is 75% of the men's in weight, their discus is only 50%; so for women the discus record matches the record in the javelin.

Event	Distances
1 Men's javelin	317ft 4in (96.72m)
2 Hammer (men only)	268ft 4½in (81.8m)
3 Women's javelin	235ft 10in (71.88m)
4 Women's discus	235ft 7in (71.8m)
5 Men's discus	233ft 5in (71.16m)
6 Women's shot	73ft 8in (22.45m)
7 Men's shot	72ft 8in (22.15m)

The table *above* lists record distances in the various Olympic throwing events. These distances are also illustrated *right*.

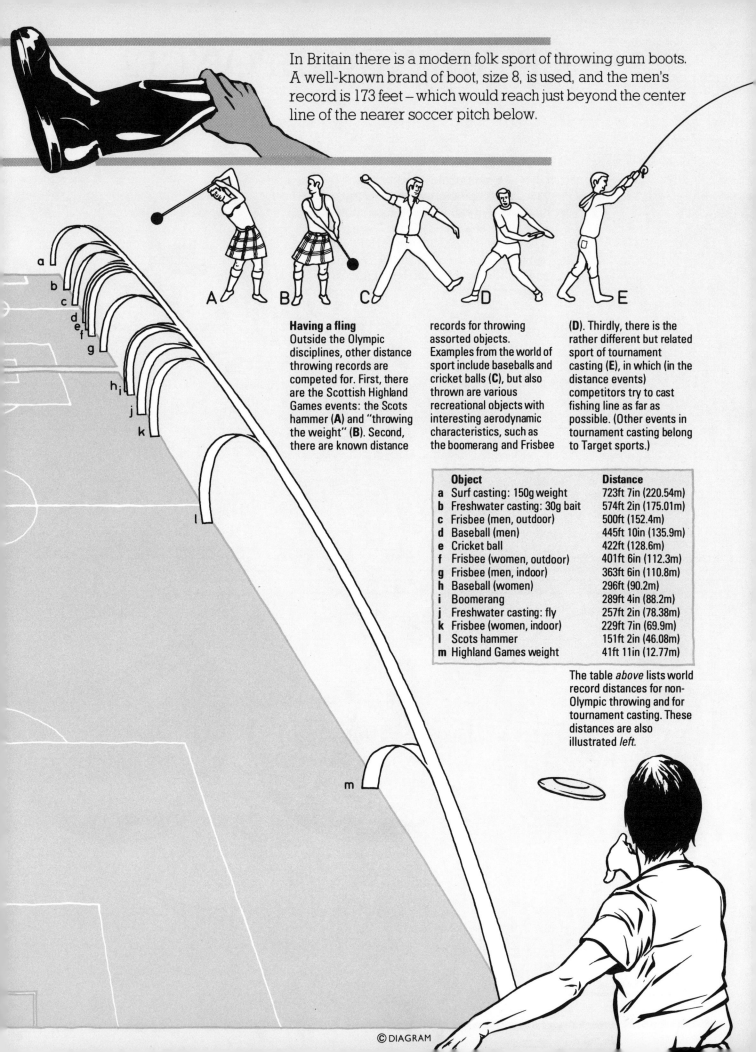

In Britain there is a modern folk sport of throwing gum boots. A well-known brand of boot, size 8, is used, and the men's record is 173 feet – which would reach just beyond the center line of the nearer soccer pitch below.

Having a fling
Outside the Olympic disciplines, other distance throwing records are competed for. First, there are the Scottish Highland Games events: the Scots hammer (**A**) and "throwing the weight" (**B**). Second, there are known distance records for throwing assorted objects. Examples from the world of sport include baseballs and cricket balls (**C**), but also thrown are various recreational objects with interesting aerodynamic characteristics, such as the boomerang and Frisbee (**D**). Thirdly, there is the rather different but related sport of tournament casting (**E**), in which (in the distance events) competitors try to cast fishing line as far as possible. (Other events in tournament casting belong to Target sports.)

	Object	Distance
a	Surf casting: 150g weight	723ft 7in (220.54m)
b	Freshwater casting: 30g bait	574ft 2in (175.01m)
c	Frisbee (men, outdoor)	500ft (152.4m)
d	Baseball (men)	445ft 10in (135.9m)
e	Cricket ball	422ft (128.6m)
f	Frisbee (women, outdoor)	401ft 6in (112.3m)
g	Frisbee (men, indoor)	363ft 6in (110.8m)
h	Baseball (women)	296ft (90.2m)
i	Boomerang	289ft 4in (88.2m)
j	Freshwater casting: fly	257ft 2in (78.38m)
k	Frisbee (women, indoor)	229ft 7in (69.9m)
l	Scots hammer	151ft 2in (46.08m)
m	Highland Games weight	41ft 11in (12.77m)

The table *above* lists world record distances for non-Olympic throwing and for tournament casting. These distances are also illustrated *left.*

© DIAGRAM

JUMPING: DISTANCE

Distance jumping in sport includes various forms of jumping proper (major and minor human events and a few animal sports), plus ramp jumping, in which the "jump" is created by an inclined ramp. Here we look at distance records in all of these, and notice how achievement in the long jump itself has improved over time.

Making great strides
In 1874 John Locke of Ireland achieved a long jump of 23ft 1½in. So the present men's world record *right* marks an improvement of 26% on this (**a**). In a much shorter period women have achieved an improvement of 28% (**b**), from a mark of 18ft 2in set in 1921.

The distant past? One of the few sport records we have from ancient times is a long jump of 23 feet 1½ inches by the Greek athlete Chionis in the 7th century BC – a feat not equalled until 1874.

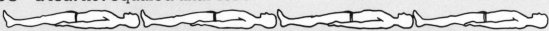

Long jumping

Left and *below* we illustrate the current long jump records in different areas of sport, and compare them with some achievements by animals.

1 Skateboard jumping 17ft (5.18m)
2 Frog jumping: single jump 17ft 6¾in (5.35m)
3 Women's long jump 23ft 3¼in (7.09m)
4 Horse long jump over water (official world record) 27ft 6½in (8.4m)
5 Men's long jump 29ft 2½in (8.9m)
6 Greyhound: long jump during hunting 30ft (9.14m)
7 Ice skating: barrel jumping 32ft (9.75m)
8 Horse long jump over water (Australian record) 32ft 10in (10m)
9 Red kangaroo c.40ft (12.2m)
10 Snow leopard c.50ft (15.24m)
11 Triple jump (men only) 58ft 8½in (17.89m)

9
10
11

© DIAGRAM

Ramp jumping

Below we illustrate record distances for jumps made from inclined ramps – and compare the distances with the lengths of two adjacent soccer pitches. In these various events, cars (**C**) and motorcycles (**D**) naturally provide their own power; water skiers (**A,B**) are pulled on to the ramp by powerboats going at set maximum speeds (36mph for men, 30mph for women); while for skiers (**E,F**) the power comes, of course, from the steep downhill incline of the ski-jump slope. The car and motorcycle events are often looked at in terms of numbers of parked cars cleared, but we give distances to allow easier comparison. (The car event is sometimes called a T-bone dive.) The drawing also shows to the same scale, in one corner of the first field, the long jumping records given above.

A Women's water ski jump 135ft 2in (41.2m)
B Men's water ski jump 196ft 4in (59.84m)
C Automobile T-bone dive 196ft 5in (59.86m)
D Motorcycle jump 212ft (64.6m)
E Women's ski jump 321ft 6in (98m)
F Men's ski jump 590ft 6in (180m)

F

JUMPING: HEIGHT

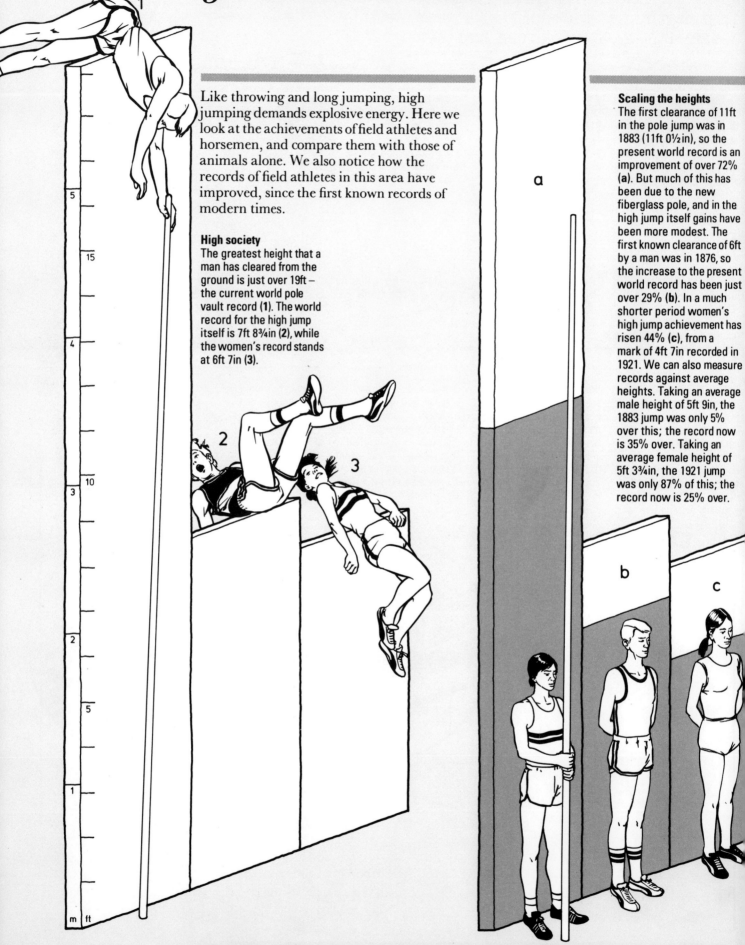

Like throwing and long jumping, high jumping demands explosive energy. Here we look at the achievements of field athletes and horsemen, and compare them with those of animals alone. We also notice how the records of field athletes in this area have improved, since the first known records of modern times.

High society
The greatest height that a man has cleared from the ground is just over 19ft – the current world pole vault record (**1**). The world record for the high jump itself is 7ft 8¾in (**2**), while the women's record stands at 6ft 7in (**3**).

Scaling the heights
The first clearance of 11ft in the pole jump was in 1883 (11ft 0½in), so the present world record is an improvement of over 72% (**a**). But much of this has been due to the new fiberglass pole, and in the high jump itself gains have been more modest. The first known clearance of 6ft by a man was in 1876, so the increase to the present world record has been just over 29% (**b**). In a much shorter period women's high jump achievement has risen 44% (**c**), from a mark of 4ft 7in recorded in 1921. We can also measure records against average heights. Taking an average male height of 5ft 9in, the 1883 jump was only 5% over this; the record now is 35% over. Taking an average female height of 5ft 3¾in, the 1921 jump was only 87% of this; the record now is 25% over.

Going up in the world? If the world high jump record holder went to the moon, the weaker gravity would allow him to jump to 48½ft – high enough to clear the combined height of three London double-decker buses with 5ft to spare.

Event	Record height
1 Pole vault (men only)	19ft 2in (5.84m)
2 Men's high jump	7ft 8¾in (2.36m)
3 Women's high jump	6ft 7in (2.01m)
4 Horse high jump – Australian record	8ft 4in (2.54m)
5 Horse high jump – official record	8ft 1¼in (2.47m)
6 Horse high jump – bareback record	6ft 7in (2.01m)

Riding high *below*
An Australian record for horse high jumping stands at 8ft 4in (**4**), but the official international record is 8ft 1¼in (**5**). The bareback record is 6ft 7in (**6**) – exactly equal to the current women's world high jump record.

High and mighty *right*
The highest known leap of any creature from the surface of our planet was an estimated 30ft by a Mako shark (**A**), hooked by fishermen off the coast of the USA and recorded on film. On our scale his achievement is well off the top of the page. The highest known jump by a land animal is 18ft by a puma, leaping into a tree (**B**). The best effort by a domestic animal is an 11ft 8in leap and scramble by a German Shepherd dog (Alsatian) (**C**), over a training obstacle.

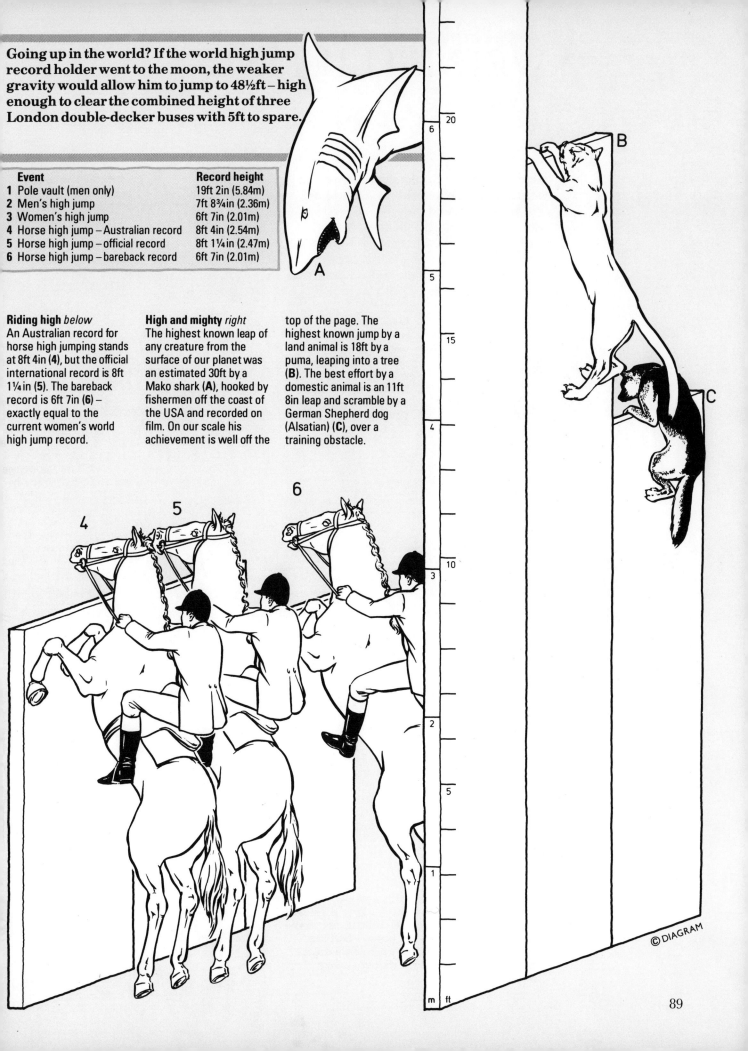

© DIAGRAM

89

WEIGHTLIFTING

Here we compare the two forms of sport weightlifting. Olympic lifting features two lifts: the snatch, and the clean and jerk. It demands coordination, balance, and flexibility, as well as strength. Powerlifting, the other form, is more a matter of pure strength, and employs three lifts: squat, dead lift, and bench press.

Lifting the standard
In the 1920 Olympics the winner in the top weight class achieved a clean and jerk of 120kg (264½lb). It would not impress anyone today, for it's less than the current flyweight record of 142.5kg (314lb).

World records *left and right* We show the current world records for each of the lifts below – in actual weight, and in terms of numbers of 18-year-old girls. (The average 18-year-old girl in the USA weighs 120lb.)

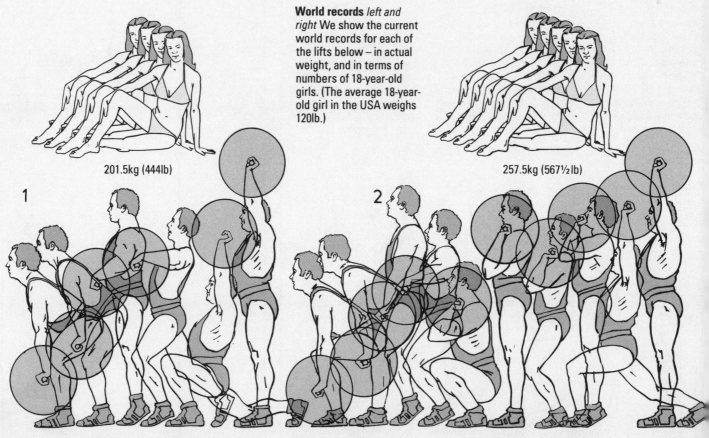

201.5kg (444lb)   257.5kg (567½lb)

1   2

Olympic lifting *above*
Snatch (**1**) The lifter must lift the bar in a single continuous movement till his arms are fully extended above his head. As the bar passes chest level, he either squats or "splits" to get beneath it. (The "split" style is shown.) He then gets upright in his own time.

Clean and jerk (**2**) First the lifter brings the bar to his shoulders, while he squats or "splits." (The usual squat style is shown.) He then recovers to upright position; splits to get his arms fully extended above his head; and finally recovers again to upright.

The larger a creature is, the less efficient it is as a weightlifter. An Asiatic elephant can support 1 ton on its back – but that is only a quarter of its own bodyweight. An ant can lift 50 times its own body bodyweight!

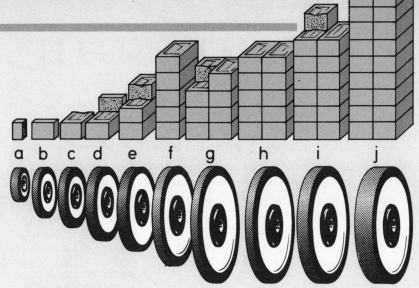

The weights

Only disk barbells are used in weightlifting. The barbell and its fittings weigh 25kg (55lb 2oz), and the disks are marked with their weights in kilograms. *Left* we compare the various disks used with their equivalent weight in bricks. An average building brick weighs about 2kg (4lb 6½oz).

a 0.25kg (0.55lb)
b 0.5kg (1.10lb)
c 1.25kg (2.76lb)
d 2.5kg (5.51lb)
e 5kg (11.02lb)
f 10kg (22.05lb)
g 15kg (33.07lb)
h 20kg (44.09lb)
i 25kg (55.11lb)
j 50kg (110.23lb)

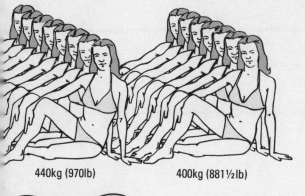

440kg (970lb)   400kg (881½lb)

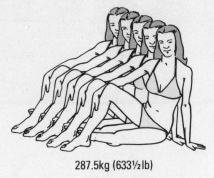

287.5kg (633½lb)

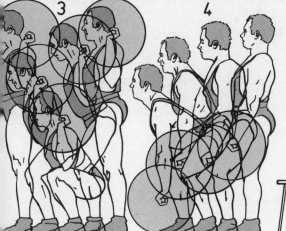

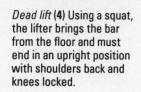

©DIAGRAM

Powerlifting *above*
Squat (**3**) The lifter begins with the bar across his shoulders at the back of the neck. He does a deep knee bend, then recovers to an upright position. At the low point of his squat, his thighs must pass the horizontal.

Dead lift (**4**) Using a squat, the lifter brings the bar from the floor and must end in an upright position with shoulders back and knees locked.

Bench press (**5**) Lying on a bench, the lifter begins with the bar held at arm's length. He lowers the bar until it touches his chest, and then must return it to its original position.

Weight classes
Weightlifters only compete against others of similar bodyweight. *Below* we list the weight categories used. Olympic

weightlifting and powerlifting share the same categories, but the names given are only used in Olympic lifting.

Class	Maximum weight
Flyweight	52kg (114½lb)
Bantamweight	56kg (123½lb)
Featherweight	60kg (132¼lb)
Lightweight	67.5kg (148¾lb)
Middleweight	75kg (165¼lb)
Light heavyweight	82.5kg (181¾lb)
Middle heavyweight	90kg (198¼lb)
First heavyweight	100kg (220½lb)
Second heavyweight	110kg (242½lb)
Super heavyweight*	110+kg (242½+lb)

*powerlifting has a further top weight class: 125+kg (275½+lb).

OTHER STRENGTH SPORTS

We now consider three other sports in which strength is the main element – though skill, of course, also plays its part. The tug-of-war is a mainly European form of sport, and steel strandpulling mainly British, while the event known as "tossing the caber" is peculiar to the tradition of the Scottish Highland Games.

Tug-of-war *below*
Teams of eight tug at opposite ends of a long rope, each trying to pull the other out of position. The winner is decided on the best of three pulls. Competitions may be on a knock-out basis, or on points with group winners proceeding to a final. During a pull, the pullers must keep their feet ahead of their knees at all times. Boots worn must have heels flush with the soles, and no knots or loops in the rope or special grips are allowed (except for the anchor man – end man –

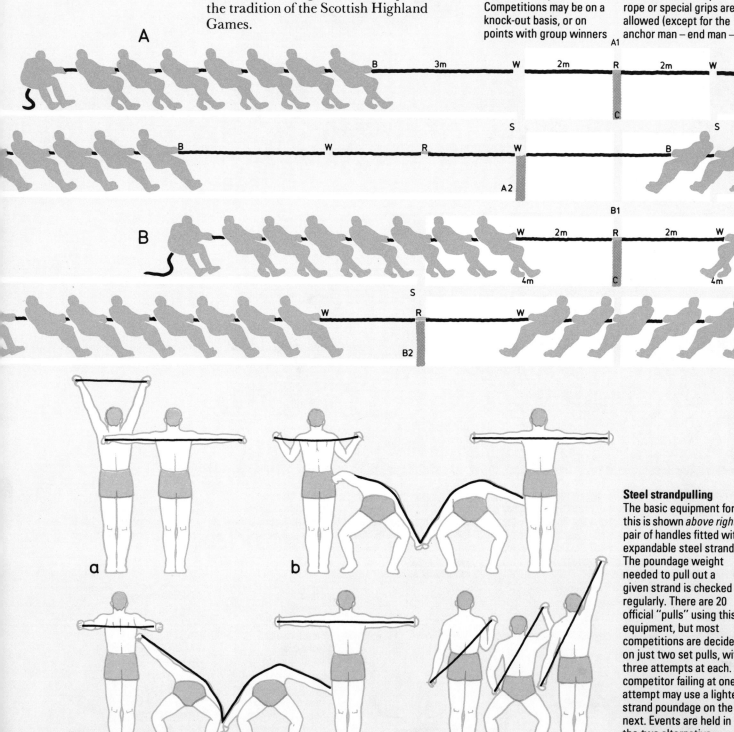

Steel strandpulling
The basic equipment for this is shown *above right:* a pair of handles fitted with expandable steel strands. The poundage weight needed to pull out a given strand is checked regularly. There are 20 official "pulls" using this equipment, but most competitions are decided on just two set pulls, with three attempts at each. A competitor failing at one attempt may use a lighter strand poundage on the next. Events are held in the two alternative bodyweight classifications ("stone" and "half-stone")

The caber used at the Highland Games at Braemar in Scotland is 19ft 3in long – making it equal to the height of three average men and one woman standing on one another's shoulders!

who may pass the rope around his body in a specified way). Events are in weight classes based on the total weight of all team members. International weight classes are 560kg (1234½lb), 640kg (1411lb), and 720kg (1587¼lb) National events often include further weight divisions and an unlimited (catchweight) class. Ground and rope markings for outdoor (**A**) and indoor (**B**) events are illustrated *below left* and listed in the key *below right*. The nearest member of each team must grip the rope within 30cm (11¾in) of its outermost mark (the blue tape on the outdoor rope, the white on the indoor). The pull begins with the center tape of the rope in line with the ground center line (**A1, B1**). A pull of 4m (13ft 1½in) is needed to win. In outdoor events, this is achieved when one of the white tapes on the rope is pulled over the opposite ground sideline (**A2**). In indoor events, it is when the center tape is pulled over one of the ground sidelines (**B2**).

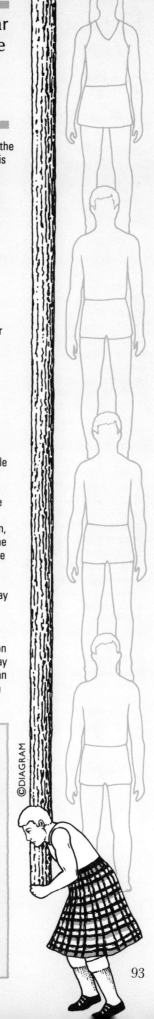

Rope markings
R central red tape
W white side tape
B blue side tape (outdoor only)
Ground markings
C center line
S sideline

Tossing the caber *right*
The caber is a section of tree trunk, of considerable length and weight. (The record length is 25ft, the record weight 280lb.) The competitor cradles the caber's base, makes a run, and tries to pitch it into the air. The aim is to make the caber turn on itself longitudinally, and land with its base pointing away from the thrower ("12 o'clock toss"). Each competitor has three attempts, and is judged on the best. A new caber may be shortened if no one can toss it, but once tossed a caber may never be cut.

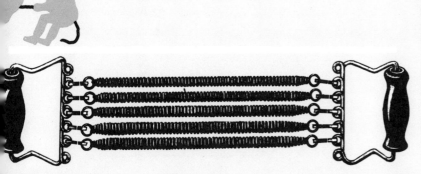

given in the table *right*. If two competitors in a weight category achieve equal poundages on a pull, the lighter man wins (but competitors with a short arm reach have a penalty deduction against the poundages they pull). The diagrams *left* show the Championship pulls in the British Open (the effective world championship).The 'stone-class" pulls are a overhead downward knuckles in a backpress anyhow. The "half-stone" class pulls are c dislocation anyhow d right arm push.

"Stone" class*	"Half-stone" class
84lb (6 stone)	77lb (5½ stone) mosquitoweight
98lb (7 stone)	91lb (6½ stone) paperweight
112lb (8 stone)	105lb (7½ stone) flyweight
126lb (9 stone)	119lb (8½ stone) bantamweight
140lb (10 stone)	133lb (9½ stone) featherweight
154lb (11 stone)	147lb (10½ stone) lightweight
168lb (12 stone)	161lb (11½ stone) middleweight
182lb (13 stone)	175lb (12½ stone) light heavyweight
196lb (14 stone)	189lb (13½ stone) middle heavyweight
217lb (15½ stone)	217lb (15½ stone) heavyweight
217+lb (15½+ stone)	217+lb (15½+ stone) superheavyweight

*"stone" class categories do not have names, except for the 15½-stone category (heavyweight) and the 15½+-stone category (superheavyweight).

© DIAGRAM

DISPLAY EVENTS

We now come to a group of sports which we have called the "display events" – those in which competitors are judged by observation of how well they perform some skill. The events cover a wide range, but a number deal with the movement of the human body, and here some interesting comparisons can be made.

Degrees of difficulty
In many display events, a competitor has some choice of which maneuvers to attempt. In these cases, his final score needs to reflect not only how well he succeeded in what he tried to do, but also how difficult the feat was that he attempted. Because of this, many of these sports list "degrees of difficulty" or "tariff values" for all the various recognized maneuvers, and these are used in calculating a competitor's score.

Patterns
In some display events, the aim is to use the human body to form patterns in various ways. In some cases, these are static patterns, made by a group of human figures. For example, in the various team free-fall events in sport parachuting (a) the patterns are in a horizontal plane, although the team as a whole is of course falling vertically toward the ground. Similarly in synchronized swimming (b) some static horizontal patterns are included.
By contrast, the canopy display events of sport parachuting aim at vertical human patterns (c), and these also appear in sports acrobatics (d). In other display events, we are looking at patterns formed by the movement of a single human figure – whether in a horizontal plane, as in figure skating (e), or in a vertical one, as in the example shown from synchronized swimming (f).

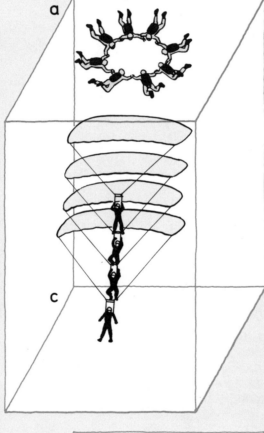

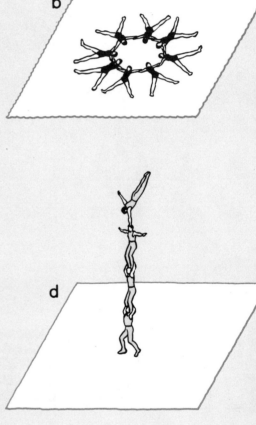

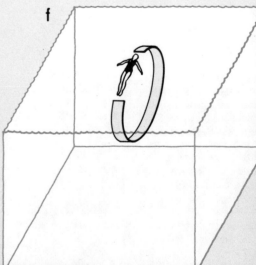

Movements

In another aspect of the display events, the emphasis is not on the pattern formed, but on the movement itself: the achievement of an action by the body through one or more planes. Often the same movement occurs in very dissimilar sports. Perhaps the most obvious example is the somersault or tumble (**A**), which occurs in sports as different as sports acrobatics (**1**) and barefoot water skiing (**2**). Equally common are twisting movements of the body (**B**), whether through the air as in diving (**3**) or through water as in synchronized swimming (**4**). Spins (**C**) can occur either about a vertical axis (**a,b,c**) or about a horizontal one (**d**). Those about a vertical axis are featured especially in ice skating (**5**) and roller skating (**6**), and also in movements on the pommel horse in artistic gymnastics (**7**). Those about a horizontal axis also occur in artistic gymnastics, in typical moves on the bars and rings. In other cases the competitor is aiming to achieve a certain body posture as he moves through the air (**D**) – as in the "pikes" (**a**) and "tucks" (**b**) of trampolining (**8**), diving, and freestyle skiing (**9**). In still others he is aiming to "flip" abruptly from one body posture to another (**E**): both sports acrobatics and freestyle skiing provide examples. Finally, in some display events, one aim is simply to make a certain sequence or pattern of steps across a floor (**F**), as in modern rhythmic gymnastics (**10**) or in the ice dancing event in ice skating.

GYMNASTICS 1

Gymnastics routines are based on balletic and acrobatic movements, performed either with or without the use of specialized equipment. Each of the four main forms of the sport emphasizes different aspects of these movements. Here we look at the various pieces of apparatus, and at the sizes of the floor areas used in competition.

Artistic (Olympic) gymnastics

This is probably the best known form of gymnastics, and includes separate competitions for men and women. The gymnasts perform a series of balletic and acrobatic movements, either within a set floor area or on the various pieces of fixed apparatus shown to scale *below*. Men compete on the following.
a Floor: 12x12m (39ft 4½inx39ft 4½in) mat
b Rings: 18cm (7in) in diameter, hanging 50cm (20in) apart, and 2.50m (8ft 2in) above the ground.

The supporting frame is 5.50m (18ft) high, and 2.80m (9ft 2in) wide at the base.
c Pommel horse: 1.10m (3ft 7in) high, 1.63m (5ft 4in) long, 35cm (13½in) wide. The pommels are 12cm (4¾in) high, 28cm (11in) wide, and set 45cm (18in) apart in the center of the horse.
d Vaulting horse: 1.35m (4ft 5in) high. Remaining measurements as pommel horse, excluding pommels.
e Parallel bars: two bars, 3.50m (11ft 5in) long, set 42cm (17in) apart, and 1.60m (5ft 3in) above the ground.
f Horizontal bar: 2.40m (7ft

10in) long, set 2.55m (8ft 5in) high.
The floor area used in the women's competition is the same as that used by the men (**a**). The three pieces of apparatus used by women competitors are as follows.
g Balance beam: 5m (16ft 3in) long, 1.20m (3ft 11in) high, 10cm (4in) wide.
h Vaulting horse: 1.10m (3ft 7in) high. Other dimensions as men's vaulting horse (**d**).
i Asymmetric bars: lower bar 1.50m (4ft 11in) high, upper bar 2.30m (7ft 6in) high. Both bars are 3.50m (11ft 3in) long, and they are set 43cm (17in) apart.

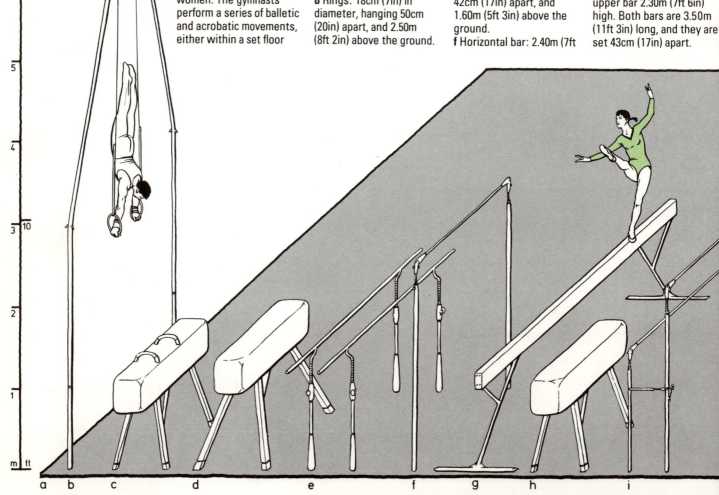

The maximum distance allowed for the approach run to the vault in men's artistic gymnastics is 20m (65ft 7½in) — half the length of the 40m (131ft 3in) track used for the solo events in sports acrobatics.

The 6m ribbon used in modern rhythmic gymnastics is only 11in shorter than the combined heights of four average women gymnasts.

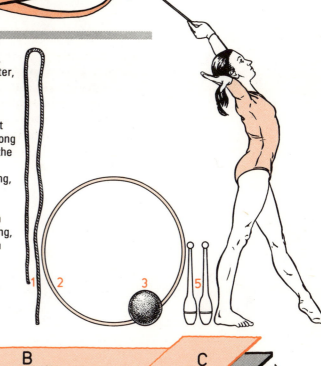

Modern rhythmic gymnastics

This form of gymnastics is for women only; there are events for individuals, and for groups of six. All the exercises are performed on a 12x12m floor area (**a**); competitors may choose between two areas, one covered with a mat and one without. The gymnasts carry out a series of balletic movements, based on a variety of steps, pivots, jumps, and flexions of the body; acrobatic movements are forbidden. Individual competitors perform one routine without apparatus, and one routine with each of the pieces of hand apparatus shown to scale *right*. Competitors in the group competition may choose which piece of apparatus they use, provided that it is identical for all members of the team.

1 Rope: the length of the hemp rope is proportional to the gymnast's height. When the gymnast stands on the center of the rope, the ends should reach to her armpits; a 5ft 2in tall woman would use a rope approximately 8ft 9in long.

2 Hoop: wood or plastic, 80-90cm (31½-35½in) in diameter

3 Ball: rubber or plastic, 18-20cm (7-7⅞in) diameter, minimum weight 400g (14oz)

4 Ribbon: satin, 4-6cm (1⅝-2⅜in) wide, 6m (19ft 8in) long, but doubled along a length of 1m (39in) at the stick end. The stick is 50-60cm (19⅝-23⅝in) long, maximum diameter 1cm (⅜in)

5 Clubs: two clubs, each 40-50cm (15¾-19⅝in) long, minimum weight of each club 150g (5¼oz)

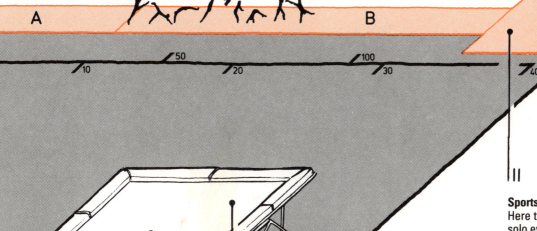

A   B   C

10   50   20   100   30   40

©DIAGRAM

II

I

Trampolining

Here the competitors perform series of acrobatic aerial movements between bounces on the trampoline bed. Individual, team, and synchronized competitions are held for men and women separately. The individual and the team competitions are run concurrently; each individual's score counts toward his team's overall score. In the synchronized competition, two gymnasts perform identical routines at the same time and in the same rhythm on separate trampolines, parallel and 2m (6ft 6in) apart.

Both men and women use the same size of trampoline (**I**), shown to scale *above left*. The central woven part, the bed, is 3.60-4.30m (11ft 10in-14ft 1½in) long, and 1.80-2.15m (5ft 11in-7ft 1in) wide. The frame is 0.95-1.05m (3ft 1in-3ft 5in) high. Competitions are held in a hall which is at least 8m (26ft 3in) high.

Sports acrobatics

Here there are separate solo events for men and women; events for men's, women's, and mixed pairs; and events for groups of three women or four men. Gymnasts perform a series of acrobatic maneuvers, including tumbling (a sequence of acrobatic jumps and somersaults performed in immediate succession) and balancing (building human pyramids). Solo events are held on a track covered in matting (**II**), shown *above*. The lengths of the sections are: approach run (**A**), 10m (32ft 9½in); horizontal sprung section (**B**), 25m (82ft); touchdown area (**C**), 5m (16ft 5in). Pair and group events are held on a 12x12m area of floor covered by a mat (**a**).

GYMNASTICS 2

On the previous page we compared the various types of equipment used in the main forms of gymnastics. Here we look at the exercises performed on the fixed pieces of apparatus used in artistic gymnastics and trampolining. On subsequent pages we go on to look at floor exercises and exercises using hand apparatus.

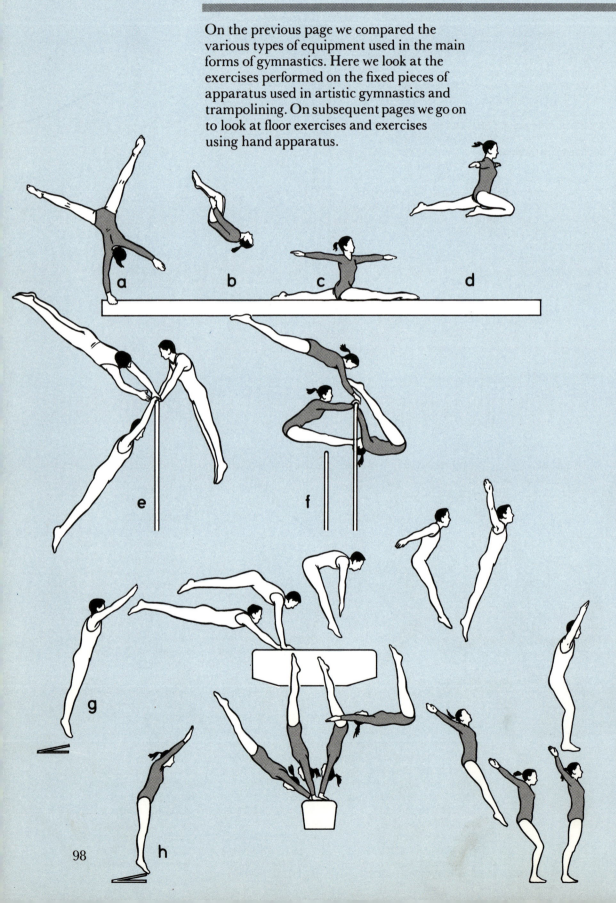

Balance beam *below left*
The exercise, which lasts 80–105 seconds, must make use of the full length of the narrow beam. Gymnasts perform a linked series of jumps, somersaults, balances, and horizontal and vertical turns. The ways in which they mount and dismount from the beam are also considered by the judges. We show examples of some of these movements:
a vertical turn, e.g. one-arm cartwheel
b somersault
c balance, e.g. splits
d jump, e.g. stag leap

Horizontal and asymmetric bars *left*
In both the men's horizontal bar exercise (**e**) and the women's asymmetric bars exercise (**f**), the emphasis is on continuous vertical swinging and circling movements, and on changes of grip on the bar. Men must include at least one movement in which they release both of their hands from the bar simultaneously, and then regrasp the bar with both hands at the same time. Women must display good use of both bars.

Vaulting horse *left*
Men vault the length of the horse, and women across the width. In vaulting, the emphasis is on aerial movement; gymnasts are judged on their lift, flight through the air, and overall balance. The three main types of vault are the horizontal vaults, such as the Hecht vault (**g**); the handstand vaults, such as the Yamashita (**h**); and vaults which include turns in the air. The gymnast's hands must always be placed on the horse during the vault. Each competitor has two vaults in each round.

A form of vaulting horse was in use during the time of the Roman Empire – cavalrymen used a wooden horse to practice jumping in and out of the saddle.

Parallel bars *below* **and rings** *right*
These exercises are based on swinging and holding movements, and must also include an element of strength. On the parallel bars (**i**), the vertical swinging movements should predominate; the gymnast must include at least one movement in which he releases and then regrasps the bars simultaneously with both hands. In the exercises on the rings (**j**), swinging, strength, and holding movements should all be included. The gymnast is required to perform two handstands, one of which should be dependent on swinging movements, and the other on strength. The rings should remain stationary throughout the exercise.

Pommel horse *below*
Here again the emphasis is on continuous swinging and circling movements, but this time in a horizontal plane. Double leg circles (**k**) should predominate, although other possible movements are undercuts, single leg circles, and scissors movements (**l**). Gymnasts may use one or both pommels to support themselves, and must make good use of all parts of the horse.

Trampoline *right*
Again the emphasis is on aerial movement: the gymnasts perform series of twists and somersaults in the air between springing from the bed of the trampoline and landing on it again. Men and women each perform 10 linked maneuvers in each round of a competition. These maneuvers may include both single and multiple somersaults, performed straight or with twist, pike, or tuck, using a variety of different starting and landing positions. Shown *right* is a somersault with 2½ twists landing in a back drop (**m**). Competitors must land on their feet after the tenth movement, and remain standing for at least three seconds.

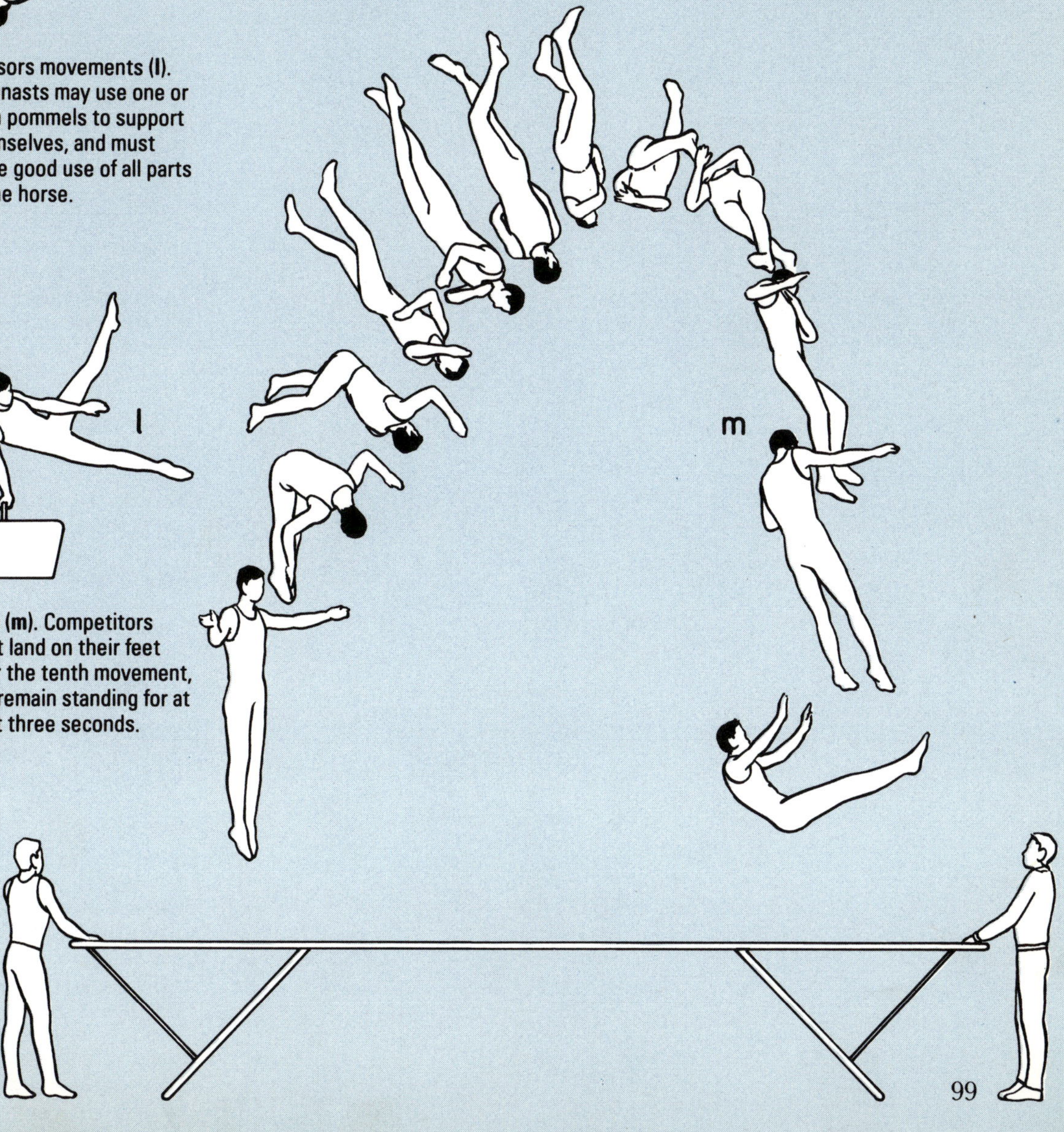

99

GYMNASTICS 3

Floor exercises in gymnastics range from the balletic movements of modern rhythmic gymnastics to the rapid series of aerial somersaults which make up the tumbling runs in sports acrobatics. In artistic gymnastics the floor exercises combine elements of both types of movement.

Modern rhythmic gymnastics
Gymnasts competing in the individual event perform six exercises, to music of their own choice. The first demonstrates body technique (**a**), and is in the nature of a dance routine. It should include rhythmic step sequences, jumps with or without turns, body flexions and waves demonstrating extreme suppleness of the spine, balances on various parts of the body, and pivots of 360° or more on the toes of one foot.

The five exercises with hand apparatus combine these body movements with the techniques appropriate to the piece of apparatus used. In the rope exercise (**b**), the emphasis is on skipping over the rope (demonstrating as many variations as possible), and on body movements accompanied by swings and throws of the rope. Swings and throws are likewise characteristic of the hoop exercise (**c**), as are rolling the hoop along parts of the body or along the floor. Gymnasts may also jump over the rolling hoop, or pass through it while it is moving. Work with the ball (**d**) will include rolling it along the floor or on parts of the body, throwing, catching, and bouncing it, and balancing it on one hand. The clubs (**e**) are used to extend the line of the arm and emphasize large swinging and circling movements. They may also be thrown and caught, and used to describe small circles or to beat rhythmic patterns on the floor or against each other. In the ribbon exercise (**f**) the emphasis is on the various patterns formed by the ribbon – circles, spirals, figures of eight, and waves. Throwing and catching may

also be included.
The group exercise (**g**) is also performed to music. The gymnasts have their own choice of apparatus, but each member of the team must use an identical piece of equipment. As well as demonstrating body technique and the characteristic techniques of the apparatus chosen, the routine must include at least six formations or floor patterns, such as circles, lines, and triangles. The gymnasts must also exchange the apparatus between themselves in at least four different ways.

Artistic gymnastics
Here the floor exercises are for individuals: there is no group event. The women's exercises (**h**) are performed to music; the gymnasts combine the balletic types of movement used in modern rhythmic gymnastics with acrobatic movements and elements of tumbling. A typical routine could therefore include step sequences, handsprings, cartwheels, balances, pivots, and a variety of somersaults. Although the men's exercise (**i**) must be rhythmic and harmonious, it is not performed to music. The routine should emphasize acrobatic skills with a variety of leaps and somersaults. It should also include strength movements, and balances which must be held for at least two seconds.

Until the 1930s, the gymnastics floor exercises in the Olympic Games were usually mass performances. All members of a team had to perform the same exercise simultaneously – and a team could include as many as 100 gymnasts!

Sports acrobatics

In the individual event, the emphasis is on tumbling. Competitors perform three tumbling runs – sequences of at least three different somersaults or saltos (somersaults in the air) linked by acrobatic jumps. In the first routine, the straight run (**j**), any turns must be of 180° or less; in the second, the twisting run (**k**), turns must be a minimum of 180°. The third routine, the combined run, includes both straight and twisting elements.

The exercises for the pairs and for the women's trio are accompanied by music. Again there are three routines. In the first, the balance routine (**l**), the gymnasts create a series of linked pyramids and balances, supporting each other on different parts of the body. The second, the tempo routine (**m**), mainly emphasizes flight through the air, but must also include tumbling elements and linking choreographic movements. The third is a combined routine, and includes both balance and tempo elements.

The men's fours perform only two routines, a tempo routine and a balance routine. The tempo routine is similar to that for the pairs and the women's trio, but the balance exercise (**n**) is somewhat different. There is no music, and the gymnasts are expected to create only one or two pyramids, which must be held for a minimum of four seconds.

Time limits

Most floor exercises must be performed within a set period of time. In modern rhythmic gymnastics each individual exercise, with or without apparatus, lasts 1-1½ minutes. The group exercise lasts for 2½-3 minutes; an extra 15 seconds are allowed for positioning the gymnasts on the floor before the exercise begins. In artistic gymnastics, the men's floor exercise lasts for 50-70 seconds, the women's for 1-1½ minutes. There are no time limits for the individual tumbling runs in sports acrobatics. The tempo and balance routines for the pairs and for the women's trio each last for a maximum of 2½ minutes; the maximum for the combined routine is 3 minutes. The men's fours tempo exercise also lasts for 2½ minutes; there is no time limit on the men's fours balance routine.

SKATING

The two skating display events – figure skating and ice dancing – are the same for both ice and roller skaters. Solo figure skaters perform a program of compulsory figures, followed by two different free-skating programs; pairs figure skaters only perform the freestyle sections. Ice dancing is an event for pairs only.

Edges and steps *left*
The ice skates (A) used in figure skating and ice dancing have hollow ground blades. As a result, each blade has two edges: the inside edge (i.e. on the inside of the foot), and the outside edge. The roller skating equivalents are the inside and outside pairs of wheels. All the skating movements are performed on one edge or the other. Each specific step is described in terms of the foot used (L, left; R, right); the direction (B, backward; F, forward); and the edge used (O, outside edge; I, inside edge). So RBI

indicates a step that is to be skated backward on the right foot using the inside edge of the skate.

Compulsory figures
The patterns formed by these figures are based on two or three linked circles; the figure shown *above right* is a double three. In performing the figures ice skaters leave tracings on the ice which are examined by the judges; roller

skaters skate over circles painted on the rink. Figures may be skated with either forward or backward steps, on the left or the right foot, on one or the other edge, or in various combinations of these. In competition, three figures, each with a prescribed sequence of

steps, are selected by lot from those on a previously announced list; each skater repeats each figure three times. They are judged on technical merit; the judges check the tracings for any signs of faulty execution.

1

4

Free skating
There are two free-skating sections in competitions: the short program, and the free (or long) program. Both sections are marked on technical merit and artistic impression. The short program is based on a number of prescribed

free-skating movements; there are six compulsory elements for pairs, and seven for solo competitors. Skaters may arrange these movements in any sequence they choose within the two-minute time limit, to music of their own choice.

The free program is also performed to the skater's own choice of music. As the name implies, there are no restrictions on the elements which skaters may include in their free program. The women competitors skate for four minutes, men competitors

and pairs for five minutes. Most typical free-skating elements fall into one of the following groups. *Above* and *opposite* we show an example of each.
1 Jumps, e.g. lutz
2 Spins, e.g. camel spin
3 Lifts, e.g. three jump lift
4 Spirals, e.g. death spiral

5 Step sequences, e.g. scissors backward cross-over
6 Glides, e.g. spread eagle
7 Shadow skating (pairs skaters performing the same elements at the same time, but without being in contact with one another)

A standard 60 x 30m (196ft 10in x 198ft 5in) competition ice rink has an area of 19,374½ft². So one ice dancing couple needs the same amount of space as more than a dozen *corps de ballet* – the area of stage used for ballet at London's Royal Opera House is only 1600ft².

a

b

Dancing

Ice and roller dancing competitions are in three separate sections: the compulsory dances; the original set pattern dance; and a four-minute free program. In the three compulsory dances (which are chosen by lot from a previously announced list), skaters are judged on their accuracy, rhythm, and presentation of the set step sequences that make up the dance. Shown *above* are (a) the first few steps from one typical compulsory dance, the Westminster Waltz, and (b) the pattern formed on the rink by its complete step sequence. Each of the compulsory dances is repeated a set number of times – three in this case. The original set pattern dance also consists of repeated step sequences. The rhythm for the dance is set annually, but each couple choose their own tempo, music, and pattern of steps, repeating them for three circuits of the rink. In the free program, couples choose their own non-repeating sequences of steps and dance movements, and perform to music of their own choice. They may include some free-skating movements, but these must be strictly limited. Both the original set pattern dance and the free program are marked on technical merit and artistic impression.

2

3

5

©DIAGRAM

6

7

SKIING 1

We traditionally think of skiing as a racing event. But here we consider a much more recent form of the sport – freestyle skiing, which emphasizes acrobatic and balletic movements. In water skiing, it is the freestyle – "tricks" – event which is the more established, water ski racing being the comparative newcomer.

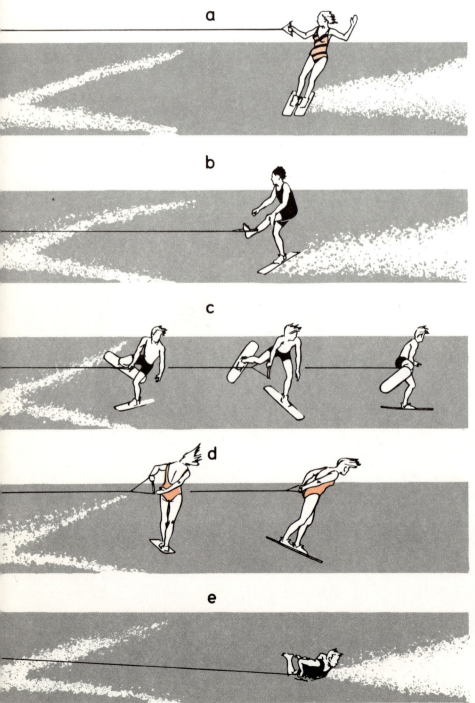

a

b

c

d

e

Tricks *below left*

Each water skiing trick has a set points score; the more difficult the trick, the higher the score it carries. If a competitor completes a trick correctly, he is awarded the points; he is not judged on style or presentation. Competitors each choose their own program, putting together a series of tricks in the attempt to score as many points as possible within the time allowed. But if a competitor falls during the performance of any trick his run is automatically concluded.

Tricks may be performed on one ski or two, and may be water turns (performed on the surface of the water) or wake turns (performed while moving across the wake of the boat with air visible between the skis and the water). An example of each type of trick is shown *left*:

a Water turn on two skis, e.g. two-ski side slide

b Water turn on one ski, e.g. toe-hold side slide

c Wake turn on two skis, e.g. wake step front to back

d Wake turn on one ski, e.g. wake 360°

The reverse of a trick also scores providing it follows on immediately from the trick itself.

The tricks used in barefoot water skiing are very similar; they may be wake or water turns performed on one foot or both feet. However, if a barefoot skier falls, he may recover his position by means of a tumbleturn (**e**) and then continue his run, although he will not score for the trick in which he fell. Tumbleturns are also tricks in their own right.

Aerials *opposite*

These are acrobatic leaps from prepared snow jumps. Aerials may be upright, e.g. the backscratcher (**1**); upright rotational, e.g. the helicopter (**2**); or inverted (front or back single or multiple somersaults with or without twist) e.g. tucked front somersault (**3**). Each maneuver has a degree of difficulty value used in calculating the final score. Skiers are judged on their performance of the maneuver, on the height achieved in the jump, and on the style of their takeoff and landing.

Ballet *opposite*

Ballet skiers perform a free program of maneuvers in harmony with their choice of music. Broadly speaking, there are four types of maneuver; we show an example of each:

4 Jumps, e.g. axel

5 Spins, e.g. one-ski 360°

6 Step sequences, e.g. reverse crossover

7 Somersaults with the poles, e.g. gut flip

Skiers are judged on their overall performance (including choreography), the degrees of difficulty of the maneuvers, and the style and fluidity of their movement.

Moguls *opposite*

Skiing short sharp turns down a steep snow slope creates a series of bumps called moguls. Mogul competitions are held on courses densely covered with these bumps. Skiers are judged on the aerial maneuvers (**8**) they perform off the tops of the moguls, and on the technique and style of the turns (**9**) which they make around them. Competitors are also timed over the course, and awarded further marks for speed. (Somersaulting is forbidden, as the speed of the event would make it a dangerous maneuver.)

8

9

105

SKIING 2

Tricks events in both water skiing and barefoot water skiing use courses marked out with buoys on stretches of calm water. But the courses for the three freestyle snow skiing events are very different from one another, ranging from the smooth, relatively gentle slope used for ballet to the steep, rough-surfaced mogul course.

Water skiing
The courses used in the tricks events need to be symmetrical, as they are run in both directions. Similar course layouts are used for water skiing (**I**) and barefoot water skiing (**II**), but the distances involved differ. The two courses are shown to scale *below left*. For water skiing, the two entrance buoys at each end are 15m (49ft) apart. The left- and right-hand second entrance buoys are separated by approximately 175m (574ft) of water. In barefoot water skiing, the entrance buoys are in pairs, forming gates that are approximately 2m (6ft 6½in) wide. The two gates at each end are 31m (102ft) apart, and the left- and right-hand second entrance buoys are separated by about 400m (1312ft) of water.

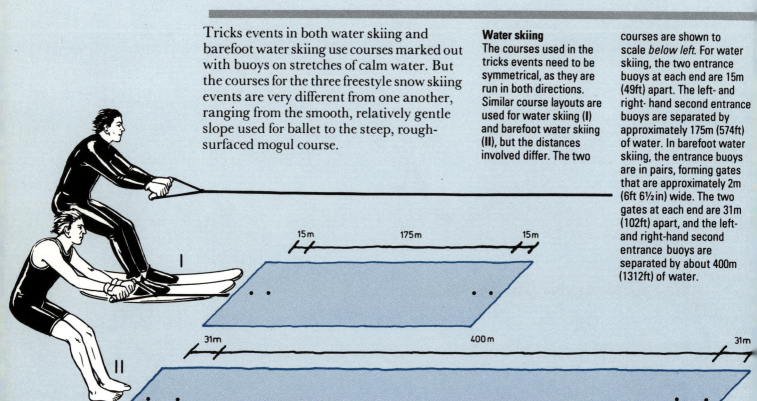

Ballet
The course, shown to scale (**A**), is covered in smooth, firm snow, free of any obstacles. The skiing area is 200-250m (656-820ft) long, and 30-40m (98-131ft) wide. The course slopes as evenly as possible, at an angle of 12°-20°.

Moguls
This is the only skiing course where smooth snow is not required! Instead, the skiing area, shown to scale (**B**), should be heavily and evenly covered in moguls. The course is a minimum 200m (656ft) long, and 20-35m (66-115ft) wide. It slopes steeply at an angle of 28°-45°. Three control gates, 8-15m (26-49ft) wide, mark the center of the course. Competitors may choose their own line over the moguls provided that they ski through these gates.

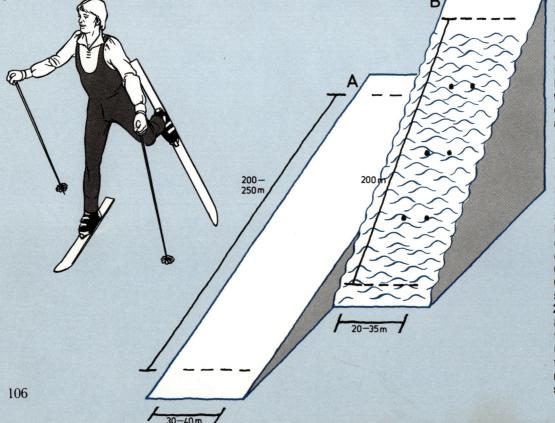

If only they could skate on a slope, six ice dancers could perform their routines in the space used by one ballet skier. The 200x30m minimum-size ballet course is over three times the length of a 60x30m competition ice rink.

Aerials

The jumps and landing hill of the aerial course, shown to scale (**C**), are built up with snow on the natural contours of the hill. There are three jumps: the small kicker (**a**), used for single somersaults; the floater (**b**), used for upright and upright rotational aerials; and the large kicker (**c**), used for double and triple somersaults. The small kicker is a minimum 1.5m (4ft 11in) high, and sited a minimum 4m (13ft 1½in) from the knoll (**d**). The floater and the large kicker are both a minimum 1.7m (5ft 7in) high, and sited a minimum 8m (26ft 3in) from the knoll. The floater is less steeply inclined than the large kicker.

The knoll area slopes at an angle of 10° toward the landing hill (**e**). This is a minimum 30m (98ft) long and 15m (49ft) wide, slopes at approximately 37°, and is covered in at least 60cm (2ft) of softened snow. There are no prescribed dimensions for the runs into the jumps; skiers may chose their own starting points on these "inruns."

Times and trials

Water skiers and barefoot water skiers are judged on two runs, one in each direction of the course. They have 20 seconds in which to perform as many tricks as they choose. The timing begins when a competitor passes the second entrance buoy or gate, or when he makes his first movement toward a trick when he is between the first and second entrance buoys or gates. Water skiers have a three-minute interval between their two runs, barefoot water skiers have a two-minute interval.

Aerial skiers are judged on two jumps, which must be different from one another. Ballet skiers are judged on one run down the course; there is no time limit, and no limit to the number of maneuvers they may perform. Mogul skiers are also allowed one run, and they are usually expected to perform two aerials. Because mogul competitions are partly judged on speed, the skiers will obviously try to travel as fast as possible.

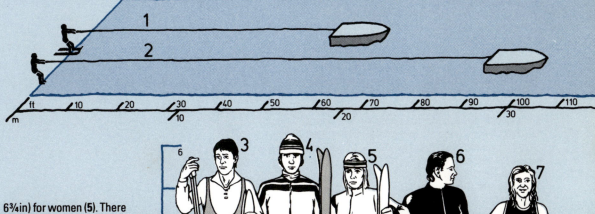

Tows

Shown to scale *right* are the lengths of towlines used in tricks events. The average length used in water skiing (**1**) is 30-50ft; in barefoot water skiing (**2**), the maximum length allowed is 26m (85ft) including the handle. Whether using skis or barefoot, the water skiers have their own choice of boat speed, usually averaging 15-20mph.

Skis and poles

These are shown to scale *right*. The flexible skis used in ballet events (**3**) must be a minimum of 81% of the skier's height; so a 6ft tall skier would use skis which were at least 4ft 10¼in long. His long ski poles would be restricted to 6ft; ski poles must not be longer than the skier! The minimum length for mogul skis is 1.80m (5ft 10¾in) for men (**4**), and 1.70m (5ft 6¾in) for women (**5**). There are no restrictions on the skis used in the aerial event, and the use of ski poles is optional. Water skiers may use one or two skis of any length; short, wide skis are the most usual. On average, a man would use skis about 42in long (**6**); a woman, skis about 40in long (**7**). Barefoot water skiers obviously perform their tricks with no skis at all!

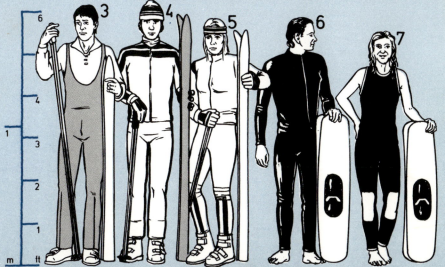

©DIAGRAM

SYNCHRONIZED SWIMMING

Synchronized swimming, which has been described as ballet in water, is a sport in which only women compete. As in many other display events, competitions include both a set-figure event and a freestyle program of the swimmer's own choice. Here we look at some of the maneuvers that are typical of each section.

Figure competition
Every four years, six groups of six figures each are chosen (from over 100 possibilities) for use in this solo competition; each group includes figures of a similar range of degrees of difficulty. The group that is to be performed in a competition is chosen by lot 24 hours before the event begins. Nearly all the figures are swum "on the spot" – that is, the swimmer remains in the same position relative to the edges of the pool, and there is little or no horizontal movement

a 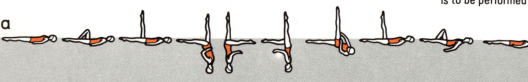 b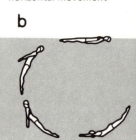

d  e

Routine competition
In this event solos, duets, and teams of between four and eight swimmers perform freestyle routines to music. The time limits are 3½ minutes for solos; 4 minutes for duets; and 5 minutes for teams. These limits include 20 seconds for movements around the sides of the pool before the swimmers enter the water. There are no restrictions on the figures or strokes that the competitors may use in their routines; some typical patterns that may be used are shown *right*. Patterns may be vertical, e.g. the fishtail (**A**), or horizontal, e.g. the star (**B**). They may also be static, e.g. the ballet leg circle (**C**), or moving, e.g. the dolphin (**D**). The judges consider the patterns made in the pool, the synchronization of the swimmers with one another, the interpretation of the music, and the variety of strokes and figures used. In the team competition, teams with more than four members automatically gain extra points.

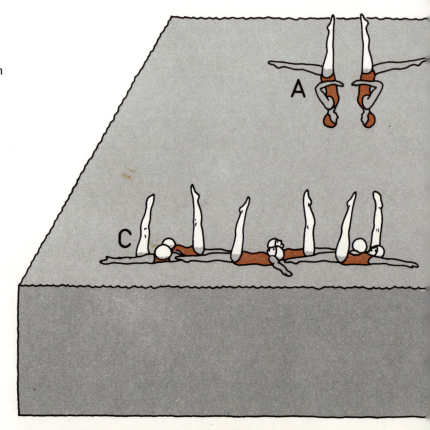

The minimum water area for the synchronized-swimming figure event is 12 x 12m (39ft 4½in x 39ft 4½in) – the same size as the mat for gymnastics floor exercises. But you could stack over 66 of the 4.5cm (1¾in) thick gymnastics mats in the required 3m (9ft 10¼in) minimum depth of water.

through the water. Each part of each figure must be clearly defined, and the performance must be slow and controlled and take place high in the water. In the illustration *below* we show six of the figures that are currently used in competition. The castle (a) starts with one of the most basic movements, the ballet leg, and also includes a half twist (i.e. rotating the body 180° about a vertical axis). A number of the movements are based on somersaults: in an arched position in the dolpholina (b); tucked, in the kip (c); and piked, in the somersub (d). The somersub also includes a vertical movement upward through the water; in the kip, the vertical movement is downward. The sword-fish straight leg (e) features a splits position and a "walkout"; the high-tower (f) emphasizes vertical patterns in the water. Other figures may include twisting and spinning movements; for example, the kip can be performed with 180° or 360° twists, or with a variety of spins. (Spins are twists that are performed while the swimmer is descending vertically through the water).

c

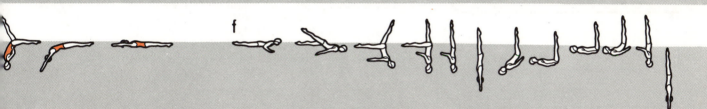

f

©DIAGRAM

B

D

DIVING

The main emphasis in competition diving is on performing somersaults in the air. Springboard divers gain the height they need for this by projecting themselves upward into the air from a flexible and resilient board. Highboard divers make their dives from a fixed platform and (at international level) from a greater height.

Diving boards
Listed in the table *below* are the height above the surface of the water (**a**), length (**b**), and width (**c**) of the diving boards shown to scale *below left*. (In competition, divers at international level use only the 3m springboard and the 10m platform, as dives from these boards attract the highest scores.) The recommended depth of water in the pool is 5m (16ft 4¾in).

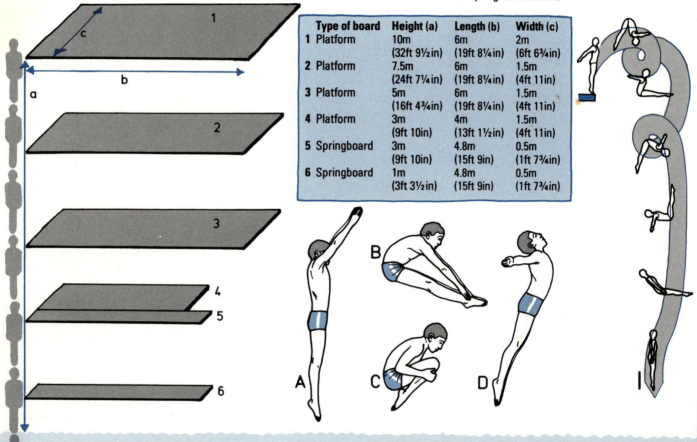

Type of board	Height (a)	Length (b)	Width (c)
1 Platform	10m	6m	2m
	(32ft 9½in)	(19ft 8¼in)	(6ft 6¾in)
2 Platform	7.5m	6m	1.5m
	(24ft 7¼in)	(19ft 8¼in)	(4ft 11in)
3 Platform	5m	6m	1.5m
	(16ft 4¾in)	(19ft 8¼in)	(4ft 11in)
4 Platform	3m	4m	1.5m
	(9ft 10in)	(13ft 1½in)	(4ft 11in)
5 Springboard	3m	4.8m	0.5m
	(9ft 10in)	(15ft 9in)	(1ft 7¾in)
6 Springboard	1m	4.8m	0.5m
	(3ft 3½in)	(15ft 9in)	(1ft 7¾in)

Body positions
Illustrated *above* are the four positions in which a diver may carry his body during his passage through the air. In all of them his legs and feet must be together, and his toes pointed, but the position of his arms is his own choice. In the straight position (**A**), the body may not be bent at the knees or at the hips. In the pike position (**B**), the body is bent at the hips, but must be kept straight at the knees. In the tuck position (**C**) the body is bent at the knees and hips into a compact ball; the hands are usually on the shins. In the free position (**D**) the body position is optional, providing that the legs and feet are kept together. This position may only be used in group V and VI dives.

The earliest form of competitive diving was called "plunging." The winner was the diver who floated the furthest distance in 60 seconds, after a headfirst standing dive from the side of the pool. The event was included in the 1904 Olympics.

Professional divers at Acapulco in Mexico regularly dive into 12ft of water from rocks 118ft high – rather like diving into the Thames at low tide from the high level footways of London's Tower Bridge!

Types of dive
Competition dives are classified into six groups. Groups I-V are for both springboard and platform divers; group VI is for platform divers only. In the illustrations *below* we give an example of a dive from each group. The group V dive is shown from a 3m springboard, the dives of other groups from a 10m platform.
Group I Forward dives with body facing the water, e.g. forward double somersault.
Group II Backward dives with body facing the platform, e.g. flying back somersault.
Group III Backward dives with body facing the water, e.g. reverse 1½ somersault.
Group IV Forward dives with body facing the platform, e.g. flying inward 1½ somersault.
Group V Twist dives, e.g. back 1½ somersault 2½ twists.
Group VI Armstand dives, e.g. armstand somersault.

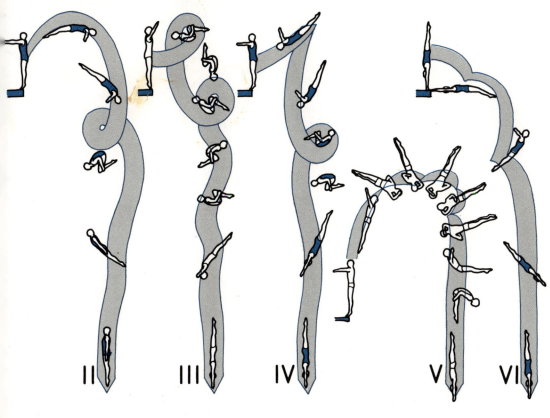

I   II   III   IV   V   VI

Mixed pairs high diving
above right This is a spectacular minority sport in which a man and woman dive simultaneously from two very high rigid platforms. On average, the platforms are 70-90ft above the surface of the water, with the upper platform 10ft above the lower. The man and woman may perform identical or different dives, but they always aim to enter the water at the same moment. If they succeed, they automatically score three extra marks. These marks are added to their basic score for the dive, which is the dive's tariff value multiplied by the judges' marks.

Diving competitions
Each dive has a tariff (degree of difficulty) value which, multiplied by the judges' marks, gives the score for that dive. Each competition round is in two parts, with a set number of dives in each. (The highest scoring divers in the first round go on to the final, where they repeat the same dives in the same order.) The first part of each springboard round is the same for men and women; they have to perform five dives valued up to 9.5. choose their own dives, but each dive must be selected from a different group. In the second part, men perform six dives and women five. Again each dive must be chosen from a different group, but here there is no limit to the total tariff value. In the first part of each highboard round, men and women perform four dives with a total tariff up to 7.6; in the second part men perform six dives without limit, and women perform four. Each dive in each part must be chosen from a different group.

Diving belle? In 1885, Sarah Henley jumped from the 250ft high Clifton Suspension Bridge, which crosses the River Avon in England. She landed unhurt – her crinoline had acted as a parachute.

BOARD CONTROL 1

These sports fall into two main groups, involving quite different kinds of skill. First we look at those sports in which the emphasis is on performing tricks on a flat surface – whether a strip of concrete or a calm stretch of water. So we contrast a water sport – freestyle boardsailing – with the land sport of flatland skateboarding.

Freestyle boardsailing
This sport features several types of trick, including:
a) normal sailing, but with the competitor in an unusual sailing position;
b) "rail rides," in which the board is sailed on edge;
c) unusual maneuvers with the sailboard;
d) acrobatics on the board.
Advanced tricks may cover elements of more than one of these. We show some typical examples at competition level.
A Lying down position
B Leeside reverse rail ride, back to sail
C Tail sink
D Head dip

Events may be open or in one-design classes. As the sport is still developing, competition rules vary. But generally there is an elimination round, in which set tricks have to be performed, and then a three-minute final in which competitors perform maneuvers of their own choice.

One very new sport is boardsailing on land – "landsailing" – and some of the trick maneuvers possible here are very similar to their waterborne originals. But, not having to fight the resistance of water, landsails build up much more speed (despite being up to 75% heavier). So a crash helmet is a good idea, even if no lifejacket is needed!

Flatland freestyle skateboarding *above*
Unlike skateboard bowl-riding (over the page) the main emphasis in flatland freestyle is on performing tricks using only your own energies. Maneuvers fall into four main categories, and we show one example of each.

1 Tricks with the board in its natural position: e.g. headstand.
2 Tricks with the board on edge: e.g. railer.
3 Tricks with one set of wheels off the ground at a time: e.g. one foot tail 360s.

4 Flying turns and flips: e.g. heli-pop.
5 Tricks with the board passing through an upside down position: e.g. 50/50 Casper.

Competition rules vary, but they typically involve a compulsory routine of 45-60 seconds and a free routine of 1½-2 minutes. (Background music may be used.) Tricks are scored on technical merit and artistic presentation.

One impressive skateboard trick is the automobile high jump. The skateboarder leaps from the board over the top of a car – and hopes to land back on the board as it emerges on the other side.

©DIAGRAM

113

BOARD CONTROL 2

Now we turn to those board sports in which conditions automatically give the board movement in three dimensions – whether on the face of a breaking wave or the curved side of a concrete bowl. Here the emphasis is on staying on the board and using the three-dimensional possibilities to the full. Again we can compare land and water events.

Surfing
A surfer attempts to ride waves as they approach the shoreline. His impetus comes from using the power of the wave. Most serious events are solo, and are either for full-size (malibu) boards (**A**) or for the shorter kneeboards (**B**). A competitor scores for the following maneuvers:
a "making" waves, i.e. getting into a surfing position on the face of a wave
b beating sections, i.e. cutting ahead of a breaking section of the wave and continuing on the wave
c tube rides, i.e. riding under the crest of a breaking wave
d turns, cutbacks, and reentries, i.e. turning movements on the face of the wave.
Only a competitor's best waves are scored.
There are also occasional tandem events for man/woman pairs. Competitors aim to achieve various acrobatic lifts on the board while surfing. Rules govern the ratio of the woman's bodyweight to the man's. Marking is for both gymnastic and surfing skills.

In addition to standard surfing events, some areas have competitions for bodyboards, ridden lying down, and for body surfing, using no board at all!

1

2

3

4

©DIAGRAM

Bowl riding

Here skateboarders use a concrete bowl or pool to perform acrobatic feats. The downward curve of the bowl's face provides the impetus, as the power of the wave does in surfing. Maneuvers fall into four main categories, and we show one example of each.

1 Aerials, in which the competitor has clear air between himself and the top of the bowl: e.g. backside air.

2 Handplants and footplants, in which the competitor is above the bowl but is supporting himself with a hand or foot: e.g. extended Andrecht handplant.

3 "Coping" maneuvers, in which the board is angled against the lip of the bowl or pool: e.g. rock'n'roll.

4 Surf-style maneuvers, in which the competitor stays on the face of the bowl, like a surfer on the face of a wave: e.g. layback. Competition rules vary, but typically involve a compulsory routine of 30-45 seconds and a free routine of 45-60 seconds.

d

Not all surfers ride on water! But sandboarders and snowboarders have only gravity to help them along – not the force of the breaking wave. So compared with true surfers, they are limited in the maneuvers they can perform.

AERIAL SKILLS 1

A number of display events involve a demonstration of aerial skill of some kind. Some feature the making of "patterns" in various ways, and these we postpone for consideration on subsequent pages. Most of the others – discussed here – emphasize some form of accuracy, whether in navigation, target landing, or precision control.

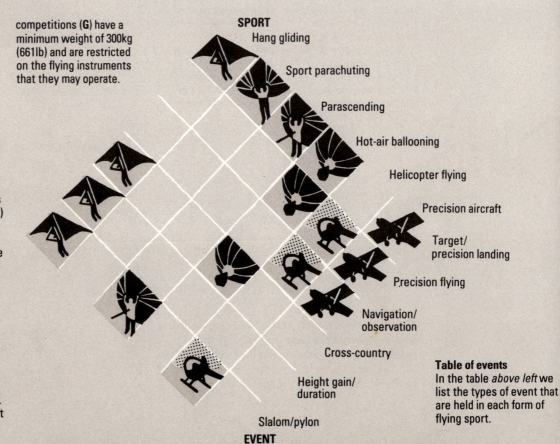

Flying circus
Across the top of these two pages we show the various forms of flying for which there are display events. Hang gliders are divided into two classes: those controlled only by the pilot shifting his bodyweight (**A**), and those with movable control surfaces as on an aircraft (**B**). Parachutes are used both by sport parachutists (who jump from an aircraft) and by parascenders, who are in effect human kites, towed into the air on a line pulled by a land vehicle or water craft. Both use similar canopies: the ram-air type (**C**) is the more common, but round parachutes (**D**) are also used. Hot-air balloons (**E**) and helicopters (**F**) vary considerably in size, but are not grouped into classes for display events. The single-engined aircraft used in precision flying competitions (**G**) have a minimum weight of 300kg (661lb) and are restricted on the flying instruments that they may operate.

SPORT
- Hang gliding
- Sport parachuting
- Parascending
- Hot-air ballooning
- Helicopter flying
- Precision aircraft

EVENT
- Target/precision landing
- Precision flying
- Navigation/observation
- Cross-country
- Height gain/duration
- Slalom/pylon

Table of events
In the table *above left* we list the types of event that are held in each form of flying sport.

Display events
Apart from those events that involve making patterns, aerial-skill competitions are of six main types:
a) target and precision landing events;
b) precision flying events;
c) navigation and flight observation events;
d) cross-country events;
e) height and duration events;
f) slalom and pylon events.
All these are considered here, except for the last group which are dealt with on pp. 120-121.

Target and precision landing
All these events involve landing accuracy, except in hot-air ballooning, where competitors drop markers as near as possible to their goal, rather than actually landing. In hang gliding, sport parachuting, and parascending, the aim is to touch down at the center of a target. (In hang gliding, this event often serves to complete some other test.) In the aircraft landing event, the aim is to touch down exactly on a line across a runway.

Precision flying
There are events in this category for helicopters, hot-air balloons, and aircraft. The hot-air balloon "elbow task event" tests general direction control only: entrants fly a dogleg route in any direction and (by their choice of flight altitudes) aim to maximize the angle between the two sections of the flight. The aircraft and helicopter events are very precise tests of both flight path and timing. The helicopter events involve reaching and landing at a specified airfield or (over a much shorter distance) following a line marked on the ground. The aircraft event involves planning and following a cross-country route.

Navigation and observation
In the helicopter event of this type, competitors are given a surprise route, and questions that are to be answered from aerial observation. Observation is also tested in the aircraft precision flying event just described.

Cross-country
These events, in hot-air ballooning and hang gliding, simply test the ability to reach a distant goal. In the hang gliding event, the goal is set by the organizers. However in the ballooning "hare and hounds" event the goal is selected by a non-competing balloon that sets off first and which competitors "chase" to its eventual landing place.

Height gain and duration
There are recognized records for altitude and duration in most forms of flying, but competitions of this type only occur in hang gliding. In duration events, competitors simply aim to travel as far as possible from a given starting place. In height gain events, they try to gain as much altitude as possible, as recorded on a sealed barograph.

117

AERIAL SKILLS 2

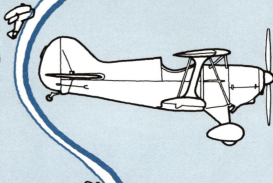

Two sports involve aerial pattern-making: aerobatics and parachuting. They provide some interesting contrasts. Aerobatics and solo free-fall parachuting feature patterns of movement. But certain other parachuting events aim either at a single static pattern, or at sequences of static patterns with minimal movement in between.

A

B

Aerobatics
Aerobatics competitions use a performance "box" measuring 1000 x 1000m horizontally and, at international level, 900m vertically (from 100m to 1000m altitude). The usual aircraft, the Pitt S-1S, is shown *above*. Its small size

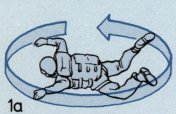

1a

1b

1c

Free-fall parachuting
Competitions here include one solo and several team events. Video recording equipment is used for judging.
1 Solo ("style") events *left*. These are jumped from 2000m (6562ft), giving about 27 seconds' working time. Each contestant gives four set displays, showing different set sequences of horizontal turns (**1a, 1b**) and vertical backloops (**1c**). Jumps are timed, and time penalties added for errors.
2 Four-way relative work *right*. These events are jumped from 2750m (9022ft), giving about 35 seconds' working time. Each team gives 10 displays: five of set sequences, five of sequences as drawn by chance from a previously announced list of patterns. If the working time on a jump allows, a team completing its sequence can begin it again and go on scoring. We illustrate (**2a, 2b**) short sections from two set sequences, with the prescribed interchange positions.
3 Eight-way relative work *opposite*. These events are jumped from 3250m (10,663ft), giving about 50 seconds' working time.

Rules are as for the four-way event. We show a short section of one set sequence.
4 Ten-way relative work *opposite below*. These events are no longer held at top international level, but are still important in some national and local competitions. They are jumped from 2295m (7530ft), giving about 35 seconds' working time. The aim is simply to form a single formation as quickly as possible: a circle ("star") of all 10 team members. The formation need not be perfectly circular, but must be held for five seconds.

Canopy display events
Competitive events in "canopy relative work" are very new. Rules are not finalized, but the aim is to make a single formation – a stack of all team members – and then to rotate the position of team members in the stack. Events involve the two separate forms of stacking illustrated (**5a, 5b**).

2a

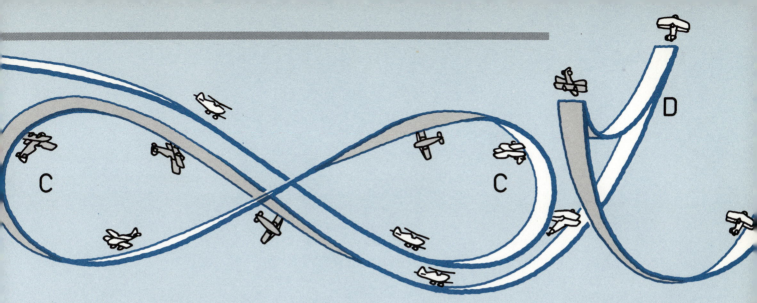

and low stall speed allow maximum use of the available space.
A typical competition consists of four programs. All entrants fly the first three, and the top scorers then fly program four.
Program one: a compulsory program announced at least six months in advance; time limit for climbing and program, 11 minutes.
Program two: a free program of up to 25 figures, submitted by entrants at least 24 hours in advance; no time limit, but a limit on the total degree of difficulty of the figures.
Program three: a compulsory program announced only 24 hours in advance, with no practicing allowed; time limit as for program one.
Program four: a free program with no limit on the number or difficulty of figures; time limits, four minutes climbing, four minutes program.
Programs one to three are marked on the precision of individual figures and on positioning. Program four is marked only on the program as a whole, and takes into account its rhythm and harmony, versatility, and originality.
Opposite and *above left* we show four typical aerobatic figures.
A Barrel roll
B Vertical "S"
C Cuban eight
D Tailslide "canopy up"

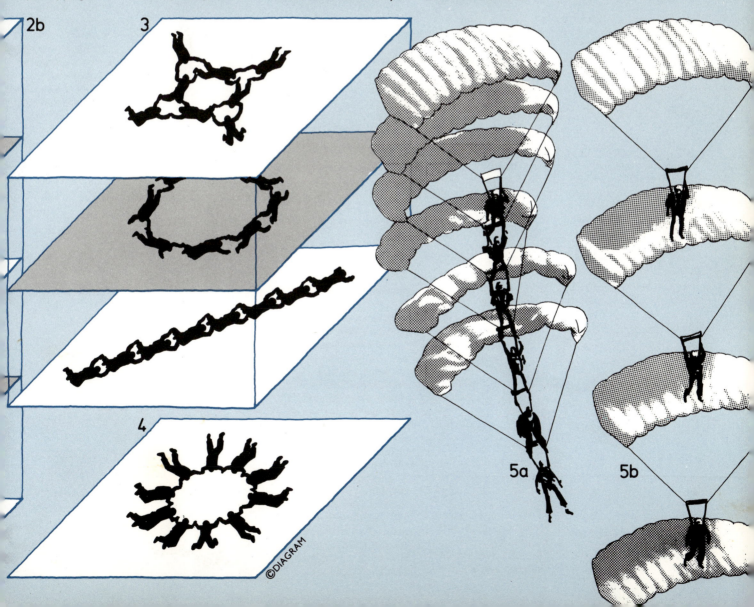

SLALOM SKILLS

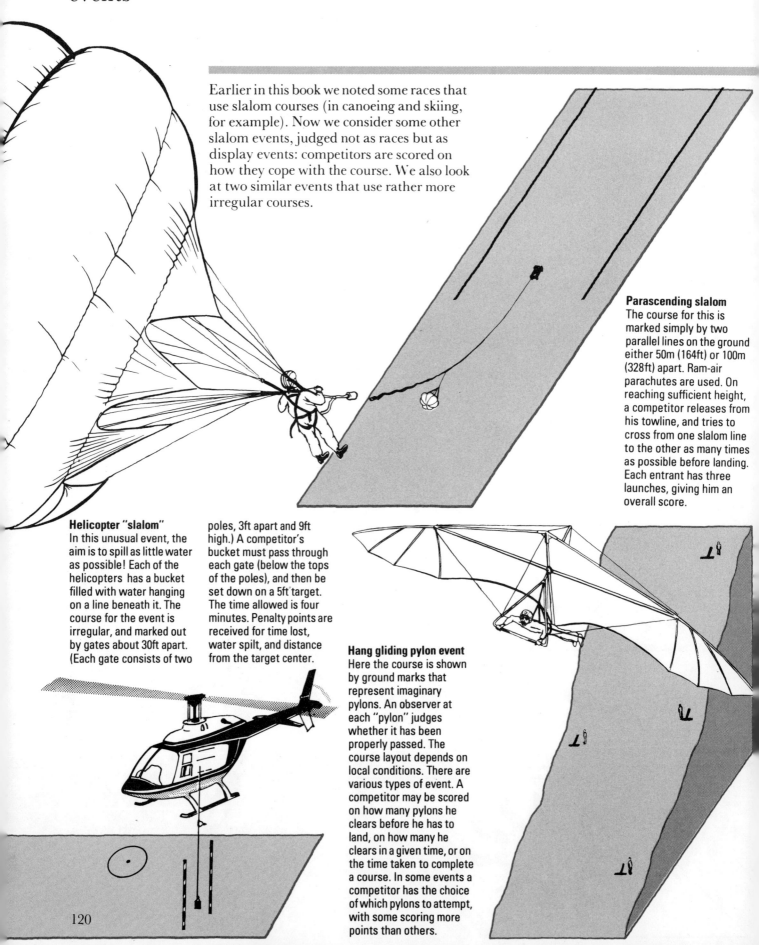

Earlier in this book we noted some races that use slalom courses (in canoeing and skiing, for example). Now we consider some other slalom events, judged not as races but as display events: competitors are scored on how they cope with the course. We also look at two similar events that use rather more irregular courses.

Parascending slalom
The course for this is marked simply by two parallel lines on the ground either 50m (164ft) or 100m (328ft) apart. Ram-air parachutes are used. On reaching sufficient height, a competitor releases from his towline, and tries to cross from one slalom line to the other as many times as possible before landing. Each entrant has three launches, giving him an overall score.

Helicopter "slalom"
In this unusual event, the aim is to spill as little water as possible! Each of the helicopters has a bucket filled with water hanging on a line beneath it. The course for the event is irregular, and marked out by gates about 30ft apart. (Each gate consists of two poles, 3ft apart and 9ft high.) A competitor's bucket must pass through each gate (below the tops of the poles), and then be set down on a 5ft target. The time allowed is four minutes. Penalty points are received for time lost, water spilt, and distance from the target center.

Hang gliding pylon event
Here the course is shown by ground marks that represent imaginary pylons. An observer at each "pylon" judges whether it has been properly passed. The course layout depends on local conditions. There are various types of event. A competitor may be scored on how many pylons he clears before he has to land, on how many he clears in a given time, or on the time taken to complete a course. In some events a competitor has the choice of which pylons to attempt, with some scoring more points than others.

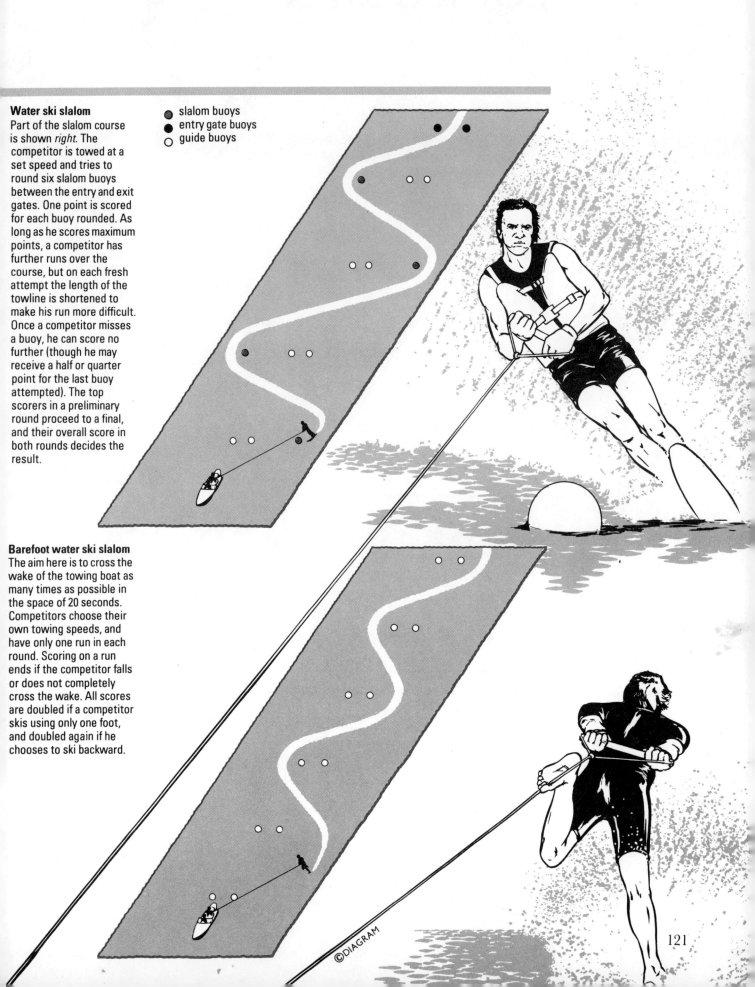

Water ski slalom
Part of the slalom course is shown *right*. The competitor is towed at a set speed and tries to round six slalom buoys between the entry and exit gates. One point is scored for each buoy rounded. As long as he scores maximum points, a competitor has further runs over the course, but on each fresh attempt the length of the towline is shortened to make his run more difficult. Once a competitor misses a buoy, he can score no further (though he may receive a half or quarter point for the last buoy attempted). The top scorers in a preliminary round proceed to a final, and their overall score in both rounds decides the result.

● slalom buoys
● entry gate buoys
○ guide buoys

Barefoot water ski slalom
The aim here is to cross the wake of the towing boat as many times as possible in the space of 20 seconds. Competitors choose their own towing speeds, and have only one run in each round. Scoring on a run ends if the competitor falls or does not completely cross the wake. All scores are doubled if a competitor skis using only one foot, and doubled again if he chooses to ski backward.

©DIAGRAM

121

EQUESTRIAN SKILLS 1

Sports of equestrian skill cover both horse riding and team driving (that is, the control of horses pulling a vehicle). In both cases, the abilities tested are general horsemanship (dressage), the negotiation of obstacles (jumps or driving obstacles), and endurance. Here we compare the various forms of competition.

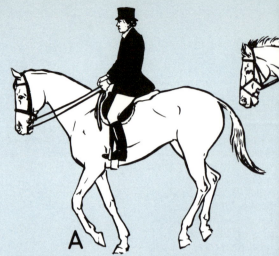

A

Events, arenas, distances
We begin *right* by looking at the basic principles of the various events. Then we compare arenas and distances. Some events involve specified arenas, described *below,* and some specified distances, described *far right.*

A) Dressage
The dressage competition tests the skills of horse and rider through a series of prescribed movements in an empty arena. These include: paces (various forms of walk, trot, and canter); halts and changes of direction; lateral movements; pirouettes and half pirouettes; and figures – large circles, small circles (voltes), serpentines, figures of eight. Judges award a points score. Penalty points are given for errors and for exceeding the time allowed.

Room for maneuver
Illustrated *above* and listed in the table *right* are the dimensions of the various arenas used in equestrian skill events. The dressage dimensions apply both to the dressage event and to the dressage stage of the three-day event. The show-jumping arena has no prescribed length or width, only a minimum area. Also shown to the same scale, for comparison, is an American football field, area 5351m² (6400yd²).

Event	Dimensions	Area
a Dressage*	60x20m (65.6x21.9yd)	1200m² (1435.2yd²)
b Show jumping†	—	2500m² (2990yd²)
c Driving: dressage*	100x40m (109.4x43.7yd)	4000m² (4784yd²)
d Driving: obstacle driving†	120x70m (131.2x76.6yd)	8400m² (10,046.6yd²)

*set dimensions †minimum dimensions

In American rodeo, a competitor in the bareback bronc-riding simply has to try to stay on his mount for eight seconds, while holding on with only one hand!

B) Show jumping
Horse and rider face a course of jumps, in an indoor arena or on an outdoor course. The jumps are of various heights, spreads, and designs. Possible errors include: refusal by the horse at a jump; knocking down part of a jump; horse or rider falling; failure to take the jumps in prescribed order; and failure to complete the course in the time limit. Scoring is usually on the number of penalties incurred, with a jump-off against the clock deciding ties for first place.

C) Three-day event
This is in three separate parts on consecutive days: dressage, endurance, and show jumping. In dressage and show jumping, the usual basic principles apply. The endurance stage is run on a time basis, and consists of four phases: roads and tracks; steeplechase; roads and tracks again; and cross-country (with jumps). The second and last phases need to be ridden at a gallop. Scoring covers time penalties, time bonuses, and faults at obstacles.

D) Driving
Most events are for teams of four horses pulling a four-wheeled carriage. The different competitions are: presentation/dressage; obstacle driving; driving marathon; and combined events. The presentation and dressage uses an empty arena, and tests appearance and control. Obstacle driving features marker cones, bridges, and water obstacles, again in an arena. The marathon has a course of 22-35km (13.7-21.7mi) over roads and tracks, with obstacles such as gates, sharp turns, steep hills, and water.

Distances
Listed *right,* and shown to two separate scales *below,* are specified course lengths for the various obstacle events (jumping and obstacle driving) (**1-5**) and the two endurance events (**6,7**). Courses for international show jumping vary greatly in length, so figures given are for some major competitions. (The Nations' Cup is the world team jumping competition. Derby events feature unusually high and difficult jumps, as well as having longer courses.)

Obstacle event distances
1 Driving, obstacle event, 500-800m (547-875yd)
2 Show jumping, World Championships, maximums for successive rounds:
a 700m (765yd); **b** 800m (875yd); **c** 600m (656yd); **d** 500m (547yd); **e** 500m (547yd)
3 Show jumping, Nations' Cup (average length), 650-800m (711-875yd)
4 Three-day event, show jumping stage, 750-900m (820-984yd)
5 Show jumping, Derby events, 1000m (1094yd) minimum

Endurance event distances
6 Three-day event, endurance stage: **a** roads and tracks, 16-20km (9.9-12.4mi); **b** steeplechase, 3.45km, 3.795km, or 4.14km (2.1mi, 2.4mi, or 2.6mi); **c** roads and tracks, 16-20km (9.9-12.4mi); **d** cross-country, 7.4-8.0km (4.6-5.0mi)
7 Driving, marathon event, successive sections: **a** trot, 8-12km (5.0-7.5mi); **b** walk, 0.8-1.2km (0.5-0.75mi); **c** trot, 6-10km (3.7-6.2mi); **d** walk, 0.8-1.2km (0.5-0.75mi); **e** trot, 6-10km (3.7-6.2mi); total distance, 22-35km (13.7-21.7mi)

The human race
Not only horsemen compete in obstacle and endurance events! Shown for comparison in the diagrams *left* are the scale distances for two track events: the 400m hurdles (**A**) and the 10,000m (**B**).

©DIAGRAM

EQUESTRIAN SKILLS 2

Show jumping and the three-day event feature an enormous variety of jumps. Here we survey the main types and the range of their dimensions, and contrast them with the obstacles in the obstacle driving event. We also compare the speeds that contestants need to achieve, to complete the various equestrian courses in the allotted times.

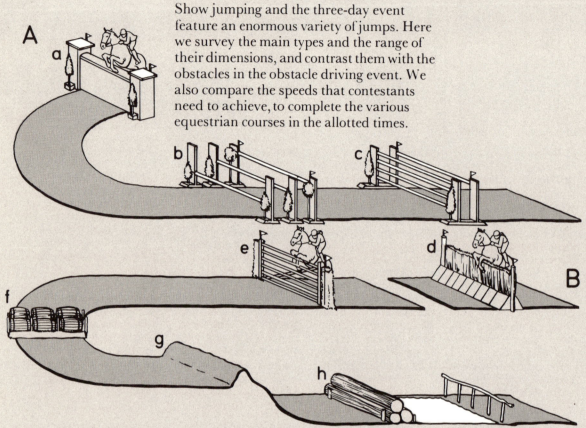

Types of jump *left*
Despite their variety, these fall into a few main categories. We show one example of each.
A Show jumping
a basic upright: stone wall
b spread jump with height increase: triple bars
c spread jump of single height: parallel bars
B Three-day event
In the endurance stage, the steeplechase has brush fences (**d**), fixed fences, and water jumps. The cross-country phase features four main types.
e basic upright: gate
f spread jump: barrels
g change of level jump: gulch
h water jump (jump into and out of water)
(Cross-country obstacles tend to be solid, whereas in show jumping they can usually be knocked down.)
In the show jumping stage, jumps are as in show jumping competitions.

Dimensions of jumps
below We illustrate to scale the maximum dimensions for the various jumping events. Maximum spreads are as follows.
A Show jumping: 2.2m (7ft 3in); water jump, 5m (16ft 5in)
B Three-day event, all

stages: 2m (6ft 7in) at highest point, 3m (9ft 10in) at base; water jumps 3.5m (11ft 6in), except the steeplechase water jump 4m (13ft 2in)
Maximum heights are as follows (we compare the height of an average man – 5ft 9in – and the current

horse high jump record).
I Three-day event, steeplechase, fixed fences, 1m (3ft 3in)
II Three-day event, cross-country (solid part of fence) and show jumping, 1.2m (4ft)
III Three-day event, steeplechase, brush

fences, 1.4m (4ft 7in)
IV Show jumping, 1.7m (5ft 7in)
V Horse high jump record, 2.47m (8ft 1¼in)
In show jumping puissance (power) events a minimum height of 1.4m (4ft 7in) is set, and there is no maximum height.

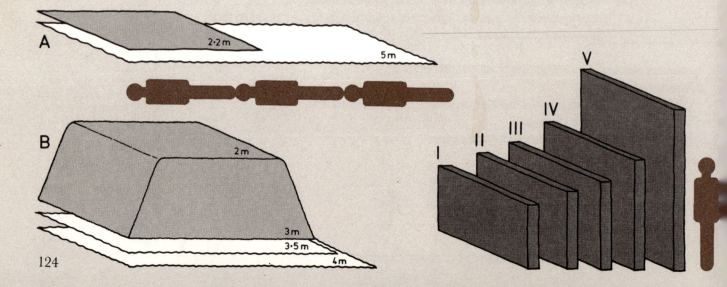

It was the enclosure of small fields, in parts of 18th century Europe, that really set off the development of horse jumping as a skill. Huntsmen chasing a fox would find their way barred by fences and hedges – and had to leap them to keep up with the hounds.

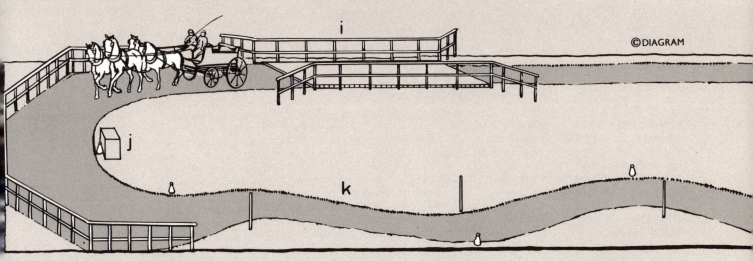

©DIAGRAM

Driving obstacles *above*
In the obstacle driving event, obstacles are built in the arena using marker cones, fence poles, etc. (Each obstacle cone has a ball set on top that is dislodged if the cone is touched.) Typical obstacles are shown: bridge (**i**), U-turn (**j**), and serpentine (**k**). Others include L-turns and water obstacles. Artificial obstacles may be used also in the driving marathon event, if there are not enough natural obstacles.

Required speeds *below*
The times allowed for completing courses in the various equestrian events imply various speed requirements, shown in the diagram below. (Note that the driving marathon is a test of regularity, and points are lost for beating the minimum time as well as for exceeding the time allowed.) We list the official metric requirement, and the equivalent in miles per hour. We also give for comparison the current world record running speeds for 400m and 10,000m athletes.
1 Driving marathon, walk

section 117m/min (4.4mph)
2 Driving obstacle event, first round, 200m/min (7.5mph)
3 Driving obstacle event, subsequent rounds, 220m/min (8.2mph)
4 Three-day event, endurance stage, roads and tracks phase, 220m/min (8.2mph)
5,6,7 Driving marathon, trotting speeds, 250m/min (9.3mph), 267m/min (9.9mph), 300m/min (11.2mph)
8 Show jumping, indoor events, 325-400m/min (12.1-14.9mph)
9 Show jumping, outdoor events, 350-400m/min

(13.0-14.9mph)
10 Show jumping, indoor Nations Cup events, 375m/min (14.0mph)
11 Three-day event, show jumping, 400m/min (14.9mph)
12 Three-day event, cross-country phase, 570m/min (21.3mph)
13 Three-day event, steeplechase phase, 690m/min (25.7mph)
A 10,000m running world record 365m/min (13.6mph)
B 400m running world record, 547m/min (20.4mph)

Dressage times
Dressage events have no speed requirements, of course, but do give an allotted performance time to each competitor. These are: dressage competition, 10min; three-day event, dressage stage, 7min 30sec; driving dressage, 10min.

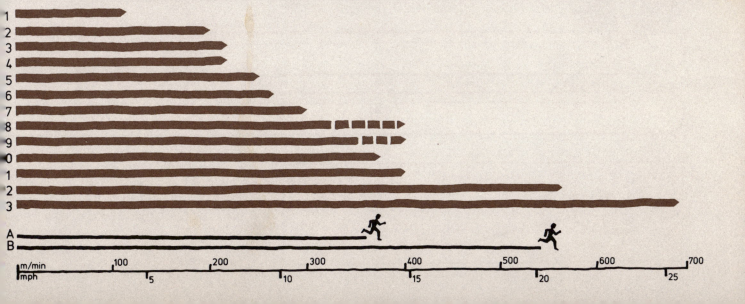

ENDURANCE RECORDS

In what we have termed the "endeavor sports," the idea of a human opponent almost vanishes. Instead the struggle is with the natural world and the challenges it presents. We begin by looking at endurance records: record journey distances for various sport activities. They are divided into "non-stop" and "expedition" categories.

Expedition records
The records listed *right* are shown as great circle distances on the globe *opposite*, with Los Angeles as starting point. Unlike non-stop records, they allow for brief breaks in the journey – for a night's sleep or a few days' camp. But not included are cycling and riding, as their longest known journeys were the side products of itinerant lives – breaks of weeks or even months were involved. Nor are sailing or rowing listed, as an effective limit in each has been achieved several times (circumnavigating

the globe by sail; crossing the Pacific by rowing boat).
A Dog sledding, longest self-supporting journey 1080mi (1738km)
B Swimming, downriver 1826mi (2938km)
C Canoeing, open sea 2170mi (3491km)
D Canoeing, on a single river 4000mi (6500km)
E Running 5110mi (8224km)
F Roller skating 5193mi (8357km)
G Canoeing, without portages 6102mi (9820km)
H Canoeing, overall record 7516mi (12,096km)
J Walking 59,651mi (96,000km)

Non-stop records
These are listed *right* and shown *below.* They cover two forms of endeavor: those where, in the nature of the activity, no stopping was possible; and those where there were only minimal pauses for physiological need.

a Surfing, on river bore 2.6mi (4.1km)
b Surf canoeing, on river bore 4mi (6.4km)
c Hang gliding 110.6mi (178.1km)
d Skateboarding 217.3mi (349.7km)
e Swimming 292mi (469.9km)
f Walking 338.2mi (544.3km)

g Running 352.9mi (568km)
h Ballooning: hot air 419.1mi (674.5km)
i Soaring 907.7mi (1460.8km)
j Water skiing 1190mi (1916km)
k Ballooning: gas and hot air 2074.8mi (3339.1km)
l Ballooning: helium 5770mi (9286km)

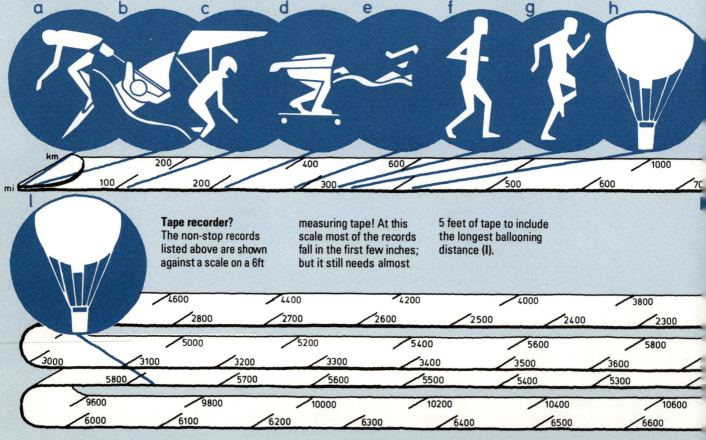

Tape recorder?
The non-stop records listed above are shown against a scale on a 6ft measuring tape! At this scale most of the records fall in the first few inches; but it still needs almost 5 feet of tape to include the longest ballooning distance (**l**).

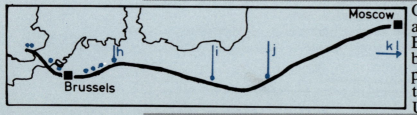

On the map we plot our non-stop records against a rail journey through Northern Europe – from London to Moscow and beyond. The shortest record distances are passed before the train gets to Brussels – the longest not until we are across the Ural Mountains.

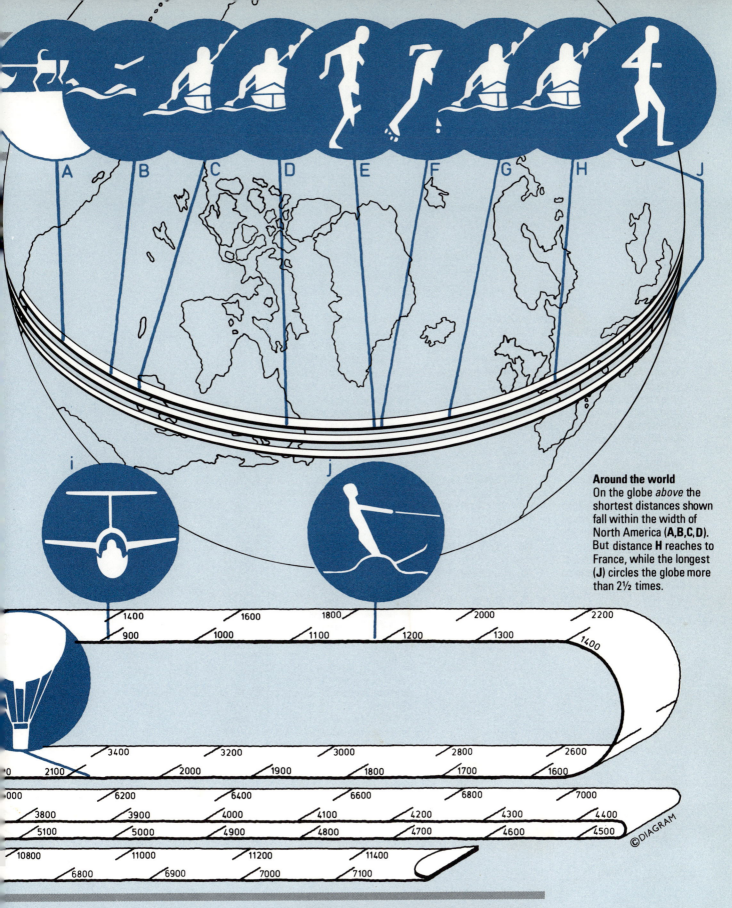

A B C D E F G H J

i j

Around the world
On the globe *above* the shortest distances shown fall within the width of North America (**A,B,C,D**). But distance **H** reaches to France, while the longest (**J**) circles the globe more than 2½ times.

| 1400 | 1600 | 1800 | 2000 | 2200 |
| 900 | 1000 | 1100 | 1200 | 1300 | 1400 |

| 3400 | 3200 | 3000 | 2800 | 2600 |
| 2100 | 2000 | 1900 | 1800 | 1700 | 1600 |

6200	6400	6600	6800	7000
3800	3900	4000	4100	4200	4300	4400
5100	5000	4900	4800	4700	4600	4500

| 10800 | 11000 | 11200 | 11400 |
| 6800 | 6900 | 7000 | 7100 |

©DIAGRAM

In 1980 a four-man team attempted to set a record by crossing the Atlantic on a sailboard. One man at a time was on the board, the rest in a boat behind. Their attempt failed only 120 miles short of its goal – when one of the team had to be rushed to hospital with acute appendicitis.

127

MOUNTAINEERING AND SPELUNKING

Climbing above ground (mountaineering) and below (spelunking or caving) share many points of equipment and technique. Unlike most sports, they offer no simple measure of achievement – a long climb may be easy, a short one difficult. But progressive height and depth records do give us some idea of the progress over time.

Altitude records

The lists *right,* and the climbing figures in our diagram, mark successive mountaineering altitude records from 1521 to 1953 (when the conquest of Everest, the highest peak in the world, ended this area of achievement). As the table shows, three separate phases can be distinguished. First, an early period, in which records began. Second, an age in which the Himalayas came to monopolize height records. Third, an age in which all records were set by successive attempts on Everest itself.

Early records

a 1521: 17,887ft (5452m) (Popocatépetl, Mexico)
b 1624: 18,400ft (5608m) (on Himalayan pass)
c 1802: 18,893ft (5758m) (on Chimborazo, Ecuador)
d 1818: 19,411ft (5916m) (in Himalayas)

The Himalayan age

e 1855: 22,260ft (6784m)
f 1892: 22,606ft (6890m)
g 1897: 22,834ft (6960m)
h 1903: 23,394ft (7130m)
i 1905: 23,787ft (7250m)
j 1907: c.23,900ft (7285m)
k 1909: 24,607ft (7500m)

The assault on Everest

l 1922: c.24,900ft (7590m)
m 1922: 26,986ft (8225m)
n 1922: c.27,300ft (8320m)
o 1924: 28,126ft (8570m)
p 1952: 28,215ft (8599m)
q 1953: 28,721ft (8754m)
r 1953: 29,028ft (8848m)

Summit conquests

Of course, climbers may set a new altitude record without reaching a new summit. So for comparison we list some major summit conquests from climbing history – marked by the mountain peaks in the diagram *right*. It can be seen that altitude records were set in the Himalayas (**b,d,e,** etc) long before a major Himalayan summit was reached (**F**).
A 1786: Mont Blanc, highest in Western Europe, 15,771ft (4807m)
B 1829: Mt Ararat, traditional site of Noah's Ark, 16,946ft (5165m)
C 1874: Mt Elbrus, highest in Europe, 18,510ft (5642m)
D 1889: Kilimanjaro, highest in Africa, 19,340ft (5895m)
E 1897: Aconcagua, highest in Americas and highest volcano, 22,834ft (6960m)
F 1907: Trisul, first major Himalayan peak, 23,360ft (7120m)
G 1936: Nanda Devi, highest peak of inter-war period, 25,646ft (7817m)
H 1950: Annapurna I, first peak over 8000m, 26,504ft (8078m)
J 1953: Mt Everest, highest peak in world, 29,028ft (8848m)

The highest land creature ever recorded was a jumping spider, found on Everest at 22,000ft.

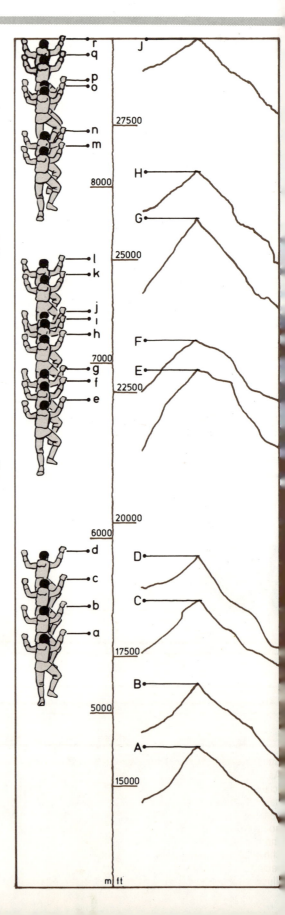

The Himalayan expedition that climbed Mt Annapurna via its south face, in 1970, used 18,000ft of rope – about 60 times the normal amount. Run vertically, this would almost equal the height of Europe's highest mountain, Mt Elbrus (18,510ft).

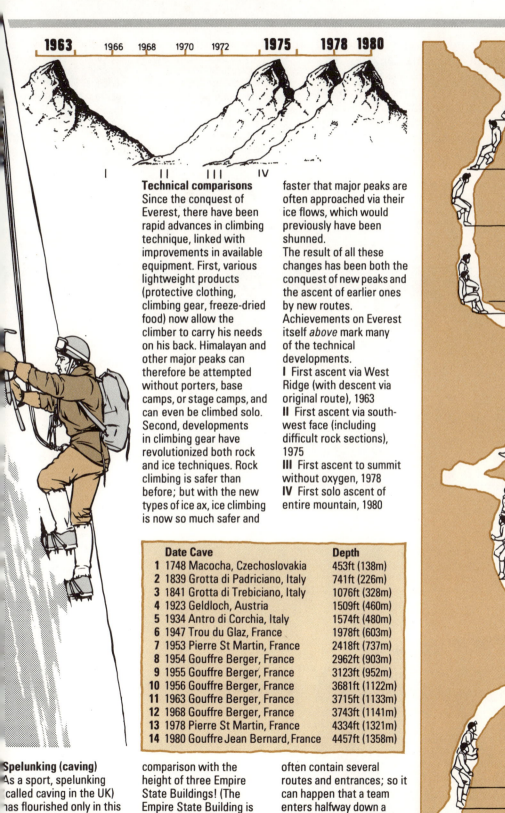

1963 1966 1968 1970 1972 1975 1978 1980

I II III IV

Technical comparisons

Since the conquest of Everest, there have been rapid advances in climbing technique, linked with improvements in available equipment. First, various lightweight products (protective clothing, climbing gear, freeze-dried food) now allow the climber to carry his needs on his back. Himalayan and other major peaks can therefore be attempted without porters, base camps, or stage camps, and can even be climbed solo. Second, developments in climbing gear have revolutionized both rock and ice techniques. Rock climbing is safer than before; but with the new types of ice ax, ice climbing is now so much safer and faster that major peaks are often approached via their ice flows, which would previously have been shunned.

The result of all these changes has been both the conquest of new peaks and the ascent of earlier ones by new routes. Achievements on Everest itself *above* mark many of the technical developments.

I First ascent via West Ridge (with descent via original route), 1963
II First ascent via south-west face (including difficult rock sections), 1975
III First ascent to summit without oxygen, 1978
IV First solo ascent of entire mountain, 1980

	Date Cave	Depth
1	1748 Macocha, Czechoslovakia	453ft (138m)
2	1839 Grotta di Padriciano, Italy	741ft (226m)
3	1841 Grotta di Trebiciano, Italy	1076ft (328m)
4	1923 Geldloch, Austria	1509ft (460m)
5	1934 Antro di Corchia, Italy	1574ft (480m)
6	1947 Trou du Glaz, France	1978ft (603m)
7	1953 Pierre St Martin, France	2418ft (737m)
8	1954 Gouffre Berger, France	2962ft (903m)
9	1955 Gouffre Berger, France	3123ft (952m)
10	1956 Gouffre Berger, France	3681ft (1122m)
11	1963 Gouffre Berger, France	3715ft (1133m)
12	1968 Gouffre Berger, France	3743ft (1141m)
13	1978 Pierre St Martin, France	4334ft (1321m)
14	1980 Gouffre Jean Bernard, France	4457ft (1358m)

Spelunking (caving)

As a sport, spelunking (called caving in the UK) has flourished only in this century; but its records do go back earlier than this. In the table *above right* we show the successive depth records achieved – and illustrate them *right* by comparison with the height of three Empire State Buildings! (The Empire State Building is 1472ft high, with mast.) The record figures used are for distances actually descended during a single expedition. This can be important, as cave systems often contain several routes and entrances; so it can happen that a team enters halfway down a system, and reaches a greater absolute depth, without having made as great an actual descent.

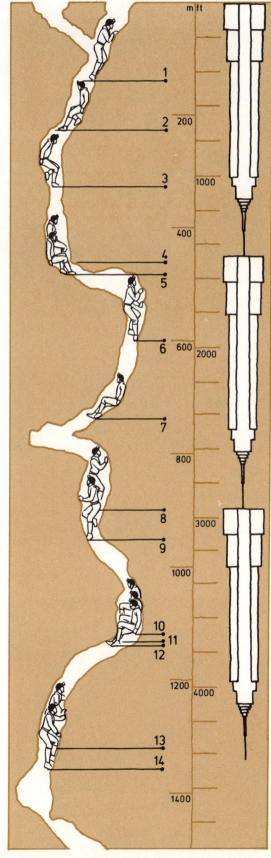

m ft
200 1000
400
600 2000
800
1000 3000
1200 4000
1400

©DIAGRAM

DEPTH AND ALTITUDE RECORDS

We have already looked at the heights and depths achieved by man on land. Now we consider similar records established in water and in the air. These are highly hazardous forms of endeavor, and on the borderline of what may be called "sport." We compare various human achievements, and also some known records for animals.

Sink or swim?
On this page we list and illustrate the various underwater depth records. The "sporting" records are those for breath-held and scuba diving, because only sports equipment was used by the diver. (But note that major medical back-up was usually available; and, more generally, that the degree of danger involved in these records is such that no endorsement of their quest is intended.) For comparison we give depth records for dives using gas mixtures – both real (commercial) and also simulated (laboratory) dives. Also shown are the greatest known depths for a bird (the long-tailed duck) and a mammal (the sperm whale) – though it is estimated that sperm whales can in fact go almost three times as deep as this. The illustration compares all these with the height of the Empire State Building (1472ft with mast). The known sperm whale record (**g**) equals 2½ Empire State Buildings. Not shown, and far beyond the range of our scale, is the record for a dive by a machine (bathyscaphe), which stands at 35,802ft – or more than 24 Empire State Buildings deep!

a Breath-held diving, women's record 147ft 6in (45m)
b Long-tailed duck, greatest recorded depth 200ft (61m)
c Breath-held diving, men's record 328ft (100m)
d Scuba diving record 437ft (133m)
e Diving with gas mixture (record following release from a diving bell) 1640ft (500m)
f Diving with gas mixture (simulated dive in dry pressure chamber) 2250ft (686m)
g Sperm whale, greatest recorded depth 3720ft (1134m)

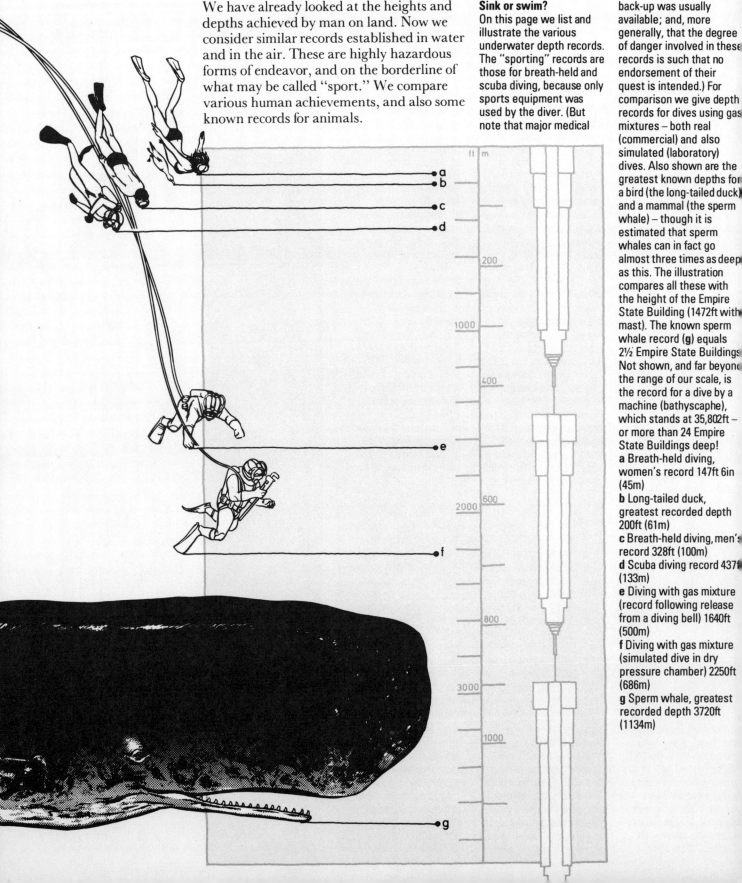

If legend is to be believed, the very first altitude record was set by Icarus, using the wings of feathers and wax invented by Daedalus, his father. Despite his father's warnings, Icarus flew higher and higher. Finally the wax melted, in the fierce heat of the sun, and Icarus plummeted into the sea.

Flying high

Illustrated *left* and listed *below* are aerial altitude records for various forms of sporting endeavor. Also included for comparison are some records that were set using military facilities and equipment (**2,4**), and the highest recorded flight by birds (**10**). In the illustration we compare all these heights with that of Mt Everest (29,028ft). The greatest of them (**1,2**) are higher than four Everests.

1 Ballooning, unofficial world record 123,800ft (37,735m) (balloonist died in attempt)

2 Powered flight, record for aircraft taking off from ground under own power 123,524ft (37,650m)

3 Ballooning, official world record 113,740ft (34,668m)

4 Parachuting, highest free-fall jump (military) 102,800ft (31,333m)

5 Ballooning, hot air balloon record 57,000ft (17,400m)

6 Soaring, highest absolute altitude record 46,266ft (14,102m)

7 Ballooning, open basket record for non-hot air balloons 38,789ft (11,822m)

8 Parachuting, highest free-fall jump (civilian) 32,000ft (9753m)

9 Hang gliding, greatest altitude descended from 31,600ft (9631m)

10 Highest recorded flight by birds (whooper swans) 27,000ft (8230m)

11 Hang gliding, height gain record 12,139ft (3700m)

©DIAGRAM

COMBINED SPORTS

In a combined sport, an athlete has to perform in a number of different events. His success in each is added together, to arrive at an overall score. Combined sports fall into two groups: those that include only track and field events (decathlon and pentathlon), and those covering a wider range (modern pentathlon and winter biathlon).

Decathlon and pentathlon
The decathlon is for men, the pentathlon usually for women. The events included in each are shown in the chart *below*.
The decathlon consists of:
day one – 100m sprint, long jump, shot put, high jump, 400m sprint;

day two – 110m hurdles, discus, pole vault, javelin, 1500m running.
The women's pentathlon consists of:
day one – 100m hurdles, shot put, high jump;
day two – long jump, 800m running.

Greek pentathlon *above*
The original pentathlon was part of the ancient Greek Olympics. It consisted of running (c.200yd sprint), long jump, discus, javelin, and wrestling. The javelin was a target event rather than a distance one; wrestling

was upright, the aim being to throw the opponent to the ground without going down oneself; and in the long jump competitors used weights, thrown backward, to increase the power of their leap.

All-round achievement
The diagrams *right* compare the achievements of combined-sports record holders with those of specialist athletes. Those on this page measure the performance of the current women's pentathlon world record holder against the women's world records in each constituent event. Opposite we do the same for the decathlon and men's world records. In each case, the record performance of the combined-sports athlete is given as a percentage of the individual world record (in the running events, as a

percentage of the speed). For example, in the long jump the decathlon record holder achieved 8 % of the world long jump record, whereas the women's pentathlon record holder achieved 95% of the women's long jump record. The performance of the decathlon record holder ranged from only 64% of the record (in the discus) to 94% of it (in the 100m sprint). That of the women's pentathlon world record holder ranged from 75% (in the shot put) to 95% (in the long jump).

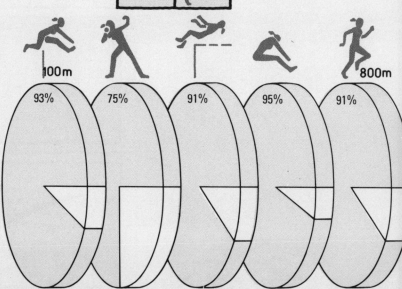

100m 93% 75% 91% 95% 91% 800m

A busy couple of days!
To achieve the same as a top decathlete, you would have to get up, run 110yd for the bus, clear the length of four men, hurl a bundle of 4½ bricks up to 50ft, jump as high as your office door, and run 440yd for your bus home. Next day you would have

to run 120yd for the bus while jumping over ashcans on the sidewalk, throw a heavy ashtray up to 160ft, pole vault into your first-floor office window, throw an 8½ft harpoon at least 220ft, and run almost a mile to catch the bus home.

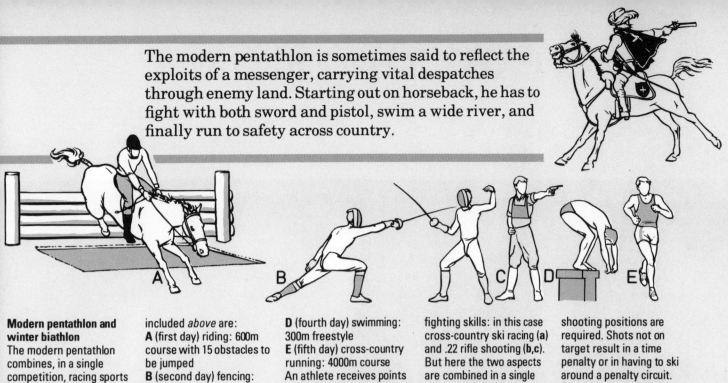

The modern pentathlon is sometimes said to reflect the exploits of a messenger, carrying vital despatches through enemy land. Starting out on horseback, he has to fight with both sword and pistol, swim a wide river, and finally run to safety across country.

A B C D E

Modern pentathlon and winter biathlon

The modern pentathlon combines, in a single competition, racing sports and sports based on fighting skills. It is usually for men, but competitions for women are now well established. The events

included *above* are:
A (first day) riding: 600m course with 15 obstacles to be jumped
B (second day) fencing: épée
C (third day) pistol shooting: .22 caliber, with standard silhouette pistol target

D (fourth day) swimming: 300m freestyle
E (fifth day) cross-country running: 4000m course
An athlete receives points for his performance in each event, and they are added to give his overall score. The winter biathlon *below* also combines racing and

fighting skills: in this case cross-country ski racing (**a**) and .22 rifle shooting (**b,c**). But here the two aspects are combined in a single event, in which the competitors ski with rifle and ammunition, and pause at set points to shoot. Both prone and standing

shooting positions are required. Shots not on target result in a time penalty or in having to ski around a penalty circuit. There are separate 10km, 20km, and team relay (4x7.5km) competitions.

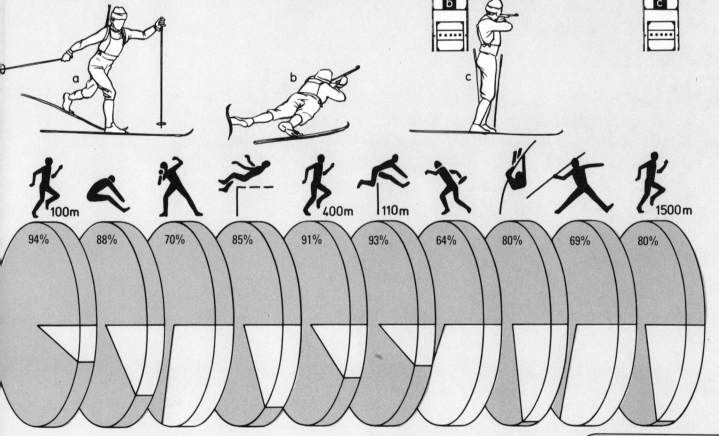

a   b   c

100m   400m 110m   1500m

94% 88% 70% 85% 91% 93% 64% 80% 69% 80%

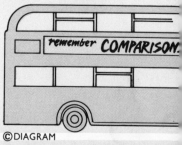

remember COMPARISON.

©DIAGRAM

PART THREE

OPPONENT AND TOURNAMENT SPORTS

COMBAT SPORTS 1

Combat sports, both armed and unarmed,
grew out of the realities of battle. Today they
are tests of skill, and strict rules govern
safety. Among the unarmed forms, a rough
distinction can be made between those in
which you strike your opponent, those where
you grapple with him and try to pin him
down, and those where you try to throw him.

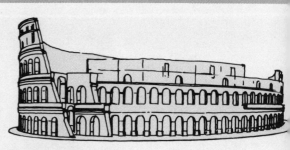

Fields of battle *right*
Drawn to scale and listed in
the table are the areas for
each form of combat sport.
Compared with many
sports they take up little
space. An American
football pitch could
accommodate 18 judo or 72
karate matches with room
to spare. Even a basketball
court has space for 14
fencing pistes, while 50
professional boxing rings
would fit on an ice hockey
pitch.

Sport	Dimensions
1 Fencing	14x2m (45ft 11inx6ft 7in)
2 Amateur boxing	4.88x4.88m (16x16ft)
3 Sumo	5.44x5.44m (17ft 10inx17ft 10in)
4 Professional boxing	6.1x6.1m (20x20ft)
5 Karate	8x8m (26ft 3inx26ft 3in)
6 Aikido	9x9m (29ft 6inx29ft 6in)
7 Kendo	11x10m (36ft 1inx32ft 10in)
8 Amateur wrestling	11x11m (36ft 1inx36ft 1in)
9 Judo	16x16m (52ft 6inx52ft 6in)

Sumo, wrestling, and judo dimensions include safety
margins. Aikido and kendo areas tend to have
additional safety margins of unspecified size. Note that
sambo (*opposite*) uses a standard amateur wrestling
area; and that the safety margin around a wrestling
area may be circular rather than square as shown.

Old and new
The most famous combat
arena of ancient times was
the Colosseum in Rome
above, with its gladiatorial
shows and room for 50,000
spectators. Most famous
today is Madison Square
Garden in New York, with
seats for 20,000 in its main
arena.

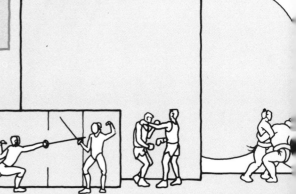

A) Boxing
Fist fighting is the most
publicized of all combat
sports. Amateurs and
professionals fight under
different rules, but in both
cases bouts are won either
on a count-out or on points
awarded for good punches.

C) Freestyle wrestling
Amateurs fight on a mat,
and use permitted holds
and throws to seek a "fall"
(when both the opponent's
shoulders are pinned to
the ground). Bouts are
often decided on points. In
the professional ring, fake
showmanship dominates.

B) Karate
This is the most forceful of
the oriental unarmed
disciplines. Karate means
"empty hand," and sport
karate contests are
sparring matches: to avoid
injury all punches, blows,
strikes, and kicks are
pulled back at contact.

D) Greco-Roman wrestling
The other main form of
amateur wrestling. Rules
are similar to freestyle,
but all leg holds and
techniques – such as
tripping – are forbidden.
Contestants may fight only
with their arms and upper
parts of their bodies.

E) Sambo
Here a fall is scored by grasping the opponent's jacket and throwing him cleanly on to his back. If both fall, the fight continues on the mat. A submission, gained by use of knee and elbow locks, will then decide the bout.

F) Sumo
The massive size of the contestants, and the ritual and ceremony of the fights, make Sumo the most spectacular form of wrestling. A match is decided when one of the wrestlers is forced out of the circle or felled within it.

G) Judo
In this sport the aim is to use your opponent's own efforts to unbalance and throw him. This may be followed by holds and locks on the ground. Judo methods can allow a skillful small fighter to overcome a much heavier opponent.

H) Aikido
Here, as in judo, force is not met with force but with avoiding action. But while judo features close-in grappling, the aikidoist tends to work at arm's length, using arm holds that act on wrist and elbow to throw his opponent.

I) Fencing
In armed combat sports, the weapon is the sword. These are contact sports, decided by the number of hits scored, so protective clothing is essential. Three types of sword are used in fencing, the foil, the épée, and the saber.

J) Kendo
Kendo derives from samurai sword fighting, and mental discipline, agility, and control are more important than mere strength. Fighters are well protected, wear traditional dress, and follow prescribed rituals.

COMBAT SPORTS 2

In many combat sports, the competitor is striking out with a weapon – whether a sword, a punching fist, or a kicking foot. In all of them, it is his opponent's body that he must strike at or act against – a greater or lesser part of it. So these two pages look at the contrasting weapons and target areas in the different sports.

The human target
The drawings of human figures *below* show the parts of the opponent's body that may be attacked in different combat sports: that is, the parts against which a correct technique of the sport may be used. On the left-hand page are

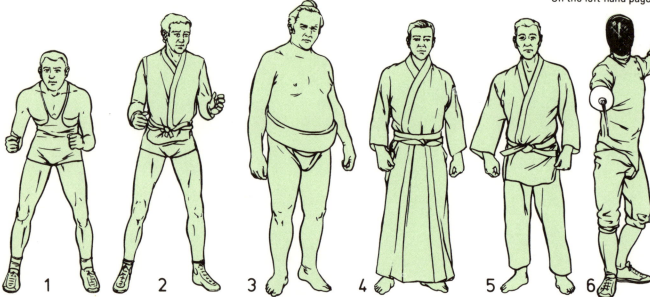

Weapons
The combat sports in which points are awarded for correctly performed blows or hits are karate, boxing, and the four swordfighting sports. In sport karate the main scoring "weapons" *right* are:
a the knuckles of the first and middle fingers of the fist
b the heel
c the side of the foot
d the ball of the foot
e the instep
In boxing the part of the glove that scores is the knuckle area illustrated *opposite* (**f,g,h**).

For the four swordfighting sports the appropriate weapons are illustrated *far right*. Their maximum overall lengths are:
A Saber 105cm (3ft 5¼in)
B Foil 110cm (3ft 7¼in)
C Epée 110cm (3ft 7¼in)
D Kendo sword (*shinai*) 118cm (3ft 10½in)
The part of the blade used for a scoring blow in each case is indicated by a colored line. (In kendo the point of the *shinai* scores only on thrusts to the throat.)

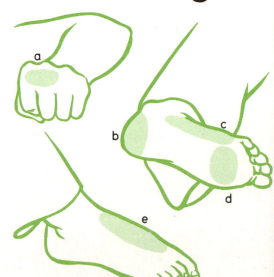

An amateur boxer is allowed up to 8ft 4in of bandage on each hand – a professional up to 18ft. So stringing a professional's two bandages together would give just enough tape for the top of a singles' tennis net!

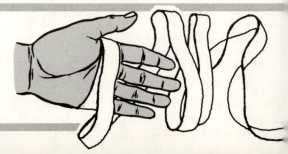

As far as we know the record for the most gladiatorial fights survived in classical times was the 51 combats won at Pompeii by a freedman named Publius Ostorius.

those sports in which the human target is virtually unrestricted. On the right-hand page, the target area becomes more and more limited as we move from left to right. Aikido is divided into its individual events as their target areas differ. (Ninin dori is a three-man fight, randori kyoghi a two-man, while tanto randori involves defense against a dummy knife attack.)

Of course, in any combat sport it is illegal to attack the opponent's eyes or genitals, or to pull at his hair.

1 Freestyle wrestling
2 Sambo wrestling
3 Sumo wrestling
4 Aikido: ninin dori and randori kyoghi events
5 Judo
6 Epée fencing
7 Greco-Roman wrestling
8 Saber fencing
9 Karate

10 Foil fencing
11 Boxing
12 Aikido: tanto randori (knife target area)
13 Kendo

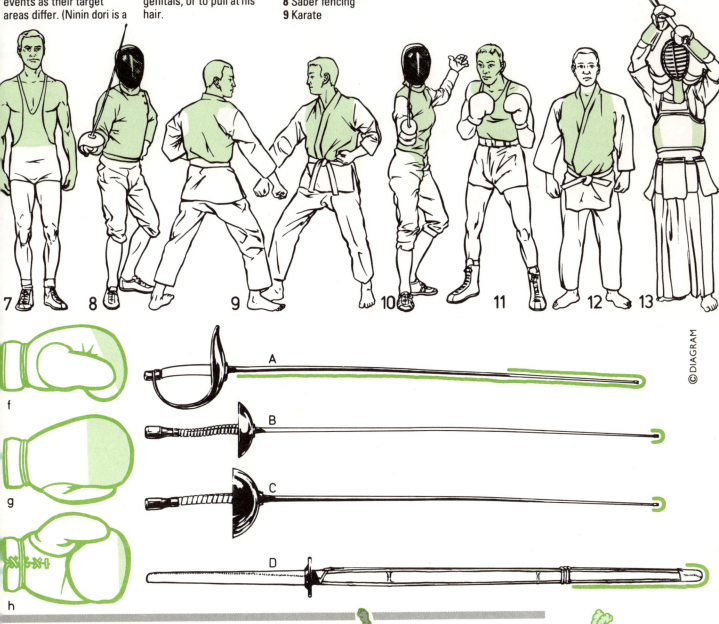

Mock armed combat was familiar in medieval times – but its principles were very different from modern fencing! With armored men on foot, the aim was to knock over the opponent, using heavy maces, swords, or battleaxes. In jousting on horseback, the goal was to break the opponent's lance.

© DIAGRAM

COMBAT SPORTS 3

Weight is a great help in most unarmed combat. Even in top-class judo, the heavier man tends to win an open fight. Similarly in a contest without time limits, fatigue generally ensures that brute force triumphs in the end. So rules on weight categories and time limits have often been vital for the preservation of the element of skill.

Weighty matters
Sport karate, as a sparring match, does not need weight divisions. Nor does aikido, where most fighting is at arm's length. In Sumo weight is very useful, but is not officially controlled. So the unarmed combat sports that use weight divisions for competition are boxing, judo, and international amateur wrestling (freestyle, Greco-Roman, and sambo). (Professional wrestling does also, but is more showmanship than sport.) *Below* we list the weight categories in these, then *right* set them out on a common scale – together with the usual weight range of Sumo wrestlers.
A Sumo wrestling
B Amateur wrestling
C Judo, men
D Judo, women
E Amateur boxing
F Professional boxing

Bricks and bantams
A typical Sumo wrestler *above* weighs the same as 63 household bricks, while (at bottom of page) it would take a similar number of top-weight bantam hens to equal the weight of the lightest bantamweight boxer.

Wrestling weight categories (B)
1	Light flyweight	48kg (106lb)
2	Flyweight	52kg (115lb)
3	Bantamweight	57kg (126lb)
4	Featherweight	62kg (137lb)
5	Lightweight	68kg (150lb)
6	Welterweight	74kg (163lb)
7	Middleweight	82kg (181lb)
8	Light heavyweight	90kg (198½lb)
9	Heavyweight	100kg (220½lb)
10	Super-heavyweight	100+kg (220½+lb)

Judo weight categories
C) Men		D) Women	
1	60kg (132lb)	1	48kg (106lb)
2	65kg (143lb)	2	52kg (115lb)
3	71kg (156½lb)	3	56kg (123½lb)
4	78kg (172lb)	4	61kg (134½lb)
5	86kg (190lb)	5	66kg (145½lb)
6	95kg (209lb)	6	72kg (159lb)
7	95+kg (209+lb)	7	72+kg (159+lb)

Boxing weight categories
	E) Amateur (IABA)	F) Professional (WBC)
Light flyweight	1 48kg (106lb)	1 49kg (108lb)
Flyweight	2 51kg (112lb)	2 51kg (112lb)
Bantamweight	3 54kg (119lb)	3 53.5kg (118lb)
Super bantamweight	—	4 55kg (121lb)
Featherweight	4 57kg (126lb)	5 57kg (126lb)
Junior lightweight	—	6 59kg (130lb)
Lightweight	5 60kg (132lb)	7 61kg (134½lb)
Light (junior) welterweight	6 63.5kg (140lb)	8 63.5kg (140lb)
Welterweight	7 67kg (148lb)	9 66.5kg (147lb)
Light middleweight	8 71kg (156½lb)	10 70kg (154lb)
Middleweight	9 75kg (165lb)	11 72.5kg (160lb)
Light heavyweight	10 81kg (179lb)	12 79kg (174lb)
Heavyweight	11 81+kg (179+lb)	13 79+kg (174+lb)

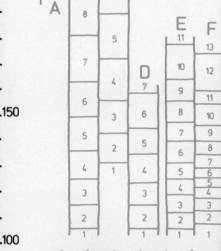

Kangaroos are noted for their boxing skills: a circus kangaroo – wearing boxing gloves – that escaped in Japan, downed three men before being captured by a Judo-trained policeman. But even the heaviest kangaroo (about 180lb) would only just qualify as a heavyweight in amateur boxing.

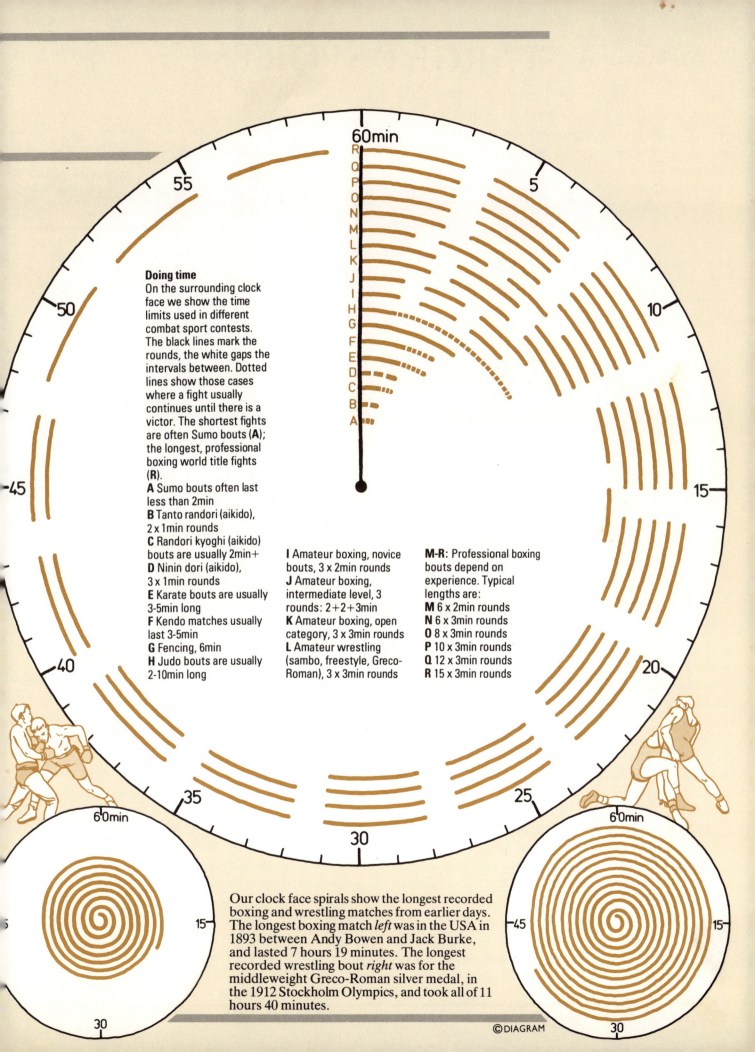

60min

55

5

50

10

45

15

Doing time

On the surrounding clock face we show the time limits used in different combat sport contests. The black lines mark the rounds, the white gaps the intervals between. Dotted lines show those cases where a fight usually continues until there is a victor. The shortest fights are often Sumo bouts (**A**); the longest, professional boxing world title fights (**R**).

A Sumo bouts often last less than 2min
B Tanto randori (aikido), 2 x 1min rounds
C Randori kyoghi (aikido) bouts are usually 2min+
D Ninin dori (aikido), 3 x 1min rounds
E Karate bouts are usually 3-5min long
F Kendo matches usually last 3-5min
G Fencing, 6min
H Judo bouts are usually 2-10min long

I Amateur boxing, novice bouts, 3 x 2min rounds
J Amateur boxing, intermediate level, 3 rounds: 2+2+3min
K Amateur boxing, open category, 3 x 3min rounds
L Amateur wrestling (sambo, freestyle, Greco-Roman), 3 x 3min rounds

M-R: Professional boxing bouts depend on experience. Typical lengths are:
M 6 x 2min rounds
N 6 x 3min rounds
O 8 x 3min rounds
P 10 x 3min rounds
Q 12 x 3min rounds
R 15 x 3min rounds

40

20

35

25

30

60min

15

30

60min

45

15

30

Our clock face spirals show the longest recorded boxing and wrestling matches from earlier days. The longest boxing match *left* was in the USA in 1893 between Andy Bowen and Jack Burke, and lasted 7 hours 19 minutes. The longest recorded wrestling bout *right* was for the middleweight Greco-Roman silver medal, in the 1912 Stockholm Olympics, and took all of 11 hours 40 minutes.

©DIAGRAM

TARGET SPORTS 1

Target sports derive from the skills of hunting and combat. In fact some of them deliberately try to preserve something of the practical conditions of their origins. Here we look at the various competitive forms of modern shooting and archery – and also at tournament casting, a less well-known target sport.

A) Rifle shooting
Events are held for bigbore and smallbore rifles. International rules distinguish between "standard" rifles (which resemble normal weapons) and "free" rifles (which have special grips to aid the competitor). Most events use static targets, but the "running game" event has a moving target seen for only a few seconds. Also most involve three firing positions (standing, kneeling, and prone), but the smallbore "English match" uses prone only, and the running game event standing only.

B) Pistol shooting
There are events for smallbore (standard and free) and center-fire (larger bore) weapons. Most use static targets, but rapid-fire/dueling events feature a human silhouette seen for only a few seconds. A standing position is used for firing.

C) Airgun shooting
Air rifle events are held with static or (sometimes) running game targets. Air pistol events use static targets. In both cases, a standing firing position is used.

D) Shotgun shooting
In shotgun events the targets are saucer-shaped clay "pigeons," shot into the air from mechanical traps. The layout of shooting positions and traps varies. The main forms are Olympic trap, skeet, and "down-the-line."

E) Practical shooting
A new target discipline, covering pistol and (more recently) rifle and shotgun. Events recreate hostile encounter situations, including rapid-fire exercises, assault courses, and other practical scenarios (e.g. hostage situations), and are always shot against time. Any firing position may be used. Courses vary greatly. Some involve tactical decisions on choice and order of targets, shooting distances, reloading time, etc; some are presented in "surprise" form; and some even involve penalty booby traps.

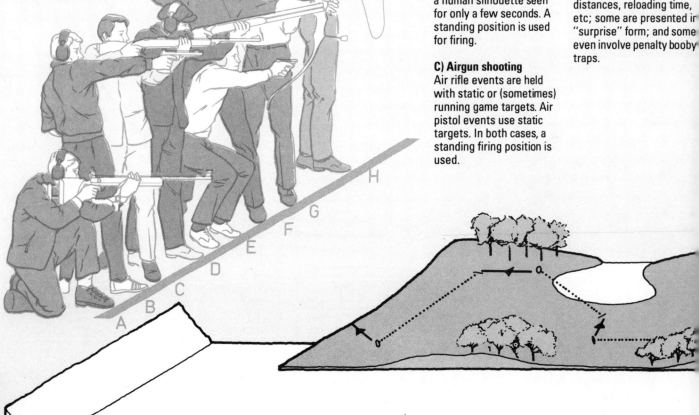

The 300m of an international rifle shooting range would be long enough to park a line of 24 greyhound buses nose to tail. But the prize for spaciousness goes to field archery: an international course needs an area of about 40 acres – equal to 30 US football pitches or 87 ice hockey rinks.

Event	Target distance
1 Airgun, 10m match X-bow	10m (32ft10in)
2 Tournament casting	6.1-24.4m (20-80ft)
3 Rapid-fire pistol	25m (82ft)
4,5 Clay pigeon shooting	not measurable
6 Smallbore rifle	50m (164ft)
7 Archery crossbow	35-65m (114ft10in-213ft3in)
8 Target archery	30-90m (98ft5in-295ft3in)
9 Field archery	15-60m (49ft3in-196ft10in)
10 Bigbore rifle	300m (984ft3in)

Target range

We show to scale *below* some of the competition areas used in target sports. The corresponding target distances are given in the table *left*. The smallbore rifle range is shown as set up for running game target shooting.

F) Archery

There are two forms. In target archery, the competitors stand side by side as on a firing range. The distance to the targets is gradually reduced according to a set program. In field archery, targets are dispersed over a course, and competitors follow a route that gives maximum variety of shooting distance.

G) Crossbow archery

Again there are two main forms. Match crossbows use bolts without feathers, shot at small paper targets over a set distance (10m or 30m). Archery crossbows use bolts with feathers, shot at archery targets over a set program of distances.

H) Tournament casting

In the accuracy events of tournament casting, competitors use various forms of angling equipment to cast at circular targets set on the ground 20-80ft away. (For the distance events, see Throwing, p.85.)

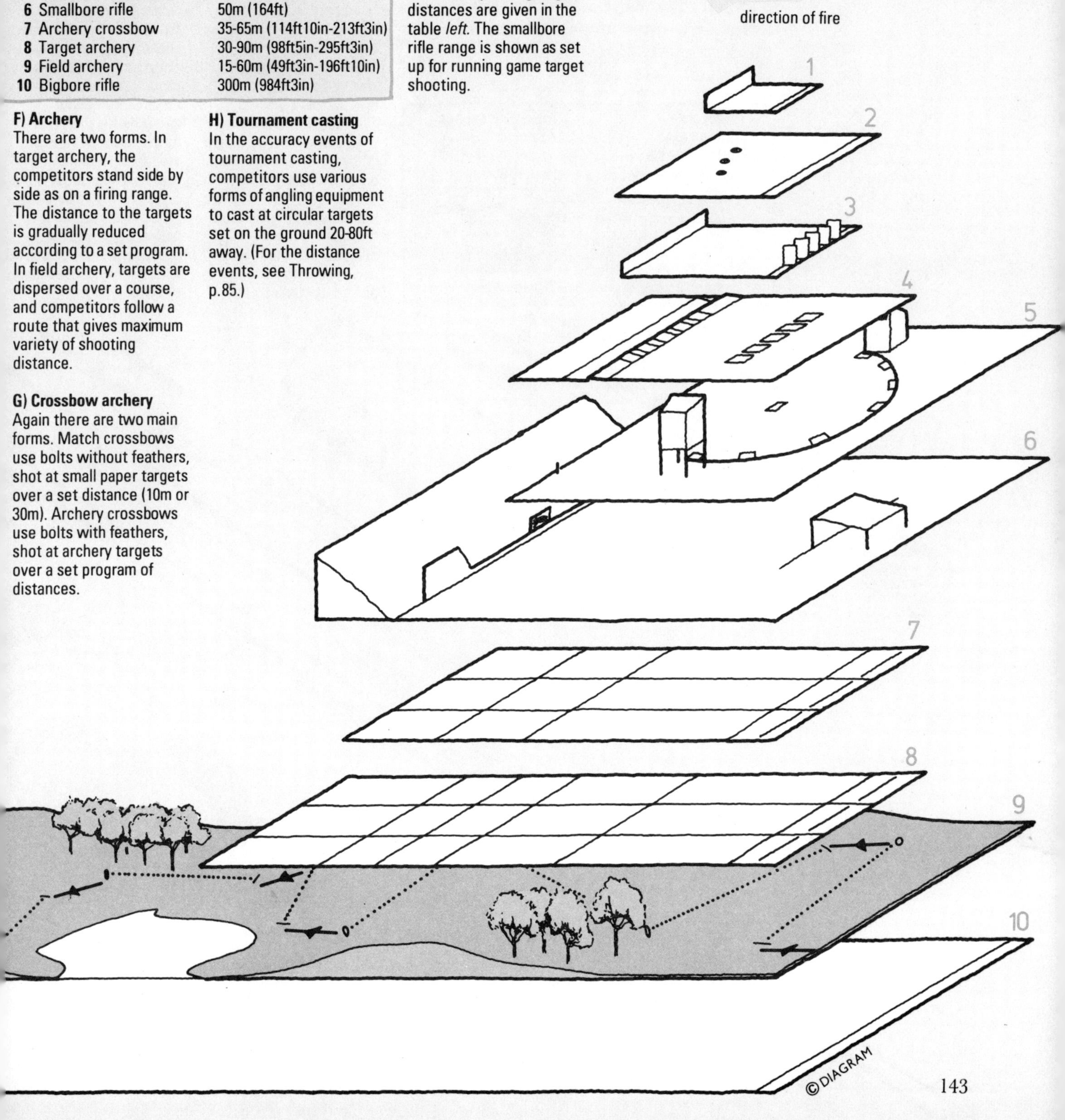

direction of fire

© DIAGRAM

143

TARGET SPORTS 2

The targets and "projectiles" used in target sports vary greatly in size, as the tables and illustrations here show. But there is also a wide range of materials involved – some highly traditional, some the fruits of modern technology – while among the targets some of the designs are interesting for their element of realism.

Projectiles *below*
The illustrations show full size some of the projectiles used in the different target sports – from airgun pellets to archery arrows. Their dimensions are given in the table: either caliber (diameter) or length. The shotgun cartridge holds lead shot of 2.5mm maximum diameter. The smallbore cartridge shown is the "long rifle" version, used in smallbore rifle events and most smallbore pistol events; but in rapid-fire/dueling events competitors prefer a cartridge with a shorter and lighter bullet.

Targets *opposite below*
Examples shown range in size from the tiny air rifle target to the 6ft target used in one of the accuracy casting events. For archery the three main designs are shown, but each in fact occurs in a range of sizes, for different shooting distances. In pistol shooting the precision target is used in free and standard pistol matches, the rapid-fire target in the rapid-fire match, and both types in center-fire and ladies' matches. The practical shooting target is usually camouflaged as shown.

Projectile	Maximum caliber
a Airgun pellet	4.5mm (0.177in)
b Smallbore bullet	5.6mm (0.22in)
c Bigbore rifle bullet	8mm (0.314in)
d Center-fire bullet	9.6mm (0.38in)
	Average length
e Shotgun cartridge	70mm (2.75in)
f Match crossbow bolt	150mm (5.9in)
g Archery crossbow bolt	343mm (13.5in)
h Archery arrow	710mm (28in)

a b c d e f

1 2 3 4 5

In the ancient Greek Olympics the javelin was a target event – not a distance one as today. The Greeks even applied the principle of "rifling" to their efforts: using a leather thong to impart spin to the javelin, as a modern gun does to a bullet.

The smallest target we show below is in reality just larger than a golf ball, but the diameter of the largest is greater than the height of an average man.

Materials

Materials used in the projectiles include lead (bullets, airgun pellets, and shotgun shot); brass (cartridge cases); cupro-nickel (jacketing for bigbore bullets); wood, aluminum, and fiberglass (archery arrows); and wood, fiberglass, and carbon fiber (crossbow bolts). Materials for targets include card, cloth, straw, canvas, metal, plastic, and even (in field archery) building board.

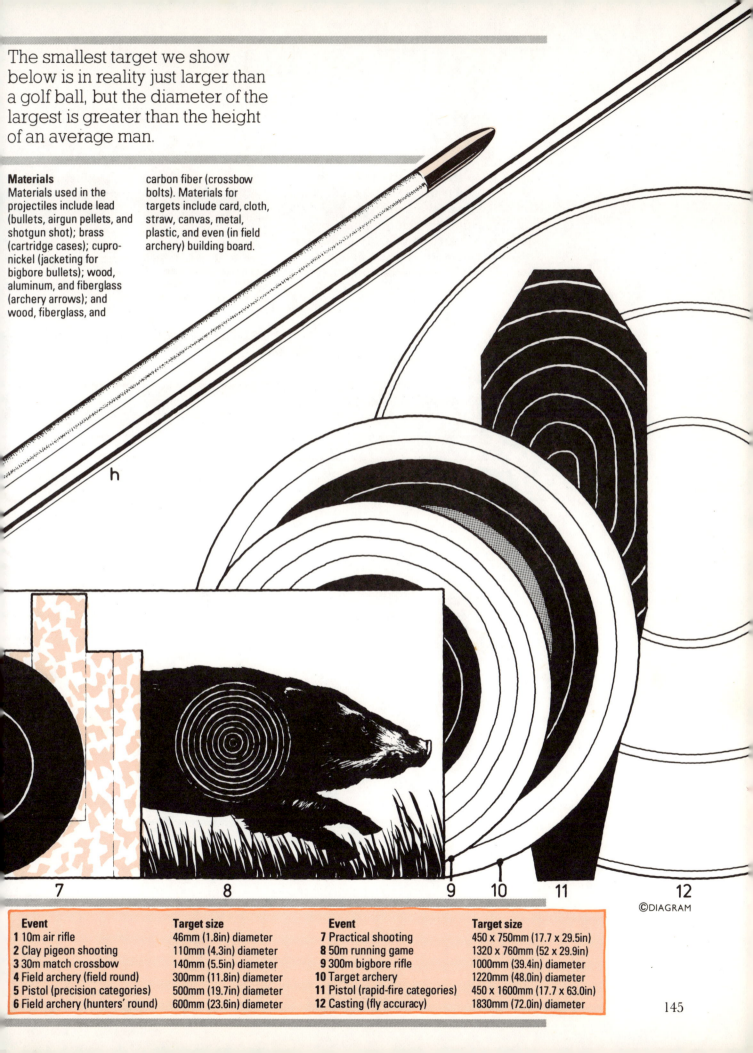

©DIAGRAM

Event	Target size	Event	Target size
1 10m air rifle	46mm (1.8in) diameter	**7** Practical shooting	450 x 750mm (17.7 x 29.5in)
2 Clay pigeon shooting	110mm (4.3in) diameter	**8** 50m running game	1320 x 760mm (52 x 29.9in)
3 30m match crossbow	140mm (5.5in) diameter	**9** 300m bigbore rifle	1000mm (39.4in) diameter
4 Field archery (field round)	300mm (11.8in) diameter	**10** Target archery	1220mm (48.0in) diameter
5 Pistol (precision categories)	500mm (19.7in) diameter	**11** Pistol (rapid-fire categories)	450 x 1600mm (17.7 x 63.0in)
6 Field archery (hunters' round)	600mm (23.6in) diameter	**12** Casting (fly accuracy)	1830mm (72.0in) diameter

TARGET SPORTS 3

The weapons used in target sports vary enormously, in both appearance and power. Here we compare these weapons, and the initial velocities they achieve – from bigbore rifle down to match crossbow. Comparison with different speeds at which man has traveled helps to make these projectile velocities more imaginable.

Weapons and velocities
Among our illustrations of weapons *below*, the bigbore (**1**) and smallbore (**3**) rifle drawings also help to show the differences between a standard rifle (**1**) and a free one (**3**). The shotgun (**2**) is of a type used for skeet. The center-fire pistol depicted (**6**) is a revolver, but semi-automatics are also used. The archery bow (**11**) is illustrated fitted with projecting stabilizers. The match crossbow (**12**) is of the 30m type.
Typical initial velocities for the various projectiles are

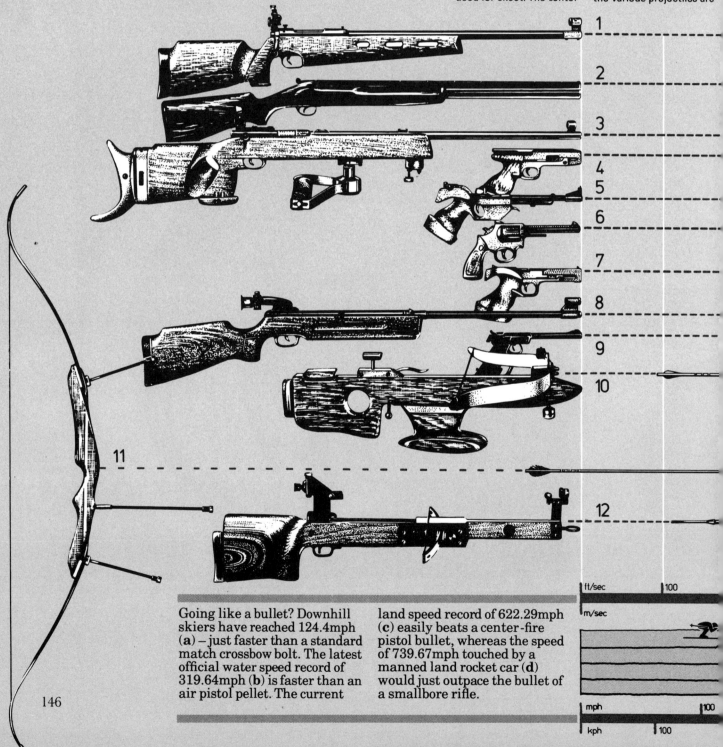

Going like a bullet? Downhill skiers have reached 124.4mph (**a**) – just faster than a standard match crossbow bolt. The latest official water speed record of 319.64mph (**b**) is faster than an air pistol pellet. The current land speed record of 622.29mph (**c**) easily beats a center-fire pistol bullet, whereas the speed of 739.67mph touched by a manned land rocket car (**d**) would just outpace the bullet of a smallbore rifle.

An estimated muzzle velocity of 54mph is credited to the human cannonball Emanuel Zacchini, performing at the Madison Square Garden in New York in 1940. He set a distance record of 175 feet.

listed in the table *right* and shown in the diagram *below*. The two fastest projectiles in the table escape our diagram. The bigbore rifle bullet (1)|has a muzzle speed more than twice that of the shotgun cartridge (2).

	Weapon	Initial velocity		Weapon	Initial velocity
1	Bigbore rifle	2850ft/sec (1943mph)	7	Rapid-fire pistol	750ft/sec (511mph)
2	Shotgun (12 bore)	1300ft/sec (886mph)	8	Air rifle	580ft/sec (395mph)
3	Smallbore rifle	1080ft/sec (736mph)	9	Air pistol	390ft/sec (266mph)
4	Standard pistol	1040ft/sec (709mph)	10	Archery crossbow	230ft/sec (157mph)
5	Free pistol	1000ft/sec (682mph)	11	Archery bow	190ft/sec (130mph)
6	Center-fire pistol	800ft/sec (545mph)	12	Match crossbow (30m)	180ft/sec (123mph)

Variations in velocity
Initial velocities can vary considerably from the figures given in the table *above* and illustrated here. The figure that is given for shotguns (2) is typical for a skeet gun, as illustrated, but guns for Olympic trap have a lower initial velocity of about 1200ft/sec. The smallbore rifle velocity (3) is correct for static target shooting, but in the running game target event a cartridge with 1350ft/sec initial velocity is often used. The figure for center-fire pistol (6) is for a .38in caliber revolver (when firing the specialized bullet used in center-fire target events); a semi-automatic would give a lower initial velocity of about 735ft/sec. Pistols for the rapid-fire events (7) are, as shown, used with a lower velocity cartridge than other smallbore pistols. This is to minimize the effect of recoil on the accuracy of successive shots. The figure for air pistols (9) is typical for a target gun – sporting guns have higher velocities. The velocity given for a 30m match crossbow (12) is for a wooden bolt with steel tip; recently developed materials such as carbon fiber can give as high as 210ft/sec. By comparison, a 10m match crossbow (not shown) has an initial velocity – using an aluminum bolt with steel tip – of about 175ft/sec.

©DIAGRAM

GOLF

Golf is a game of contrasting skills. Power is
needed to propel the ball from the tee,
accuracy and delicacy to putt it into the hole.
In between, golfers must play the ball as it
lies – on smooth turf, in a bunker (sand trap),
or in the rough. Here we compare the
equipment the golfer uses to meet these
contrasting needs.

Club	Angle of loft
Wedge (**A**)	51°
Putter (**B**)	4°

Ball size *below*
Shown actual size are a US
golf ball and a 2-wood. With
a minimum diameter of
1.68in, the US ball is
slightly larger than the UK
ball, whose minimum
diameter is 1.62in. The
maximum weight for both
balls is 1.62oz.

Ball speed
The maximum initial speed
of a golf ball is 170.5mph;
the Porsche Turbo car
shown *below* can reach
only 155mph. An average
golfer can achieve an initial
ball speed of 125mph –
about the speed of a
modern fast train.

At a stretch
Inside the ball's casing is a
thin rubber thread, wound
under tension around a
central core. The line XY
below shows to scale how
far this thread would
stretch if unwound – 279yd.
Incidentally, there are 332
dimples on a golf ball!

Clubs *above*
Golf clubs have either a
wooden head (woods) or a
steel head (irons). The
shafts are made of steel or
graphite. Golfers may use a
maximum of 14 clubs,
chosen from the four
woods (1-4), the nine
irons (1-9), and the special

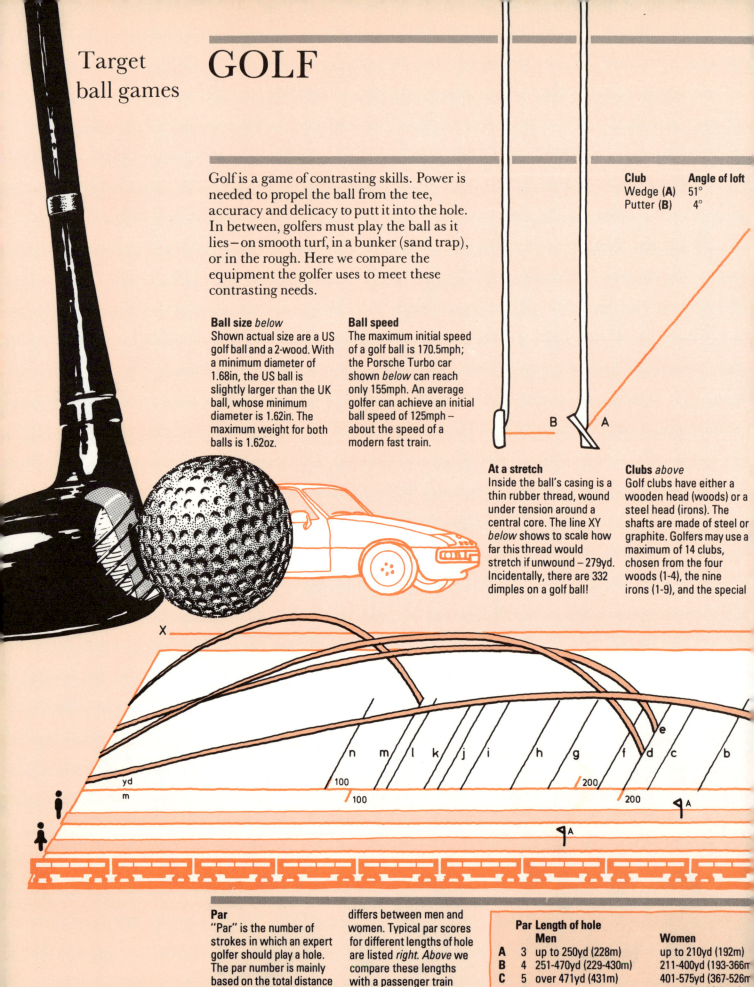

Par
"Par" is the number of
strokes in which an expert
golfer should play a hole.
The par number is mainly
based on the total distance
between the teeing
ground and green, and

differs between men and
women. Typical par scores
for different lengths of hole
are listed *right*. *Above* we
compare these lengths
with a passenger train
whose cars are 100ft long.

Par	Length of hole Men	Women
A	3	up to 250yd (228m)	up to 210yd (192m)
B	4	251-470yd (229-430m)	211-400yd (193-366m)
C	5	over 471yd (431m)	401-575yd (367-526m)
	6	—	over 576yd (527m)

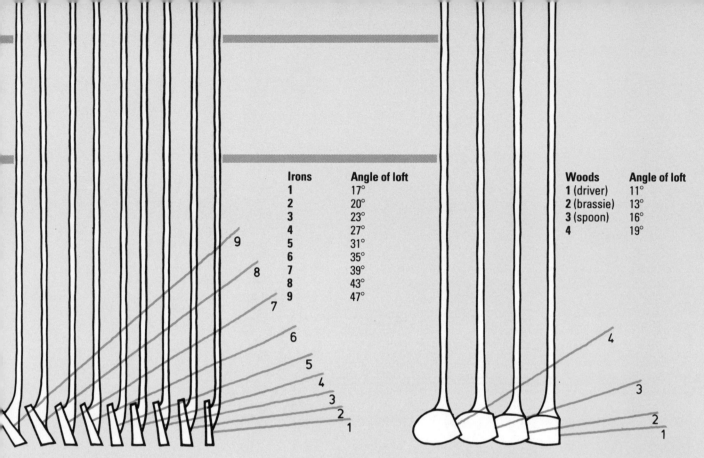

Irons	Angle of loft
1	17°
2	20°
3	23°
4	27°
5	31°
6	35°
7	39°
8	43°
9	47°

Woods	Angle of loft
1 (driver)	11°
2 (brassie)	13°
3 (spoon)	16°
4	19°

purpose clubs, which are the wedge (**A**) and the putter (**B**) Woods are used for hitting the ball over long distances, irons for the shorter, more lofted, shots. A wedge will lift the ball from rough ground or from bunkers. Putters are used on the greens.

Trajectories
The angle at which the club head is set on the shaft affects the angle at which the ball leaves the ground (the angle of loft), and the distance it travels. Listed and shown *above* is the average angle of loft for each club; the ranges of distance are listed *right* and (for men) shown *below*. Complete trajectories for the lowest and highest numbered clubs are also shown. A 4-wood has a greater angle of loft than a 1-iron, and so a higher trajectory, but the length of shot is the same.

Club		Average distances traveled by ball	
Woods		**Men**	**Women**
a	1	220-300yd (201-274m)	160-180yd (146-165m)
b	2	210-250yd (192-229m)	155-170yd (142-155m)
c	3	200-230yd (183-210m)	150-170yd (137-155m)
d	4	190-220yd (174-200m)	145-165yd (133-151m)
Irons			
e	1	190-220yd (174-200m)	145-165yd (133-151m)
f	2	180-210yd (165-192m)	140-155yd (128-142m)
g	3	170-190yd (155-174m)	135-150yd (123-137m)
h	4	155-175yd (142-160m)	125-140yd (114-128m)
i	5	140-155yd (128-142m)	115-130yd (105-119m)
j	6	125-145yd (114-133m)	110-120yd (100-110m)
k	7	120-140yd (110-128m)	100-110yd (91-100m)
l	8	110-125yd (100-114m)	90-100yd (82-91m)
m	9	90-120yd (82-110m)	70-80yd (64-73m)
n	Wedge	70-100yd (64-91m)	50-85yd (46-78m)

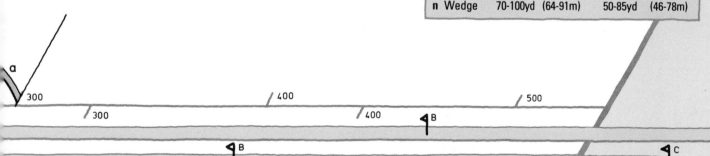

©DIAGRAM

The Old Course at St Andrews, Scotland, is probably the most famous golf course in the world. If you were to play a par round of golf there every day for a year, except Christmas Day and Thanksgiving, you would walk 1355 miles – the distance from Miami to Chicago.

CROQUET

In croquet, players use a mallet to hit balls through a course of hoops – and call on a wide range of skills and tactics in the process. Here we look at three modern croquet games: association croquet, which is played in some form in many parts of the world; roque, an American variant; and the informal game of lawn croquet.

Court sizes *below*
Shown here to scale are an association croquet lawn (**A**), measuring 84x105ft (25.6x32m), and a roque court (**B**), which measures 30x60ft (9.15x18.3m). Between them is a lawn tennis court drawn to the same scale.

A) Association croquet
Six hoops and one peg are arranged as shown, on a grass court. Four balls are always used: one player or pair takes the blue and the black balls, the other the red and the yellow. The aim is to run each hoop twice in the correct order (as shown by the arrow) and then hit the center peg. The first player or pair to do this with both balls wins. One tactical skill is in "taking croquet." If a player strikes his ball against any other (making a "roquet"), he places the striking ball so that it is touching the struck one, and hits it so both balls move ("taking croquet"). This allows him to speed his own balls or obstruct those of his opponents.

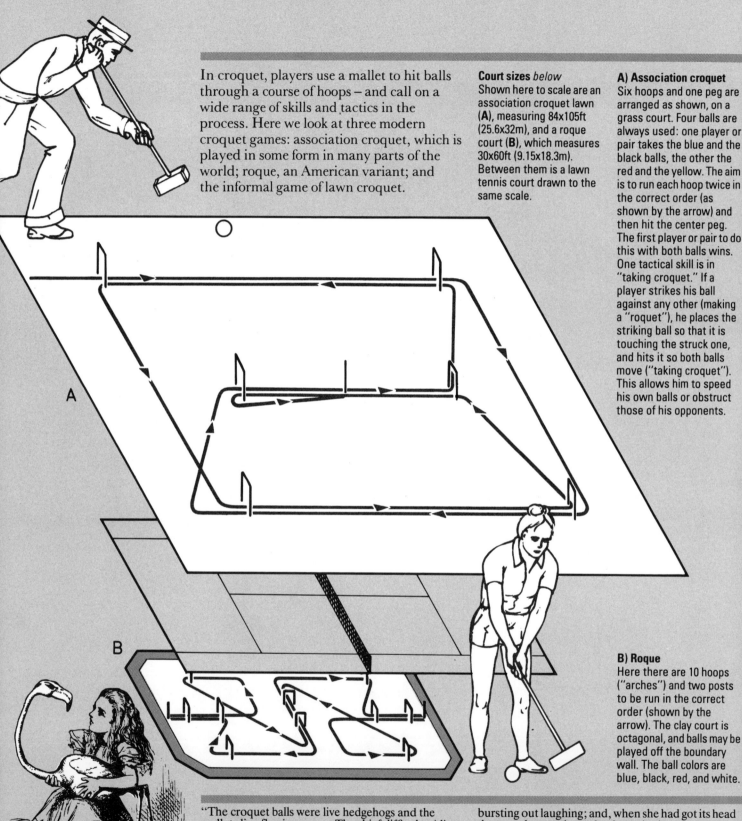

B) Roque
Here there are 10 hoops ("arches") and two posts to be run in the correct order (shown by the arrow). The clay court is octagonal, and balls may be played off the boundary wall. The ball colors are blue, black, red, and white.

"The croquet balls were live hedgehogs and the mallets live flamingoes . . . The chief difficulty Alice found at first was in managing her flamingo . . . just as she had got its neck nicely straightened out, and was going to give the hedgehog a blow with its head, it would twist itself round and look up in her face with such a puzzled expression that she could not help bursting out laughing; and, when she had got its head down and was going to begin again, it was very provoking to find that the hedgehog had unrolled itself and was in the act of crawling away. . . . Alice soon came to the conclusion that it was a very difficult game indeed."
(Extract from *Alice in Wonderland* by Lewis Carroll)

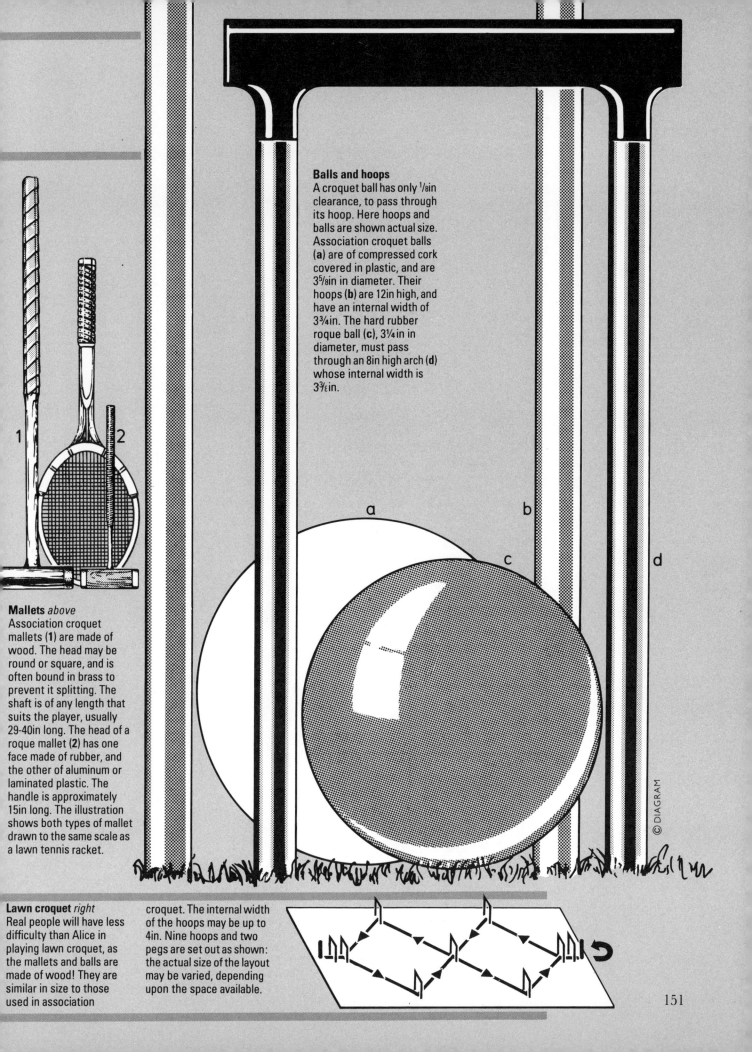

Balls and hoops
A croquet ball has only 1/8in clearance, to pass through its hoop. Here hoops and balls are shown actual size. Association croquet balls (**a**) are of compressed cork covered in plastic, and are 3⅝in in diameter. Their hoops (**b**) are 12in high, and have an internal width of 3¾in. The hard rubber roque ball (**c**), 3¼in in diameter, must pass through an 8in high arch (**d**) whose internal width is 3⅜in.

Mallets *above*
Association croquet mallets (**1**) are made of wood. The head may be round or square, and is often bound in brass to prevent it splitting. The shaft is of any length that suits the player, usually 29-40in long. The head of a roque mallet (**2**) has one face made of rubber, and the other of aluminum or laminated plastic. The handle is approximately 15in long. The illustration shows both types of mallet drawn to the same scale as a lawn tennis racket.

Lawn croquet *right*
Real people will have less difficulty than Alice in playing lawn croquet, as the mallets and balls are made of wood! They are similar in size to those used in association croquet. The internal width of the hoops may be up to 4in. Nine hoops and two pegs are set out as shown: the actual size of the layout may be varied, depending upon the space available.

© DIAGRAM

151

TERRAIN GAMES

Here we compare two grass games, two ice games, and two playable over any strip of ground. Very different games, in fact. But in each you try to get nearer to a target than your opponent – by aiming nearer to it, by knocking your opponent away from it, and even, in some of these games, by knocking the target to a new position.

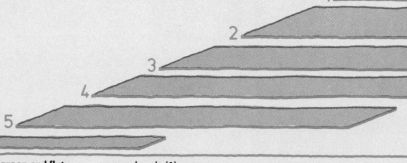

Crown green and flat green bowls
These games feature balls (bowls) (a) rolled across grass. A smaller ball, the jack (b), is rolled first to form the target. The bowls are "biased" so they run in a curve; the crown green jack is also biased. Crown green bowls (1) uses a green that rises gently from edges to center. Each new play begins from the jack's last position. Flat green bowls (2) uses a level "rink" that is one strip of a square green. Each new play begins from a different end of the rink.

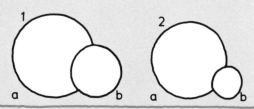

Curling and eisschiessen
These are played by sliding "stones" over ice. The target is marked on the ice, and so is not movable (though its center may be indicated by a movable wooden marker). Play is from alternate ends of the ice strip. Curling (3) is the best-known form. The stones are of granite, and brooms are used by teammates to clear the ice in front of a stone and help its run. In European eisschiessen (4) the "stone" is made of wood.

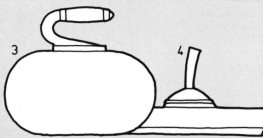

Boules and horseshoe pitching
In both these, a missile is thrown through the air at a target on the ground. In boules (5), metal balls (a) are used, with a smaller wooden jack (b) thrown first to form the target. Any strip of ground will do (dimensions shown are for the version *jeu provençal*). In horseshoe pitching (6), special "horseshoes" (a) are thrown at a target stake fixed in the ground (b). Moist clay around the stake prevents bouncing or rolling. In both games, alternate ends are used.

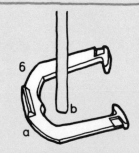

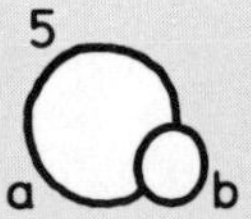

Size and weight
Shown actual size *opposite* are the various missiles used in terrain games – compared in size with a life-size house mouse. In the table *right* are given dimensions and weights for both missiles and targets.

Game		Weight (max)	Diameter (max)
1 Crown green bowls	bowl	no restrictions	no restrictions
	jack	1lb 7oz (652g)	3¾in (9.5cm)
2 Flat green bowls	bowl	3lb 8oz (1.58kg)	5¾in (14.6cm)
	jack	10oz (283.5g)	2½in (6.35cm)
3 Curling	stone	44lb (20kg)	11½in (29.21cm)
4 Eisschiessen	eisstock	13lb 3½oz (6kg)	11⅞in (30cm)
5 Boules	boule	1lb 12¼oz (800g)	3⅛in (8cm)
	jack	no restrictions	1⅜in (3.5cm)
6 Horseshoe pitching	horseshoe	2lb 8oz (1.13kg)	7¼in (18.4cm) wide

Areas
The table *right* shows the areas needed for different terrain games. A green for crown green bowls could contain four baseball infields.

	Game	Dimensions
1	Crown green bowls	144x144ft (44x44m)
2	Flat green bowls	132x19ft (40.2x5.8m)
3	Curling	138x14ft (42x4.27m)
4	Eisschiessen	138x13ft (42x4m)
5	Boules	82x13ft (25x4m)
6	Horseshoe pitching	44x6ft (13.4x1.8m)

©DIAGRAM

ALLEY GAMES

Basically, these are the games in which
skittles or pins are knocked down with a ball.
Tenpin bowling is the best-known – a US
game now played internationally. But there
are other forms, and here we compare them
with tenpin.

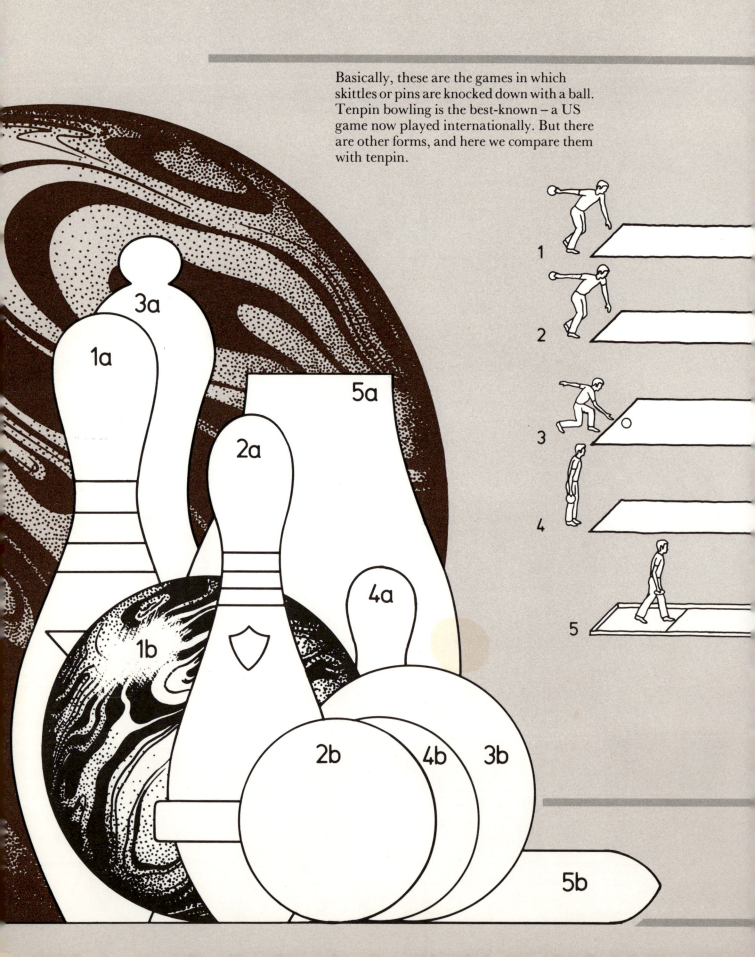

3a

1a

5a

2a

4a

1b

2b

4b

3b

5b

1

2

3

4

5

A tenpin ball weighs approximately the same as a 6-month-old baby: 16lb.

1) Tenpin bowling
This features a large ball, with fingerholes for grip. Players bowl two balls to a turn, and score for pins knocked down. There are bonuses for all pins down with the first or both balls. Pins are reset and balls returned automatically.

2) Canadian fivepin bowling
This is similar to tenpin, but uses a smaller ball and five smaller pins each fitted with a rubber deadening strip around its belly. Scoring is as for tenpin, but pins score different points according to their position.

3) European ninepin bowling
This was the ancestor of tenpin bowling. Today the main ninepin game is played on an asphalt alley, using a 6in diameter ball. One pin, the "king," is larger and heavier than the others.

4) Duckpin bowling
Played on standard tenpin alleys, this uses smaller pins and a smaller ball with no finger holes. Players have three balls to a turn. In "rubber band duckpin," a variant, the belly of each pin is fitted with a rubber strip.

5) English pub skittles
This features a short alley and bulky skittles. Players throw through the air a small ball or a flat wooden disk called a "cheese." But there are many varieties of English skittles, with rules varying from one locality to another.

©DIAGRAM

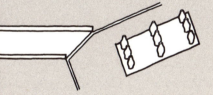

Measuring up
On the opposite page we show to scale all the targets (**a**) and "missiles" (**b**) used in the games above. Also shown, behind them, is a tenpin ball to actual size. In the table *below* we list for each game the height of the pin, the diameter and weight of the ball (or, in English skittles, the "cheese"), and the length of the alley, from pitching line to nearest target point.

	Pin (a): height	Ball (b): diameter	weight	Alley length
1 Tenpin bowling	15in (38.1cm)	8½in (21.6cm)	16lb (7.3kg)**	60ft (18.3m)
2 Fivepin bowling	12½in (31.7cm)	5in (12.7cm)	3½lb (1.6kg)**	60ft (18.3m)
3 Ninepin bowling	17in (43.2cm)	6in (15.2cm)	6½lb (3.0kg)	64ft (19.5m)
4 Duckpin bowling	9²/₅in (23.9cm)*	5in (12.7cm)	3¾lb (1.7kg)**	60ft (18.3m)
5 English skittles	14½in (36.8cm)	8¾in (22.2cm)	12lb (5.4kg)†	21ft (6.4m)
*height is for the king pin **maximum †average				

If its pin area is included, a tenpin alley is long enough to pitch a baseball in.

BILLIARD GAMES

Several forms of billiards have developed over the years. In all of them, a player uses a long wooden "cue" to propel one ball across the table, to hit another ball. His turn (or "break") lasts for as long as he goes on scoring. The differences lie in the number of balls on the table, and in how scoring occurs.

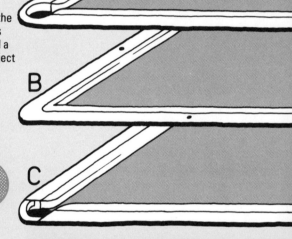

Cue balls and object balls

The ball a player strikes with his cue is called the "cue ball," the one he aims for across the table is an "object ball." *Below* we show the balls used in different billiard games. Pocket billiards (pool) and snooker use one white cue ball, played by both players, and many colored object balls. Pool (**a**) has 15 numbered object balls. (1 through 8 are in solid colors, 9 through 15 are striped.) Snooker (**b**) uses 15 red object balls, and 6 "color" ones – yellow, green, brown, blue, pink, and black. In carom billiards (**c**) and English billiards (**d**) there are two white cue balls – one marked with one or two spots. Each player keeps to one of the cue balls, and treats his opponent's cue ball and a third (red) ball as the object balls.

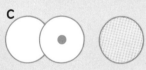

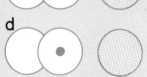

 cue balls

 red ball

colored balls

Game	Dimensions
A Pool	9ft x 4ft 6in (2.74 x 1.37m)
B Carom billiards	10ft x 5ft (3.05 x 1.5m)
C Snooker, English billiards	12ft x 6ft 1½in (3.66 x 1.87m)

Starting and scoring

The text *right* compares how you score and win in the main billiard games, while the diagrams *below* compare the starting positions. Note that in English billiards, only the first player's cue ball is on table for the opening shot.

Carom billiards

This is played on a table with no pockets. A player scores if his cue ball hits both the other balls on one stroke (called making a carom). The main form is balkline billiards *below*. Here the table is divided into several areas – large "balk" areas and small "anchor" areas. During his break, a player may score only one or (in other versions) two caroms in succession in any one area.

Pocket billiards (pool)

Here a player scores by potting the object balls – i.e. striking them with the cue ball so they fall into a pocket. He must say before each stroke which ball and pocket he intends. In the "8-ball" game, one player pots balls 1 through 7, and the other 9 through 15. The first to complete and then pocket the 8 ball wins. In the "continuous" game, players pot any ball, and when 14 balls have gone down they are replaced in triangle formation. The first player to reach an agreed target score wins.

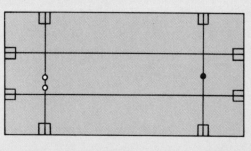

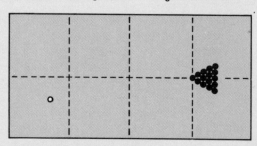

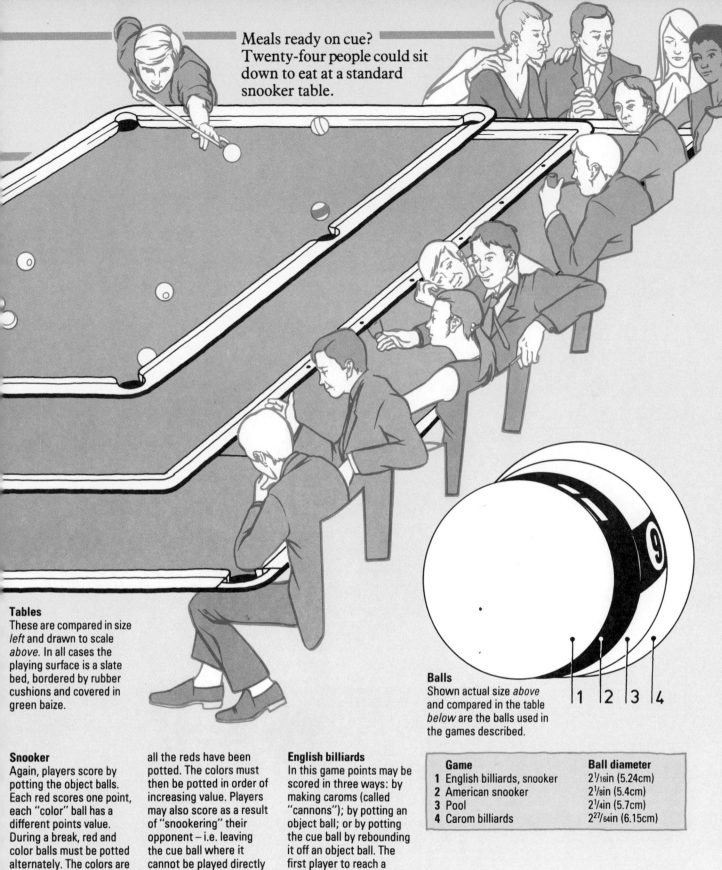

Meals ready on cue?
Twenty-four people could sit
down to eat at a standard
snooker table.

Balls
Shown actual size *above*
and compared in the table
below are the balls used in
the games described.

Tables
These are compared in size
left and drawn to scale
above. In all cases the
playing surface is a slate
bed, bordered by rubber
cushions and covered in
green baize.

Snooker
Again, players score by
potting the object balls.
Each red scores one point,
each "color" ball has a
different points value.
During a break, red and
color balls must be potted
alternately. The colors are
replaced on the table until
all the reds have been
potted. The colors must
then be potted in order of
increasing value. Players
may also score as a result
of "snookering" their
opponent – i.e. leaving
the cue ball where it
cannot be played directly
at the correct object ball.

English billiards
In this game points may be
scored in three ways: by
making caroms (called
"cannons"); by potting an
object ball; or by potting
the cue ball by rebounding
it off an object ball. The
first player to reach a
target score wins.

Game	Ball diameter
1 English billiards, snooker	2$\frac{1}{16}$in (5.24cm)
2 American snooker	2$\frac{1}{8}$in (5.4cm)
3 Pool	2$\frac{1}{4}$in (5.7cm)
4 Carom billiards	2$\frac{27}{64}$in (6.15cm)

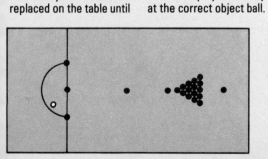

©DIAGRAM

157

NET GAMES

Net games date back to medieval times – to the simple rope strung up in village square or monastery courtyard. The tradition survives in court (real) tennis; but it was the leisured world of the 19th century country house that gave us the tennis and badminton of today. Here we compare the courts and basics of the main net games.

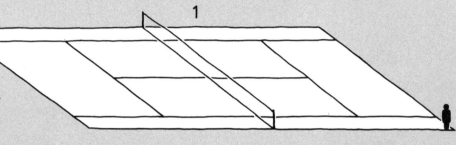

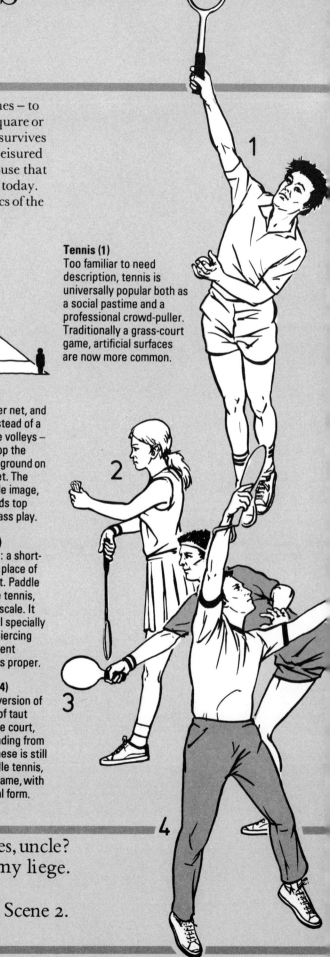

Tennis (1)
Too familiar to need description, tennis is universally popular both as a social pastime and a professional crowd-puller. Traditionally a grass-court game, artificial surfaces are now more common.

Badminton (2)
This uses a higher net, and a shuttlecock instead of a ball. All shots are volleys – a player must stop the shuttle touching ground on his side of the net. The game has a gentle image, but shuttle speeds top 100mph in top-class play.

Paddle tennis (3)
Enter the paddle: a short-handled "bat" in place of the strung racket. Paddle tennis is just like tennis, but on a smaller scale. It uses a tennis ball specially "deadened" by piercing with a pin. Excellent training for tennis proper.

Platform tennis (4)
Another paddle version of tennis. Screens of taut wire surround the court, and a ball rebounding from the court onto these is still in play. Like paddle tennis, it is mainly a US game, with doubles the usual form.

King Henry: What treasures, uncle?
Exeter: Tennis balls, my liege.

Henry V, Act I Scene 2.

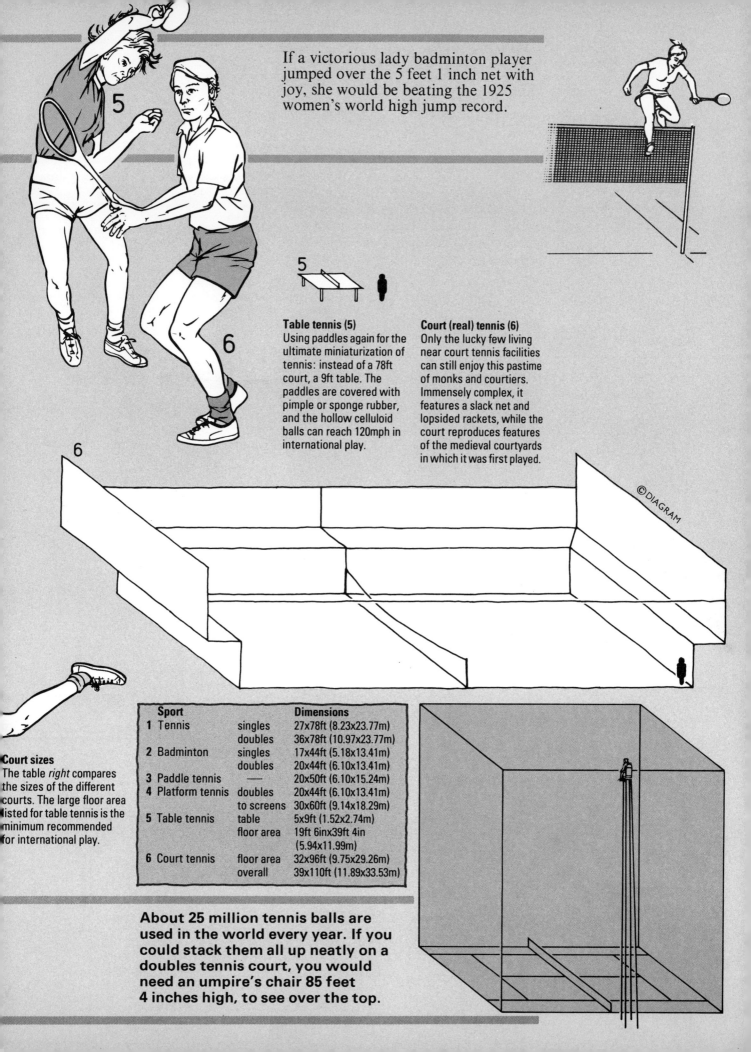

If a victorious lady badminton player jumped over the 5 feet 1 inch net with joy, she would be beating the 1925 women's world high jump record.

Table tennis (5)
Using paddles again for the ultimate miniaturization of tennis: instead of a 78ft court, a 9ft table. The paddles are covered with pimple or sponge rubber, and the hollow celluloid balls can reach 120mph in international play.

Court (real) tennis (6)
Only the lucky few living near court tennis facilities can still enjoy this pastime of monks and courtiers. Immensely complex, it features a slack net and lopsided rackets, while the court reproduces features of the medieval courtyards in which it was first played.

©DIAGRAM

Court sizes
The table *right* compares the sizes of the different courts. The large floor area listed for table tennis is the minimum recommended for international play.

Sport		Dimensions
1 Tennis	singles	27x78ft (8.23x23.77m)
	doubles	36x78ft (10.97x23.77m)
2 Badminton	singles	17x44ft (5.18x13.41m)
	doubles	20x44ft (6.10x13.41m)
3 Paddle tennis	—	20x50ft (6.10x15.24m)
4 Platform tennis	doubles	20x44ft (6.10x13.41m)
	to screens	30x60ft (9.14x18.29m)
5 Table tennis	table	5x9ft (1.52x2.74m)
	floor area	19ft 6inx39ft 4in (5.94x11.99m)
6 Court tennis	floor area	32x96ft (9.75x29.26m)
	overall	39x110ft (11.89x33.53m)

About 25 million tennis balls are used in the world every year. If you could stack them all up neatly on a doubles tennis court, you would need an umpire's chair 85 feet 4 inches high, to see over the top.

Court games WALL GAMES

In these court games, opponents share the same space, and try to keep playing the ball back onto the court's front wall. Usually, in fact, the court is like a room, and the ball can bounce off other walls on its way to or from the target wall.

Court handball, paddleball, and racquetball
These American games share identical courts and similar rules. Each has one-wall (**2**), three-wall (**3**), and four-wall (**4**) versions. Court handball (**a**) was the original game. Paddleball (**b**) and racquetball (**c**) are

more recent. Racquetball differs from squash in its short-handled racket and lively ball. Also, unlike squash, the ceiling is a part of the playing area. Paddleball is the only walled-court game played with a paddle. While racquetball emphasizes

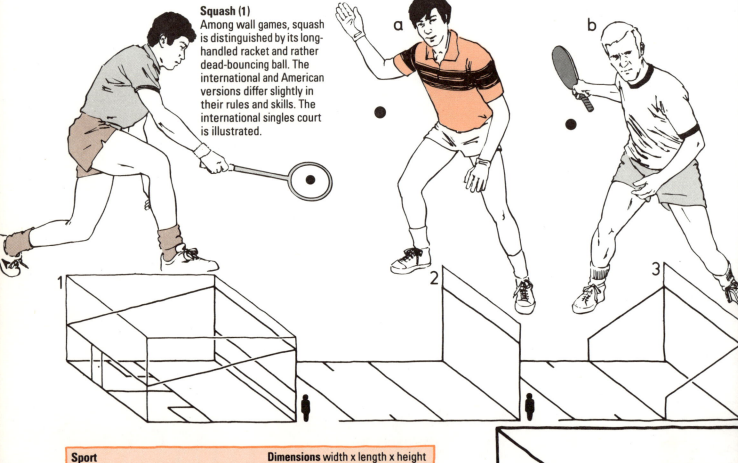

Squash (1)
Among wall games, squash is distinguished by its long-handled racket and rather dead-bouncing ball. The international and American versions differ slightly in their rules and skills. The international singles court is illustrated.

Sport		Dimensions width x length x height
Squash	international singles (**1**)	21x32x15ft (6.40x9.75x4.57m)
	American singles	18ft 6inx32x16ft (5.64x9.75x4.88m)
Court handball, paddleball, racquetball		
	one-wall (**2**)	20x34x16ft (6.10x10.37x4.88m)
	three-wall (**3**)	20x34x16ft (6.10x10.37x4.88m)
	four-wall (**4**)	20x40x20ft (6.10x12.19x6.10m)
Rugby fives (**5**)		18x28x15ft (5.49x8.54x4.57m)
Jai alai (**6**)		40x176x40ft (12.20x53.70x12.20m)

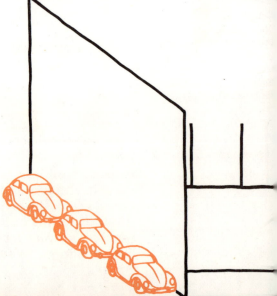

Court size *above*
Here we compare the sizes of the different courts. Width is the first of the dimensions given, then length, then height. The height given refers to the playing area only.

The little-known game of jai alai is not just the fastest of court games – it also uses the biggest court. You could park 102 Volkswagens on a jai alai *fronton* – and still have room for the drivers in the last row to get out!

Jai alai is the fastest of all court games: service speeds of 188mph have been recorded. A jai alai ball going this speed in 1927 would have beaten Lindberg across the Atlantic by 14¼ hours.

agility, paddleball – and court handball – depend more on power shots and body blocking.

Rugby fives (5)
Here, as in court handball, gloves are used to strike the ball. An unusual feature is that only the receiver of service may score. This rare game originated in the 19th century at one of England's great private schools.

Jai alai (6)
The best-known modern form of the old Basque game of pelota. Players propel the ball with a wicker basket (*cesta*) strapped to the hand. The court (*fronton*), in addition to its front wall, has a back wall but only one side wall.

©DIAGRAM

BALLS, RACKETS, PADDLES

Early court games were played with balls of leather, stuffed with hair, feathers, or cloth. Players used their bare hands; later came gloves, wooden bats, and finally strung rackets. But it was the introduction of the rubber ball that revolutionized court games, and made possible the fast and volatile sports we know today.

Ball weight
The table *right* shows set weights for the different balls used in court games, and for the badminton shuttlecock. *Below* we line them all up, from lightest to heaviest – and compare the weight of the world's smallest bird, Helena's hummingbird (0.07oz). Each bird symbol represents one hummingbird. A table tennis ball weighs just over one hummingbird – a jai alai ball almost 64 of them.

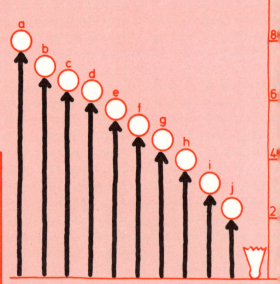

	Sport	Weight of projectile
1	Table tennis	0.085-0.09oz (2.40-2.53g)
2	Badminton	0.166-0.194oz (4.73-5.50g)
3	Squash: international	0.82-0.87oz (23.3-24.6g)
4	Squash: US doubles	1.05-1.10oz (29.77-31.18g)
5	Squash: US singles	1.10-1.15oz (31.18-32.60g)
6	Racquetball	1.4oz (39.69g)
7	Rugby fives	1.5oz (42.52g)
8	Paddle tennis	2oz (56.7g)
9	Lawn tennis	2.00-2.0625oz (56.7-58.5g)
10	Paddleball	2.3oz (65.02g)
11	Court handball	2.3oz (65.02g)
12	Platform tennis	2.47-2.65oz (70-75g)
13	Court (real) tennis	2.5-2.75oz (71-78g)
14	Jai alai	4.5oz (127g)

Ball bounce *above*
This depends on ball temperature, surface material, etc. But here we compare regulation minimum bounces in different games under control conditions. A badminton shuttlecock is effectively "dead" of course.

a Table tennis
b Racquetball
c Paddleball
d Court handball
e Tennis
f Platform tennis
g Paddle tennis
h US squash, doubles
i US squash, singles
j International squash

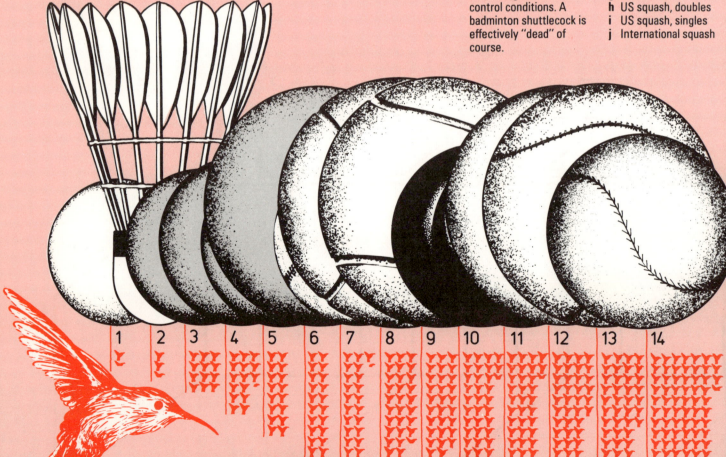

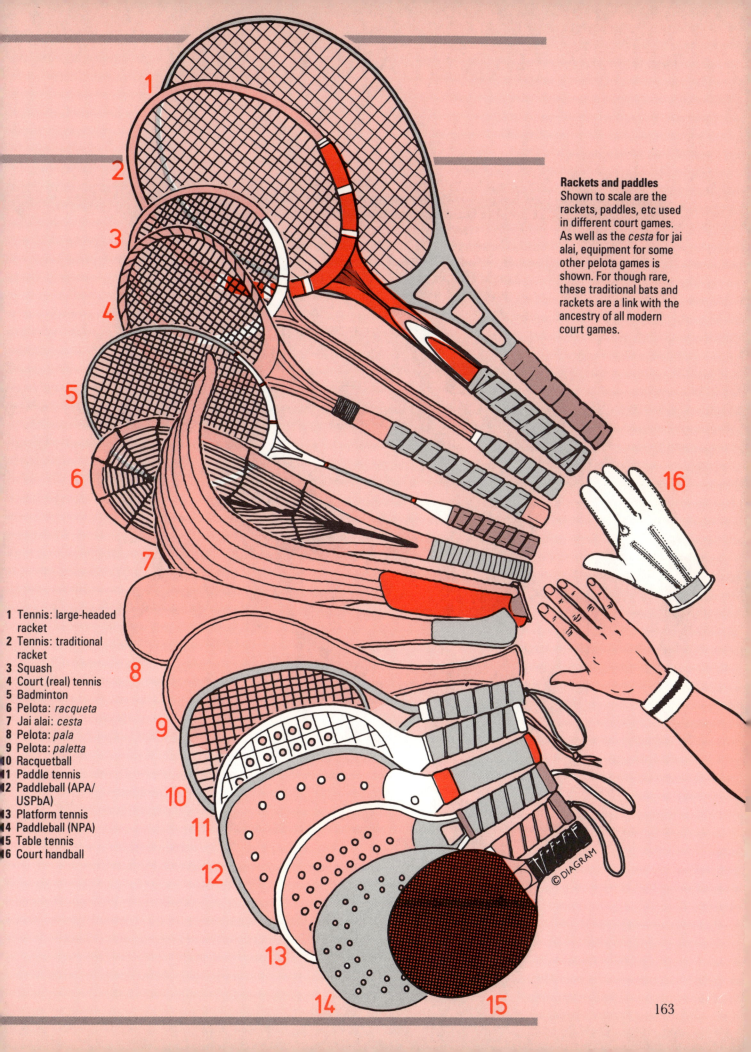

Rackets and paddles
Shown to scale are the rackets, paddles, etc used in different court games. As well as the *cesta* for jai alai, equipment for some other pelota games is shown. For though rare, these traditional bats and rackets are a link with the ancestry of all modern court games.

1 Tennis: large-headed racket
2 Tennis: traditional racket
3 Squash
4 Court (real) tennis
5 Badminton
6 Pelota: *racqueta*
7 Jai alai: *cesta*
8 Pelota: *pala*
9 Pelota: *paletta*
10 Racquetball
11 Paddle tennis
12 Paddleball (APA/USPbA)
13 Platform tennis
14 Paddleball (NPA)
15 Table tennis
16 Court handball

©DIAGRAM

HANDBALL GAMES

We now come to those sports that attract the greatest popular following, the team ball games. We begin by comparing basic principles, starting with the handball games (those in which the ball is not struck with a stick or kicked). These can be divided into three main groups, based on the scoring procedure that is used.

Basket-scoring games
These are handball games in which points are scored by throwing the ball into a basket at the opponents' end of the court.
In netball (**1**), which is usually played by women, players may not run with the ball or dribble it, and

may pass the ball only by throwing or bouncing it. The hard-surfaced court is divided into five playing areas, and a player is restricted to certain areas depending on her team position.
Korfball (**2**) is similar in the method of playing the ball,

and in the division into zones to restrict individual movement (there are two- and three-zone versions). But a korfball team is made up of equal numbers of men and women, and a grass pitch is traditional, although hard-court play is also now popular.

Basketball (**3**), the best-known of these games, is always on a hard court. Players' movements are not restricted, and they may dribble the ball (bounce it on the ground while moving), and pass it in various ways.
Pato (**4**) is a basket-scoring

game played on horseback and belongs to Argentina. Peculiarities include a windsock-shaped "basket," and a ball with six leather handles.

Hakozaki-gu no tama-seseri is a ritual handball game played at a certain Japanese temple. Each team tries to be the one to return a ceremonial wooden ball to the temple shrine, and so be assured of good fortune in the coming year. Meanwhile priests and spectators shower them with cold water!

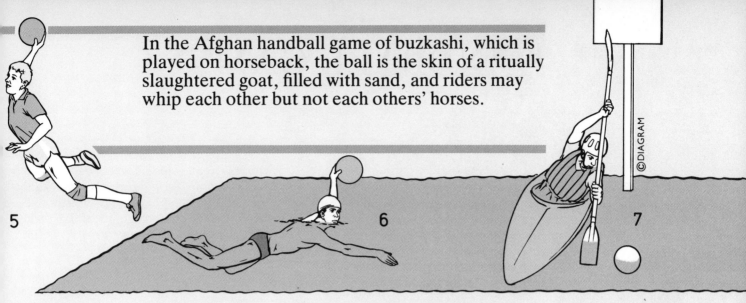

In the Afghan handball game of buzkashi, which is played on horseback, the ball is the skin of a ritually slaughtered goat, filled with sand, and riders may whip each other but not each others' horses.

©DIAGRAM

5

6

7

Goal-scoring games
Handball games of this type are not so well-known, but do include one land and three water games. Most of them favor rapid passing by limiting ball-play techniques and possession time.
In team handball (**5**), a player may not play the ball with lower legs or feet, hold it for more than three seconds without at least passing it from hand to hand, or take more than three steps without bouncing it on the ground. In water polo (**6**), a player may catch, lift, dribble, pass, or shoot the ball, but only one-handed, and may not punch it or keep it for more than 45 seconds. Canoe polo (**7**) takes two distinct forms – which we call for convenience the "pool" and "open-water" versions. The first (as played in Britain, for example) is held mainly in swimming pools, and the goals are boards against which the ball has to strike. Canoe paddles may be used to stop or deflect the ball, or to draw it across the water, but not to strike it; and when a player handles the ball he must throw it at least one meter away within five seconds. The open-water form (as played in Germany) uses a larger area of water and normal goals. Play is slower and use of the paddle less restricted (although it is still mainly a handball game).

8

9

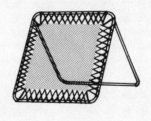

10

Other games
The remaining games are special cases with few common features. First there are two Frisbee ™ games (**8**). In the first, ultimate Frisbee, a team scores if it succeeds in passing the Frisbee to a player who is across the opponents' goal line. In the second, guts, the teams line up facing each other, and throw the Frisbee back and forth; a team scores if the opponents make a bad throw or fail to catch a good one.
The other two games are ball games. In tchouk-ball (**9**) there is a "goal" in the form of a rebound net. Basically a team scores if its shot hits the net and is not caught on the rebound by the opposing side. But the opponents score if the shot rebounds to the thrower himself, or out of court, or into a forbidden zone, or if the shot misses the net. There are two versions: one-way (with only one rebound net, used by both teams), and two-way (with rebound nets at each end of the pitch). Finally, in volleyball (**10**), we have a team game in the form of a "court" game (like tennis), with opposing teams trying to keep a ball moving back and forth over a net.

The informal American game of earthball features a ball several feet in diameter! Any number participate, and the aim is simply to push the ball over the opponents' goal line.

FOOTBALL GAMES

Football games fall into three distinct groups. On this page we first consider soccer, the one game in which all handling of the ball is forbidden; and then go on to those games that do permit handling of the ball but (because of how they restrict tackling) share with soccer an open, free-flowing style of play. Then on the opposite page we compare those football games in which handling of the ball is coupled with forceful body tackling. As a result play is frequently interrupted by "dead" or grounded balls, and so the style of play here is much more a matter of slow territorial gain.

Soccer (1)
Soccer (or Association football) is played all over the world. The basis of the game is of course very simple: to get the ball into the opponents' goal. Any part of the body may be used except hands and arms. (The goalkeeper may play the ball with hands and arms within his own penalty area.) The winning team is the one to score most goals. Fouls by a defending team within their penalty area result in a penalty kick at the goal by the attackers, with only the goalkeeper defending.

Australian football (2)
This is played on a large oval pitch (in fact, on cricket pitches during the winter season). The main technique is distance kicking of the ball—caught directly by a teammate it entitles him to a free kick. A player may also punch the ball (but not throw it), and run with it if he touches or bounces it on the ground at least every 10m (c.33ft). Scoring is by kicking the ball between goalposts, for a "goal" (between the center posts) or a "behind" (between the outer posts).

Gaelic football (3)
This is almost entirely restricted to Ireland. A player may catch, punch, bounce, or kick the ball, or strike it with his hands when it is off the ground. He may not throw it, pick it directly off the ground, or hold it for more than four steps without bouncing it. Tackling is by shoulder charging. Scoring is by getting the ball into the goal (for a "goal") or over the crossbar (for a "point").

Speedball (4)
In this North American game, players may catch, throw, or kick the ball, but not carry it or pick it up from the ground with their hands. Physical contact is also forbidden. Scoring is by kicking goals and by touchdowns.

Touchball (5)
This is also known as Finnish rugby. Players may catch or carry the ball, and pass it backward, but must release it if touched on the back by an opponent. Kicking the ball is not allowed. Scoring is by touchdowns.

Cycleball is a form of soccer played on bicycles. The front wheel is used to trap, dribble, and "kick" the ball! Although a minority sport, cycleball has in fact its own annual world championships.

The Eton wall game is a traditional and immensely complicated form of football played only at Eton, England's most famous private school. The pitch around which the game has grown includes two brick walls, a ladder, a door, and a tree!

American college football

(6) Here players may kick, carry, and throw the ball. The ball becomes dead – a "down" – if the player in possession touches the ground with any part of his body except hands or feet. Play then restarts with a scrimmage (a): the two opposing teams line up facing each other, and the team that is in possession "snaps" (passes) the ball back and tries to pass and run it through the opposing line. Passes can be made forward from behind the line of scrimmage, or laterally anywhere on the field. A team loses possession if it does not advance 10yd by running and passing in the course of four "downs." Scoring is by touchdowns and kicked goals. Penalty points are lost if a team retreats the ball and downs it in its own end zone, or plays the ball over its own end line.

American professional football

Differences in play from the college game are that a player is not "down" if he falls to the ground, as long as no opponent touches him; that if a ball is dropped on a lateral pass it can still be advanced by the opposing team; and that a pass receiver must have both feet in bounds.

Canadian football

Again, the game resembles American college football. The main differences are that teams and pitches are larger; that the goals are at the front of the end zones; that an attacking team has only three "downs" in which to gain 10yd; and that in a scrimmage, the defending players are more restricted, and attacking players less so. Also the rules on kicked balls and the details of scoring differ.

Rugby union (7)

This is the main amateur form of rugby. Players may carry or kick the ball, or pass it back. Scoring is by touchdowns ("tries") and kicked goals. If a player is grounded, the ball is released, and opposing players form a loose struggle for possession. After a minor foul such as a forward pass, a set scrum (b) for possession is held: the forwards of each team bend down, bind together, and push against their opponents, and the ball is pitched between the feet of the two front rows.

Rugby league

The main difference from rugby union is that a grounded player may keep possession: he is allowed to stand and "play the ball" by kicking or heeling it in any direction. The resulting game differs considerably in tactics.

©DIAGRAM

In South-East Asia and the Philippines they play a football game on badminton courts! Known as sepak takraw, it is like volleyball in being a team game played across a net – but hands and arms may *not* be used.

STICK-AND-BALL GAMES

These are all goal-scoring games in which the ball is normally hit with a stick, rather than kicked or thrown. They fall into four groups: those in which players run, those in which they skate, those in which they are mounted on horses or bicycles, and those played swimming in water.

Running games
Three of these games are known internationally: men's and women's lacrosse, and field hockey. Men's lacrosse (**1**) and women's lacrosse (**2**) differ in pitch, team size, and various playing rules. But in both, players use sticks fitted with nets to catch, throw, and carry the ball, and the playing area extends behind the goals. Field hockey (**3**) is more typical of stick-and-ball games, in that the ball may be struck but not caught, thrown, or carried. Also the goals are on the pitch end lines.

The three other games in this group all belong to the Gaelic tradition. In the Scottish game of shinty (**4**), the basic principles are very like those of field hockey. But in the Irish game of hurling (**5**), the ball may be struck with the hand or kicked if it is off the ground, as well as struck or carried using the stick (hurley). Camogie (**6**) is a women's version of hurling, with less body contact.

Holani is a form of hockey played in Turkey. There are apparently no time limits, no regulations about the size of the pitch, no limits on team size – and in fact very few playing rules of any kind!

Some stick-and-ball games are not widely known. Box lacrosse is a Canadian form of lacrosse, played on ice hockey rinks covered with matting; polo crosse is a horseback hybrid of polo and lacrosse; indoor hockey is a European game in which the ball may be pushed but not hit; and indoor cycle polo is a two-a-side European game played only by women.

Skating games

Ice hockey (7) is the best-known of these. The rink is edged with boards, to keep the puck in play, and play continues behind the goals. Bandy (8) is a Scandinavian equivalent, played on a larger rink with the goals on the end lines. Roller hockey (using roller skates rather than ice skates) comes in two distinct forms. The game using a ball (9) is played internationally, that using a puck is essentially a North American version of ice hockey.

Riding games

Polo (10) is played on horseback, using long-handled sticks with mallet heads. Complex rules govern the right-of-way between the opposing horsemen, and play is divided by several intervals at which players change to fresh ponies. Cycle polo (11), which also uses a mallet, occurs in several versions. That played in India and neighboring countries is closely related to polo itself; however elsewhere there has been greater modification.

Swimming games

Underwater hockey exists in various versions in different parts of the world. The best-known form (sometimes called octopush) (12) features a lead puck that is played using short, triangular-headed "pushers."

© DIAGRAM

Dakyu is a Japanese form of polo, played on a small pitch with racket-like sticks. During the course of the game, 11 balls are used: five red, five white, and one striped!

RUN-SCORING GAMES

In the run-scoring games, one team bats while the other pitches (or bowls) and fields. The batters try to hit the ball far enough away to allow runs to be scored before their opponents retrieve it. The fielders try to get the batters "out" in various ways. The roles reverse at the end of each "inning" (called an "innings" in the UK).

Pitch layout
In the run-scoring games, the infield area has set dimensions, the outfield does not. (In the outfield only fielding occurs.) Our illustrations show infields for baseball (**A**), softball (**B**), rounders (**C**), and cricket (**D**), including batting positions, pitching or bowling positions, and the route of the batter's run. (In cricket the action switches every six or eight balls between two different batting positions, each with a batsman, and two corresponding bowling positions, each with its own bowler.)

● batting position
◁ pitching position
→ batter's run

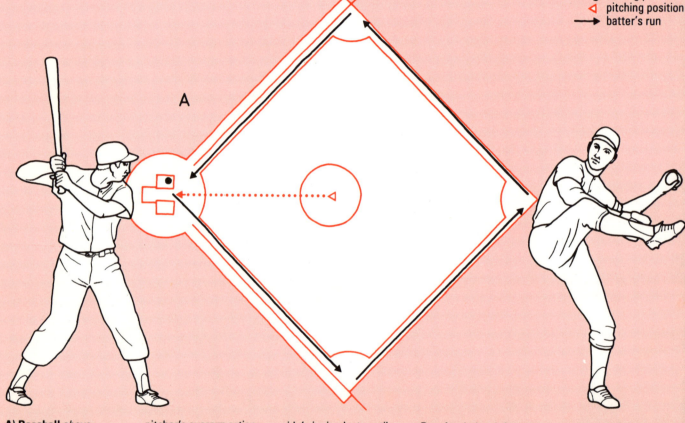

A) Baseball *above*
In a simple comparison between the various run-scoring games that are played in different parts of the world, baseball is characterized by the diamond layout of the batting (home) plate and the running bases; the pitcher's overarm action; the batter's rounded bat; the limitation of a batter's turn to three "strikes" before he must run or be out; and the scoring of a run whenever a batter gets back to home plate. A batter can bat again on his turn during an inning; a side's inning lasts until three of its batters are out; and there are several innings to a match (nine for each side in the American professional game).

Running *below left*
We compare the distances a batter must run to score one run in each of the four games.
A Baseball, 360ft (109.7m)
B Softball, 240ft (73.2m)
C Rounders, 146ft (44.5m)
D Cricket, 58ft (17.7m)
In baseball and softball, he may stop in safety at the three intermediate bases. In rounders he may do the same at the first three post – but if he does so cannot then score a run on that turn. In cricket he has no "safe base" between the two ends of the wicket.

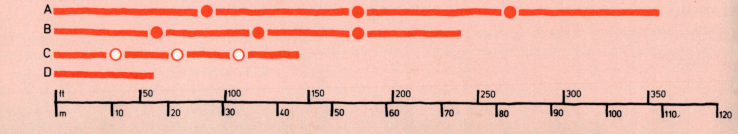

Dwyle flunking is a very rare – and very strange – English pub game. Though runs are scored, there is no bowler and no ball. Instead the batsman tries to hurl a beer-soaked rag from the end of his bat – and scores if he hits one of the opposing side!

B) Softball *below*

This is an adaptation of baseball. The field of play is smaller and the ball larger, there are only seven innings for each side, and pitching is underarm. Also, unlike baseball, players may not "steal" runs off their bases when the batter on home base is not running.

C) Rounders *below*

Here bowling is underarm, with a straight-arm action, the batter's turn lasts for only one fair ball, and a run is scored only if the batter runs the complete set of four posts in one go after hitting the ball (a half rounder is scored if he runs without hitting the ball). An inning continues until the entire side is out, and each side has two innings in a match.

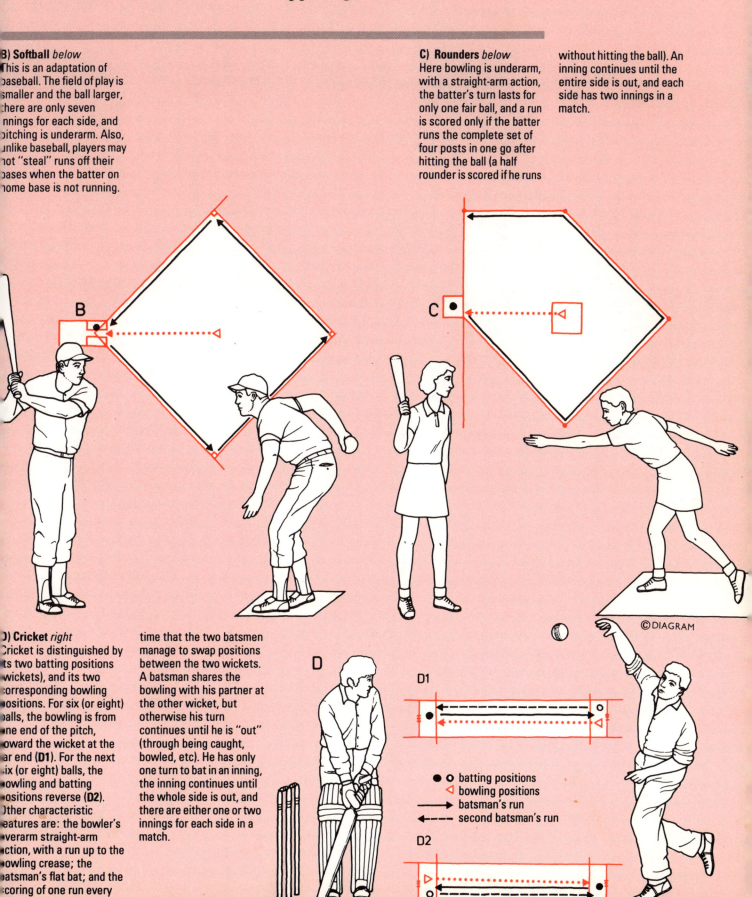

©DIAGRAM

D) Cricket *right*

Cricket is distinguished by its two batting positions (wickets), and its two corresponding bowling positions. For six (or eight) balls, the bowling is from one end of the pitch, toward the wicket at the far end (**D1**). For the next six (or eight) balls, the bowling and batting positions reverse (**D2**). Other characteristic features are: the bowler's overarm straight-arm action, with a run up to the bowling crease; the batsman's flat bat; and the scoring of one run every time that the two batsmen manage to swap positions between the two wickets. A batsman shares the bowling with his partner at the other wicket, but otherwise his turn continues until he is "out" (through being caught, bowled, etc). He has only one turn to bat in an inning, the inning continues until the whole side is out, and there are either one or two innings for each side in a match.

● ○ batting positions
◁ bowling positions
→ batsman's run
◀--- second batsman's run

PLAYING AREAS

The playing areas used in team games vary enormously, from a few square yards of swimming pool to almost 10 acres of turf. Here we compare sizes and surfaces: dimensions are listed in order of area, and illustrated on these two pages. The space needed for a water polo match would fit over 250 times into a polo field!

Playing areas

For the run-scoring games – cricket, baseball, etc – only infield measurements are given, as the outfield areas are not fixed. Puck roller hockey has no fixed dimensions and so is omitted. Figures for sports marked with an asterisk (*) are maximum dimensions.

1 Cricket (bowling pitch) 66x10ft (20.1x3.05m), 73.3yd² (61.3m²)

2 Water polo, 65ft 7inx26ft 3in (20x8m), 191.4yd² (160m²)

3 Volleyball, 59ft 1inx29ft 6in (18x9m), 193.8yd² (162m²)

4 Rounders (infield, not rectangular), 59ft 1inx39ft 4in (18x12m), 215.4yd² (180.1m²)

5 Underwater hockey, 82ftx39ft 4in (25x12m), 358.8yd² (300m²)

6 Softball (infield diamond), 60x60ft (18.3x18.3m), 400yd² (334.4m²)

7 Basketball, 85ft 4inx45ft 11in (26x14m), 435.4yd² (364m²)

8 Tchouk-ball, one-way*, 65ft 7inx65ft 7in (20x20m), 478.4yd² (400m²)

9 Netball, 100x50ft (30.5x15.2m), 555.6yd² (464.5m²)

10 Baseball (infield diamond), 90x90ft (27.4x27.4m), 900yd² (752.5m²)

11 Korfball, two-zone indoor, 131ftl3inx65ft 7in (40x20m), 956.8yd² (800m²)

12 Ball roller hockey*, as 11

13 Team handball, dimensions as 11

14 Tchouk-ball, two-way*, dimensions as 11

15 Canoe polo, pool*, 144ft 4inx62ft 4in (44x19m), 999.9yd² (836m²)

16 Guts, 137ft 9inx88ft 7in (42x27m), 1356.3yd² (1134m²) (actual width depends on arm reach of players; figure given is average for teams of four players)

17 Korfball, two-zone outdoor, 196ft 10inx98ft 5in (60x30m), 2152.9yd² (1800m²)

18 Ice hockey*, 200x100ft (61x30.5m), 2212.7yd² (1850m²); in North America, 200 x 85ft (61x 25.9m), 1879.4yd² (1718.5m²) (all area figures allow for rounding of pitch corners)

19 Korfball, three-zone, 295ft 3inx131ft 3in (90x40m), 4305.7yd² (3600m²)

20 Ultimate Frisbee, 360x120ft (109.7x36.6m), 4800yd² (4013.3m²)

21 Canoe polo, open–water, 295ft 3inx164ft (90x50m), 5382.1yd² (4500m²)

22 Touchball, 328ft 1inx164ft (100x50m), 5980.1yd² (5000m²)

23 Field hockey, 300x180ft (91.4x54.9m), 6000yd² (5016.6m²)

24 Speedball, as 23

25 American football (including endzones), 360x160ft (109.7x48.8m), 6400yd² (5351m²)

26 Men's lacrosse, 330x180ft (100.6x54.9m), 6600yd² (5518.3m²)

27 Bandy*, 360ft 11inx213ft 3in (110x65m), 8551.6yd² (7150m²)

28 Cycle polo*, 330x240ft (100.6x73.2m), 8800yd² (7357.7m²)

29 Camogie*, 360ft 11inx229ft 8in (110x70m), 9209.4yd² (7700m²)

30 Women's lacrosse, 360x246ft (109.7x75m), 9840yd² (8227.2m²)

31 Soccer*, 360ft 11inx246ft 1in (110x75m), 9867.2yd² (8250m²)

32 Rugby league* (including areas behind goals), 400ft 3inx223ft 1in (122x68m), 9922.2yd² (8296m²)

33 Canadian football (including areas behind goals), 480x195ft (146.3x59.4m), 10,400yd² (8695.4m²)

34 Rugby union (including areas behind goals), 472ft 5inx226ft 5in (144x69m), 11,883.7yd² (9936m²)

35 Gaelic football*, 479ftx298ft 7in (146x91m), 15,890.4yd² (13,286m²)

36 Hurling*, as 35

37 Shinty*, 600x300ft (182.9x91.4m), 20,000yd² (16,722m²)

38 Pato*, 721ft 9inx295ft 3in (220x90m), 23,681.4yd² (19,800m²)

39 Australian football* (not rectangular), 606ft 11inx508ft 6in (185x155m), 26,910.7yd² (22,500m²)

40 Polo, 900x480ft (274.3x146.3m), 48,000yd² (40,132.8m²)

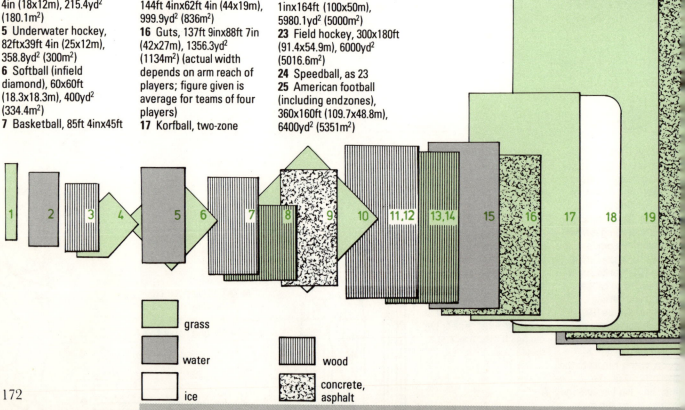

grass

water

ice

wood

concrete, asphalt

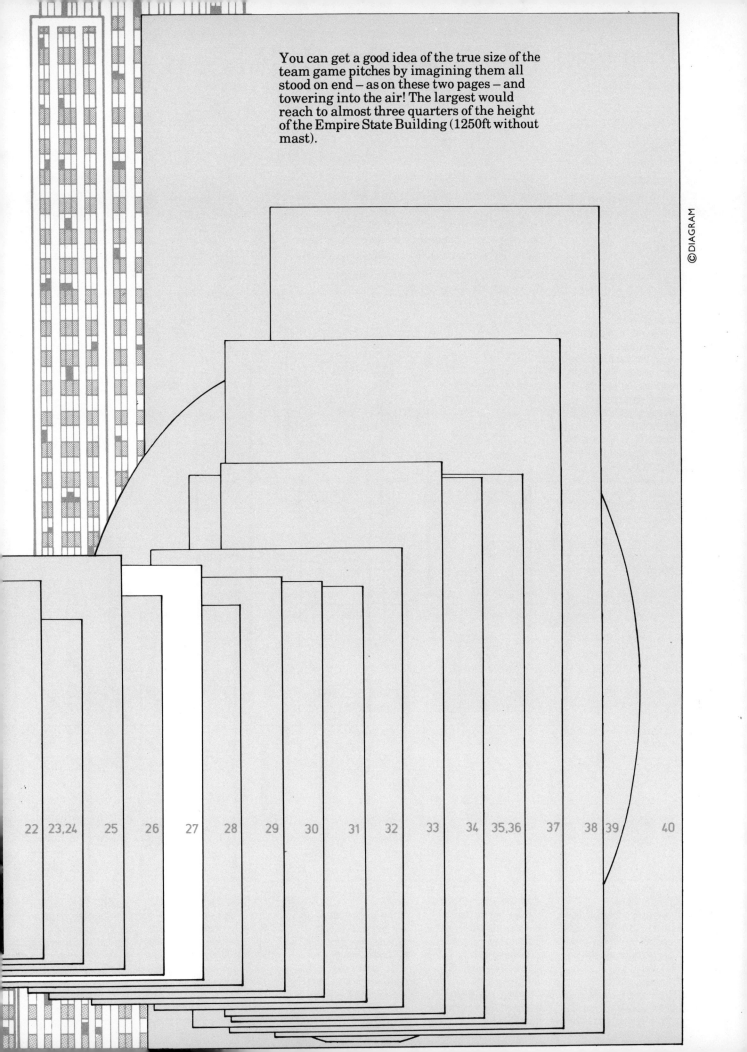

You can get a good idea of the true size of the team game pitches by imagining them all stood on end – as on these two pages – and towering into the air! The largest would reach to almost three quarters of the height of the Empire State Building (1250ft without mast).

©DIAGRAM

22 23,24 25 26 27 28 29 30 31 32 33 34 35,36 37 38 39 40

GOALS, BASKETS, BASES

The scoring procedures in team games usually involve one of three types of structure: a goal, a basket (as in some handball games), or a base or wicket (as in the run-scoring games). Within each type there are wide variations in dimensions and design. We also note those games that need no structure for scoring.

No scoring structure
A few team games use no structure for scoring: touchball and ultimate Frisbee use the end zones of the pitch, while in guts goal lines are marked on the playing surface.

Goals
Illustrated *below* and listed at the bottom of the page are all the goals used in team games. They range in size from the Australian football goal (**1**) down to the ball roller hockey goal (**24**). Some are simply structures of posts, others are fitted with nets. In addition, pool canoe polo uses a board, which the ball must strike (**25**), and tchouk-ball features a special rebound net (**26**).

Sizing them up
1 Australian football, each post 21ft (6.4m) from next, inner posts 19ft 8in (6m) high, outer posts 9ft 10in (3m) high
2 Soccer, posts 24ft (7.32m) apart, crossbar 8ft (2.44m) above ground
3 Polo, posts 24ft (7.32m)

apart and 10ft (3.05m) high
4 American football, amateur, crossbar 10ft (3.05m) above ground, upper posts 23ft 4in (7.11m) apart and at least 10ft (3.05m) high
5 Hurling, posts 21ft (6.4m) apart and 16ft 5in (5m) high, crossbar 8ft (2.44m) above

ground
6 Gaelic football, as 5
7 American football, professional, crossbar 10ft (3.05m) above ground, upper posts 18ft 6in (5.64m) apart and 30ft (9.14m) high
8 Canadian football, crossbar 10ft (3.05m) above ground, upper posts 18ft

6in (5.64m) apart and at least 10ft (3.05m) high
9 Rugby union, posts 18ft 6in (5.64m) apart, crossbar 9ft 10in (3m) above ground
10 Rugby league, posts 18ft (5.5m) apart, crossbar 9ft 10in (3m) above ground
11 Speedball, as 9 but crossbar 8ft (2.44m) above

ground
12 Camogie, posts 14ft 9in (4.5m) apart and 19ft 8in (6m) high, crossbar 6ft 6¾in (2m) above ground
13 Canoe polo, open water, posts 13ft 1½in (4m) apart, crossbar 4ft 11in (1.5m) above water
14 Shinty, posts 12ft

Volleyball is unlike other familiar team games in being set up on the lines of a court game, such as tennis or badminton. The net is 32ft wide and 3ft 3in deep, and is set so its top is more than 7ft above the ground.

Baskets *right*
A Korfball, basket diameter 1ft 3¾in (40cm), depth 9⅞in (25cm), top of basket 11ft 6in (3.5m) above ground
B Basketball, basket ring diameter 1ft 5¾in (45cm), basket depth 1ft 3¾in (40cm), top of basket 10ft

(3.05m) above ground
C Netball, basket ring diameter 1ft 3in (38cm), top of basket 10ft (3.05m) above ground
D Pato, net hoop diameter 3ft 3⅜in (1m), top of hoop 12ft 1½in (3.7m) above ground

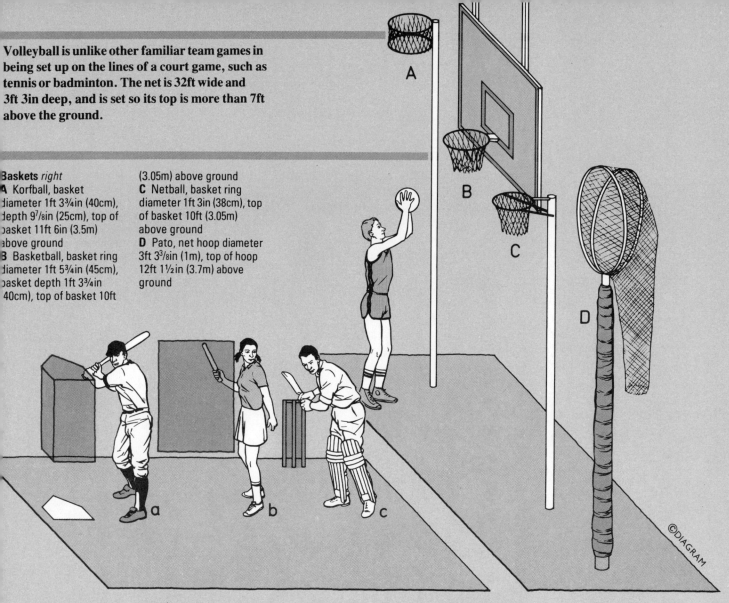

Bases and wickets *above*
In baseball and softball (**a**) the home base plate is a five-sided slab of rubber, 1ft 5in (43cm) in width and length. The area the batter must defend is the space above this from the height of his knees to his armpits. First, second, and third bases are marked by canvas bags, 1ft 3in (38cm) square. In rounders (**b**) the area the batter defends, in his square, is simply the space within his reach, from the height of his knees to the top of his head; but the run is marked by four posts, each 3ft 11in (1.2m) high. In cricket (**c**) the wicket is, overall, 9in (22.8cm) wide by 2ft 4in (71.1cm) high.

Underwater hockey
In underwater hockey the "goals" (not illustrated) are aluminum frames, placed on the bottom of the pool against the end walls. Each is shaped to form a gully 9ft 10in (3m) long and 4¾in (12cm) wide.

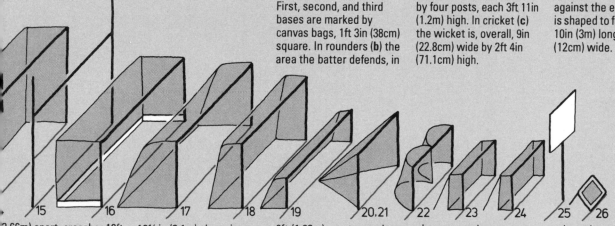

3.66m) apart, crossbar 10ft 3.05m) above ground
5 Cycle polo, posts 12ft 3.66m) apart, crossbar 9ft 2.74m) above ground
6 Field hockey, posts 12ft 3.66m) apart, crossbar 7ft 2.13m) above ground
7 Bandy, posts 11ft 5¾in 3.5m) apart, crossbar 6ft

10½in (2.1m) above ice
18 Team handball, posts 9ft 10in (3m) apart, crossbar 6ft 6¾in (2m) above ground
19 Water polo, posts 9ft 10in (3m) apart, crossbar 2ft 11½in (90cm) above water
20 Men's lacrosse, posts

6ft (1.83m) apart, crossbar 6ft (1.83m) above ground
21 Women's lacrosse, as 20.
22 Ice hockey, posts 6ft (1.83m) apart, crossbar 4ft (1.22m) above ice
23 Puck roller hockey, posts 5ft 1in (1.55m) apart, crossbar 3ft 5½in (1.054m)

above ground
24 Ball roller hockey, posts 5ft 1in (1.55m) apart, crossbar 3ft 5⅜in (1.05m) above ground
25 Canoe polo, pool, board 3ft 3in (1m) square, top of board 9ft 10in (3m) above water
26 Tchouk-ball, face of

rebound net 2ft 3½in (70cm) square, frame angled so top 2ft 6¾in (78cm) above ground

175

TEAM SIZES

It takes only four players to form a polo team, but you need 18 for an Australian football side. Here we look at team sizes, and also at the permitted number of tactical substitutes that can be brought into a team during a game – that is, the number of substitutes that can be brought on even when no player has been injured.

Teams and substitutes
At the foot of the facing page we list, for each team game, the size of a team and (in brackets) the maximum number of tactical substitutes. These figures are illustrated by the teams of players on these two pages.

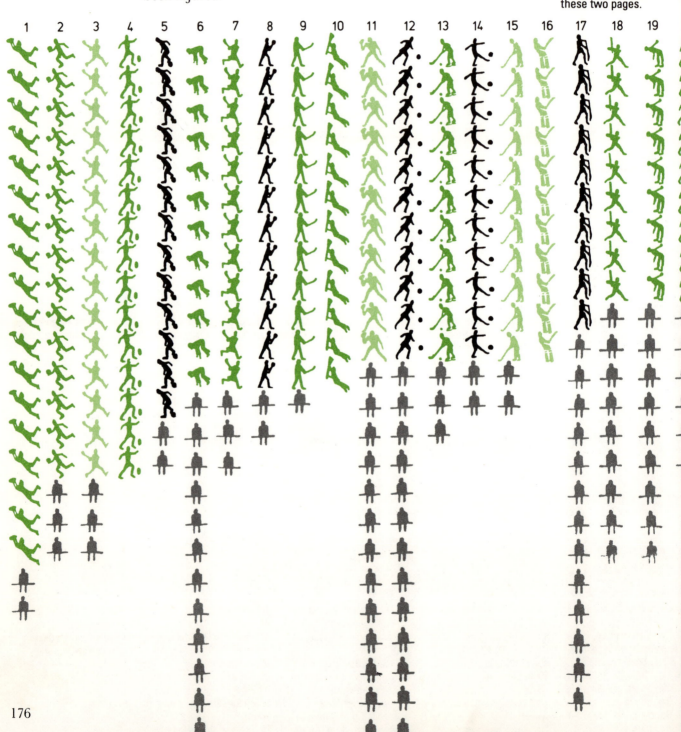

Tactical substitutes

Precise laws on tactical substitutes vary from game to game. In some cases the permitted maximum may be chosen from a larger "bench" of possible substitutes. Also in some cases substituted players are allowed to return to play later in a match – in which case a team will usually organize its pool of players into a rota of participation and rest, through a match, to maintain maximum effort. Note also that, although the number of substitutes in American and Canadian football is theoretically unlimited, in practice all leagues have their own arrangements limiting the number that are allowed to participate.

Tactical substitutes

Substitutes for injury

Rules for some team games state that a certain number of substitutions for injured players may be made. But these details are not given here, as the absence of a ruling on injury substitution is not very significant. It tends to mean only that the sport is either very unlikely to cause injury, or still too young to possess fully formalized rules.

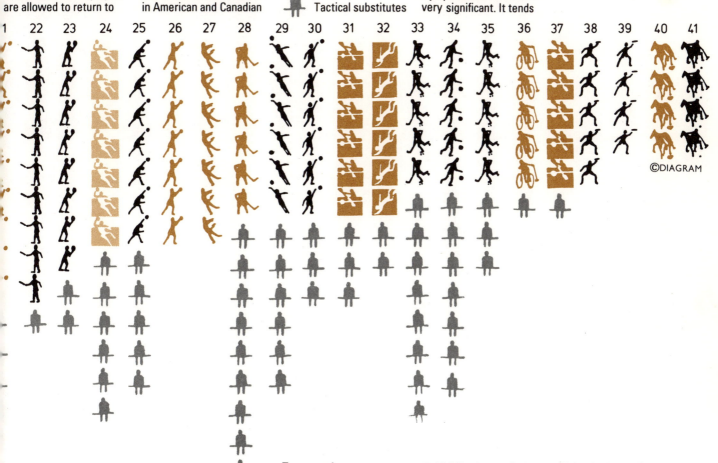

©DIAGRAM

Team numbers
1 Australian football: 18 (2)
2 Gaelic football: 15 (3)
3 Hurling: 15 (3)
4 Rugby union: 15 (nil)
5 Rugby league: 13 (2)
6 Canadian football: 12 (unlimited)
7 Camogie: 12 (3)
8 Korfball, three-zone: 12 (2)
9 Shinty: 12 (1)
10 Women's lacrosse: 12 (nil)
11 American football: 11 (unlimited)
12 Speedball: 11 (unlimited)
13 Bandy: 11 (3)
14 Soccer: 11 (2)

15 Field hockey: 11 (2, from a bench of about 5)
16 Cricket: 11 (nil)
17 Men's lacrosse: 10 (13)
18 Baseball: 9 (number unspecified)
19 Softball: 9 (number unspecified)
20 Touchball: 9 (6)
21 Tchouk-ball, two-way: 9 (3)
22 Rounders: 9 (1, from a bench of 2)
23 Korfball, two-zone: 8 (2)
24 Water polo: 7 (6)
25 Team handball: 7 (4 player substitutes and one goalkeeper substitute)
26 Netball: 7 (nil)
27 Ultimate Frisbee: 7 (nil)

28 Ice hockey: 6 (11)
29 Volleyball: 6 (6)
30 Tchouk-ball, one-way: 6 (3)
31 Canoe polo, outdoor: 6 (3)
32 Underwater hockey: 6 (2)
33 Puck roller hockey: 5 (unlimited)
34 Basketball: 5 (7)
35 Ball roller hockey: 5 (3)
36 Cycle polo: 5 (1)
37 Canoe polo, indoor: 5 (1)
38 Guts, outdoor: 5 (nil)
39 Guts, indoor: 4 (nil)
40 Pato: 4 (nil)
41 Polo: 4 (nil)

DRESS AND SAFETY EQUIPMENT

As a group the team games involve more physical contact than any other apart from the combat sports. One result has been a wide range of protective clothing, to meet different playing conditions. Goalkeepers and wicketkeepers, who must stop a speeding ball or puck, are especially in need of protection.

Dressing up

In the illustrations *below* we show some selected examples of the clothing used by players in team games, ranging from the simplest to the most protective. A water polo player (**1**) needs to wear only bathing trunks and a numbered cap. Equally, basketball (**2**) gives us an example of the simplest style of dress among land team games (shirt, shorts, and sports shoes). Similar kit is used in other low-contact hard-court games, such as volleyball, netball, and team handball. The equivalent among the grass-pitch games is typified by the soccer player's outfit of shirt, shorts, socks, and studded leather boots (**3**). With the baseball batter (**4**) we come to the first example of protective headgear. A polo player (**5**) couples this with protective kneepads, while in canoe polo (**6**) a buoyancy jacket serves to cushion against collision impacts. (A waterproof "apron" is also worn.) In the Scandinavian game of bandy (**7**) we find padded gloves and helmets with face protectors, and men's lacrosse (**8**) takes the same ideas further. Cricket (**9**) demonstrates how a game sometimes has to adjust to new conditions: the batsman shown wears not only traditional gloves and leg guards, but also a helmet and visor (and concealed thigh pads) against the speed of modern fast bowling. The ice hockey player (**10**) adds concealed shoulder and chest padding to the combination of helmet, leg pads, and gloves, but the prize for protection goes to the American footballer (**11**), with his complete "suit" of hidden padding.

a   b

1   2   3   4   5   6   7

You may need six boots to play polo! Two for yourself, of course, but also (unless you wrap his legs with bandages) four leather protectors – called "boots" – for your horse.

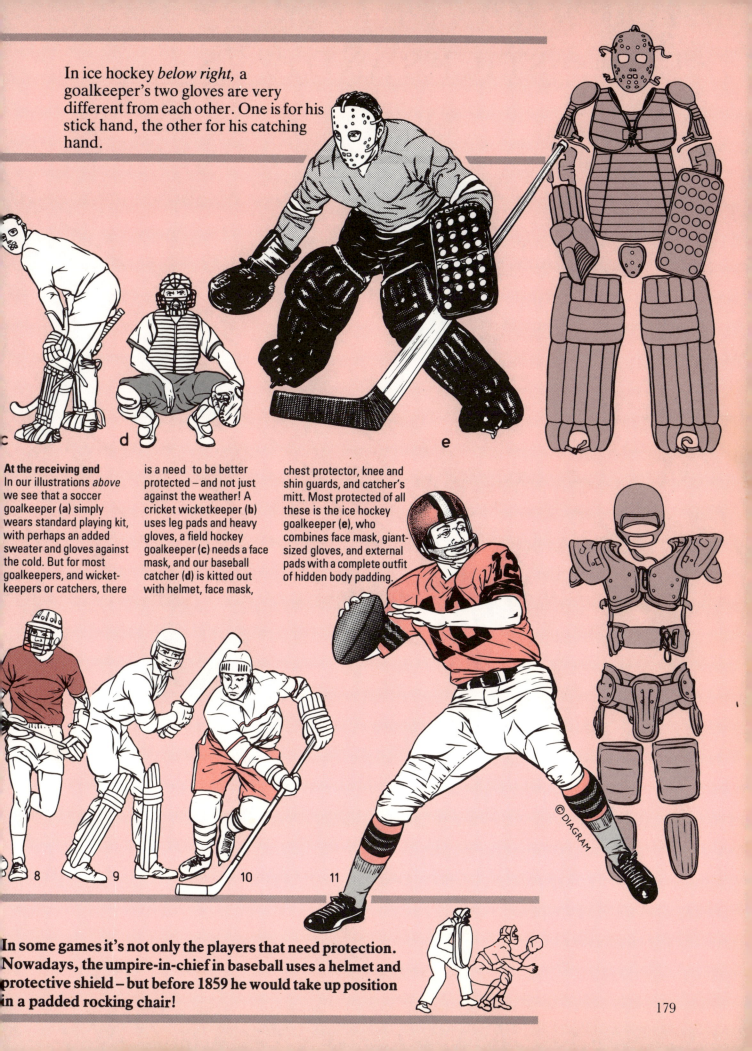

In ice hockey *below right*, a goalkeeper's two gloves are very different from each other. One is for his stick hand, the other for his catching hand.

c

d

e

At the receiving end
In our illustrations *above* we see that a soccer goalkeeper (**a**) simply wears standard playing kit, with perhaps an added sweater and gloves against the cold. But for most goalkeepers, and wicket-keepers or catchers, there is a need to be better protected – and not just against the weather! A cricket wicketkeeper (**b**) uses leg pads and heavy gloves, a field hockey goalkeeper (**c**) needs a face mask, and our baseball catcher (**d**) is kitted out with helmet, face mask, chest protector, knee and shin guards, and catcher's mitt. Most protected of all these is the ice hockey goalkeeper (**e**), who combines face mask, giant-sized gloves, and external pads with a complete outfit of hidden body padding.

8

9

10

11

© DIAGRAM

In some games it's not only the players that need protection. Nowadays, the umpire-in-chief in baseball uses a helmet and protective shield – but before 1859 he would take up position in a padded rocking chair!

STICKS AND BATS

Many team games – both goal-scoring and run-scoring – use an implement to propel the ball or puck. Here we compare the size and appearance of these various sticks and bats. Wood is their usual material, of course. But plastic is used for the underwater hockey "pusher," and often, nowadays, for the crosse head in men's lacrosse.

Measuring up
All dimensions quoted and illustrated on these two pages are permitted maximums – except where they are specifically noted as averages because no dimension rules exist. But note that with the large sticks (ice hockey, puck roller hockey, men's lacrosse), almost all players will actually use sticks of considerably smaller size.

Goal-scoring games
1 Men's lacrosse, goalkeeper's crosse, length 72in (182.9cm), inside width of head 15in (38.1cm)
2 Men's lacrosse, player's crosse, length 72in (182.9cm), inside width of head 10in (25.4cm)

3 Puck roller hockey, goalkeeper's stick, length 55in (139.7cm) from head of shaft to heel and 12.5in (31.7cm) from heel to end of blade; blade width 3.5in (8.9cm) and permitted thickening of shaft to 3.5in (8.9cm) for 24in (61cm)
4 Puck roller hockey,

player's stick, as for goalkeeper's stick but blade width 3in (7.6cm) and no thickening of shaft
5 Ice hockey, goalkeeper's stick, length 53in (134.6cm) from head of shaft to heel and 14.5in (36.8cm) from heel to end of blade; blade width 3.5in (8.9cm) and

permitted thickening of shaft to 3.5in (8.9cm) for 24in (61cm)
6 Ice hockey, player's stick, as for goalkeeper's stick but blade width 3in (7.6cm) and no thickening of shaft
7 Polo, stick, average shaft length 51in (129.5cm),

average head length 9in (22.9cm), average head diameter at center 2in (5.1cm)
8 Women's lacrosse, crosse, length 48in (121.9cm), outside width 9in (22.9cm)
9 Shinty, caman, length not to reach above hip

The game of broomball was developed by the staff of Western embassies in Moscow, and is a kind of field hockey on ice. No skates are worn by players – and the "hockey sticks" are short Russian brooms!

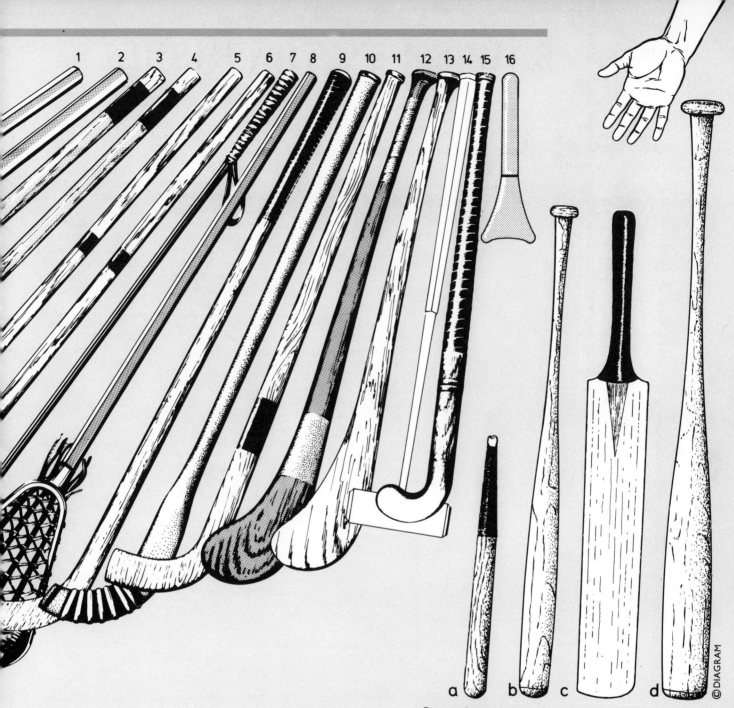

height from ground, head
must pass through 2.5in
(6.35cm) diameter ring
10 Bandy, stick, length
47.2in (120cm) along
outside of curve, width
2.4in (6cm) at widest point
11 Ball roller hockey, stick,
length 45in (114.3cm) along
outside of curve, head

must pass through a 1.97in
(5cm) diameter ring
12 Hurling, hurley, average
length 38in (96.5cm)
13 Camogie, camog,
average length 36in
(91.4cm)
14 Cycle polo, mallet, head
length 7in (17.8cm), head
diameter 2.5in (6.35cm),

average overall length 32in
(81.3cm).
15 Field hockey, stick,
average length 32in
(81.3cm), head must pass
through a 2in (5.1cm)
diameter ring
16 Underwater hockey,
pusher, length 11.8in
(30cm), width 4.7in (12cm)

Run-scoring games
a Rounders, bat, length
18.1in (46cm),
circumference 6.7in (17cm)
b Softball, bat, length 34in
(86.4cm), diameter 2.17in
(5.5cm)
c Cricket, bat, length 38in
(96.5cm), width 4.25in
(10.8cm)
d Baseball, bat, length 42in
(106.7cm), diameter 2.75in
(7cm)

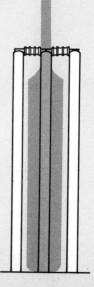

*In modern cricket, the area of the bat face
(about 110in²) is well under half the area of the
wicket that the batsman must defend.*

© DIAGRAM

BALLS, PUCKS, FRISBEES

The various team games employ an amazing variety of balls, pucks, and Frisbees. We look at the range of sizes and weights involved. We illustrate the balls full size, and compare their weights with some other familiar sports objects. All figures quoted are maximums, unless otherwise stated.

Balls

In the table *below* we list maximum permitted sizes and weights for the various balls used in team ball games. Size is given as maximum circumference. (The size of elliptical balls is given by two figures, the short circumference followed by the long circumference.) The relative sizes are shown full size in the illustrations *right,* ranging from a basketball ball (**1**) down to the ball used in bandy (**34**). The diagram *far left* plots all the maximum weights against a common scale,

Ball weight		Game	Ball circumference
22.9oz (650g)	**1**	Basketball	30.7in (78cm)
15oz (425.2g)	**2**	Gaelic football	29in (73.7cm)
19.5oz (552.8g)	**3**	Speedball	28in (71.1cm)
16.75oz (475g)	**4**	Korfball	28in (71.1cm)
16oz (453.6g)	**5**	Soccer	28in (71.1cm)
16oz (453.6g)	**6**	Netball	28in (71.1cm)
16oz (453.6g)	**7**	Canoe polo: open-water	28in (71.1cm)
15.9oz (450g)	**8**	Water polo	28in (71.1cm)
10.7oz (302.4g)	**9**	Canoe polo: pool	26.4in (67cm)
9.88oz (280g)	**10**	Volleyball	26.4in (67cm)
16.75oz (475g)	**11**	Team handball: men	23.6in (60cm)
16.75oz (475g)	**12**	Tchouk-ball	23.6in (60cm)
15.5oz (440g)	**13**	Rugby union	23.2x29.1in (59x74cm)
15.5oz (440g)	**14**	Rugby league	23.2x29.1in (59x74cm)
15.5oz (440g)	**15**	Touchball	23.2x29.1in (59x74cm)
17.6oz (500g)	**16**	Australian football	22.4x29.1in (57x74cm)
14.1oz (400g)	**17**	Team handball: women	22in (56cm)
15oz (425.2g)	**18**	American football	21.5x28.5in (54.6x72.4cm)
15oz (425.2g)	**19**	Canadian football	21.375x28.5in (54.3x72.4cm)
7oz (198.4g)	**20**	Softball	12.125in (30.8cm)
4.75oz (134.7g)	**21**	Polo	10.2in (25.9cm)
4oz (113.4g)	**22**	Cycle polo	10.2in (25.9cm)
4.6oz (130g)	**23**	Hurling	10in (25.4cm)
5.75oz (163g)	**24**	Field hockey	9.25in (23.5cm)
5.25oz (148.8g)	**25**	Baseball	9.25in (23.5cm)
5.75oz (163g)	**26**	Cricket: men	9in (22.9cm)
5.5oz (155.9g)	**27**	Ball roller hockey	9in (22.9cm)
5.31oz (150.6g)	**28**	Cricket: women	8.825in (22.4cm)
3.88oz (110g)	**29**	Camogie	8.3in (21cm)
5.25oz (148.8g)	**30**	Lacrosse: men	8in (20.3cm)
5.25oz (148.8g)	**31**	Lacrosse: women	8in (20.3cm)
3.5oz (99.2g)	**32**	Shinty	8in (20.3cm)
3oz (85g)	**33**	Rounders	7.48in (19cm)
2.2oz (62g)	**34**	Bandy	7.4in (18.85cm)

Weighing it all up

On the weight scale *left* we indicate for comparison the weights of some other familiar sports objects.

A Horseshoe pitching horseshoe, maximum weight, 2lb 8oz (1134g)

B Women's javelin, minimum weight, 1lb 5.2oz (600g)

C Tennis racket, typical weight for men's racket, 14oz (396.9g)

D Boxing glove, standard weight, 8oz (226.8g)

E Badminton racket, typical weight, 4.5oz (127.6g)

gm lb

The ball used in the Argentinian game of pato is just the same size as a soccer ball – but unlike a soccer ball it has six leather handles!

together with the weights of some other familiar items of sports equipment. Again the range is from basketball ball to bandy ball; but it can be seen that the order of weight is not always the same as the order of size.

Pucks and Frisbees
In the drawing *below* we show to scale the various pucks and Frisbees used in team games. A soccer ball is drawn to the same scale to show the relative sizes involved. Weights of these pucks and Frisbees are also plotted with those of the balls on the scale *far left*.
a Puck roller hockey, diameter 2.9in (7.37cm), thickness 1in (2.54cm), average weight 3.25oz (92.1g).
b Ice hockey, diameter 3in (7.62cm), thickness 1in (2.54cm), weight 6oz (170g)
c Underwater hockey, diameter 3.15in (8cm), thickness 1.18in (3cm), average weight 52.9oz (1500g)
d Guts, diameter 9.41in (23.9cm), weight 3.78oz (107.3g)
e Ultimate Frisbee, diameter 11in (28cm), weight 5.82oz (165g)

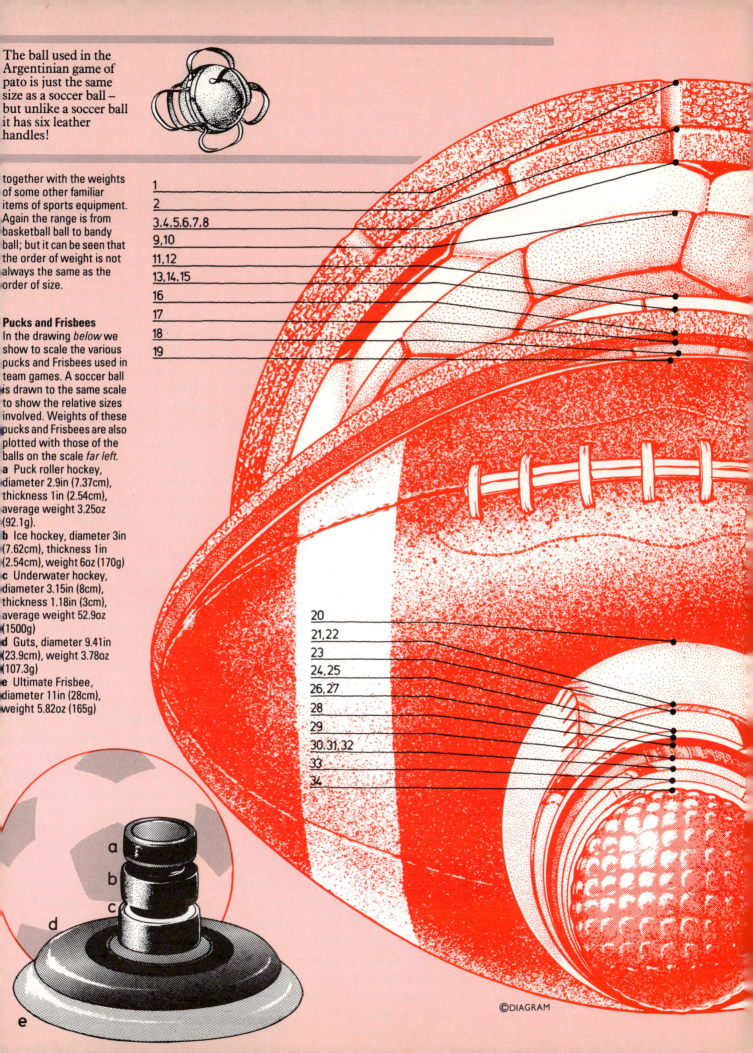

1
2
3,4,5,6,7,8
9,10
11,12
13,14,15
16
17
18
19

20
21,22
23
24,25
26,27
28
29
30,31,32
33
34

a
b
c
d
e

©DIAGRAM

DURATION, STARTING, AND SCORING

There is great variation among team games in how long they last, how they are started, and how scoring occurs. Here we look into these matters. Run-scoring games are not included, because their durations depend on what happens during play, they have no special starting procedures, and their scoring methods are quite different (see pp.170-171).

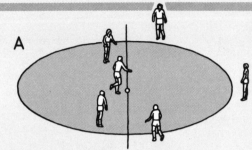

A

Playing times *below*
The clock face *below left,* and the table at the foot of the page, show playing periods, intervals, and total match times for various team games.

Starting *above*
Run-scoring games need no separate starting procedure, but other team games do, and the four methods used are shown *above* and *opposite.* The table at the foot of the opposite page indicates the method used in each game.
A The ball is given to one side, who start the match by a kick-off or throw-off. (Usually a toss of a coin decides, with the winner choosing ends or ball possession.)

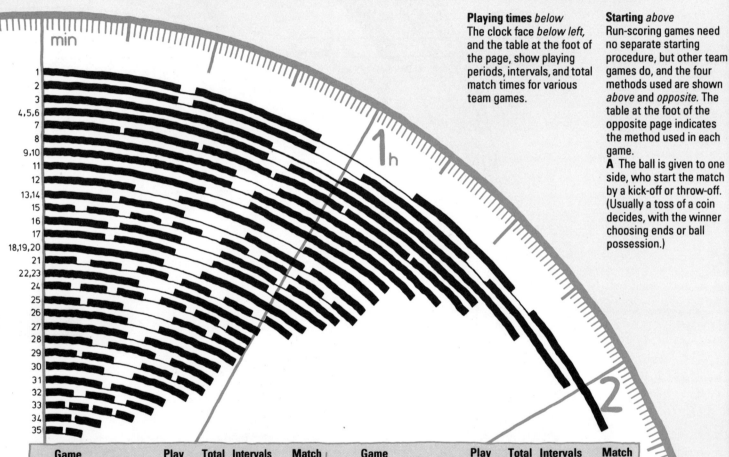

min

	Game	Play	Total	Intervals	Match
1	Australian football	4x25m	100m	3, 20, 5m	128m
2	Lacrosse (men)	4x25m	100m	3, 10, 5m	118m
3	Korfball	2x45m	90m	15m	105m
4	Shinty	2x45m	90m	5+m	95+m
5	Soccer	2x45m	90m	5m**	95m
6	Bandy	2x45m	90m	5m	95m
7	Cycle polo	6x15m	90m	1, 1, 1, 1, 1m	95m
8	Gaelic football	2x40m	80m	10m	90m
9	Rugby league	2x40m	80m	5m	85m
10	Rugby union	2x40m	80m	5m	85m
11	Field hockey	2x35m	70m	5-10m	80m*
12	Ice hockey	3x20m	60m	10, 10m	80m
13	American football	4x15m	60m	1-2, 15, 1-2m	79m*
14	Canadian football	4x15m	60m	1-2, 15, 1-2m	79m*
15	Polo[1]	8x7m	56m	3,3,3,5,3,3,3m	79m
16	Netball	4x15m	60m	3, 10, 3m	76m
17	Touchball (men)	4x15m	60m	2, 10, 2m	74m
18	Canoe polo, o/water	2x30m	60m	10m	70m
19	Hurling[2]	2x30m	60m	10m	70m
20	Team handball	2x30m	60m	10m	70m
21	Pato	6x8m	48m	4, 4, 4, 4, 4m	68m
22	Camogie	2x25m	50m	10m	60m
23	Lacrosse (women)	2x25m	50m	10m	60m
24	Polo[3]	6x7m	42m	3, 3, 5, 3, 3m	59m
25	Speedball	4x10m	40m	2, 15, 2m	59m
26	Ultimate Frisbee	2x24m	48m	10m	58m
27	Ball roller hockey	2x25m	50m	5m	55m
28	Tchouk-ball (men)	3x15m	45m	5, 5m	55m
29	Touchball (women)	4x10m	40m	2, 10, 2m	54m
30	Basketball	2x20m	40m	10m	50m
31	Puck roller hockey	2x20m	40m	3m	43m
32	Tchouk-ball (women)	3x10m	30m	5, 5m	40m
33	Water polo	4x7m	28m	2, 2, 2m	34m
34	Underwater hockey	2x10m	20m	2m	22m
35	Canoe polo, pool	2x7m	14m	1m	15m

[1] outside Europe and USA
[2] 2x40m in major matches
[3] in Europe and USA
*maximum **under international rules

In international (Test match) cricket, a game may last up to five 6-hour days. This would be enough time for 22 American football matches – or 120 games of pool canoe polo!

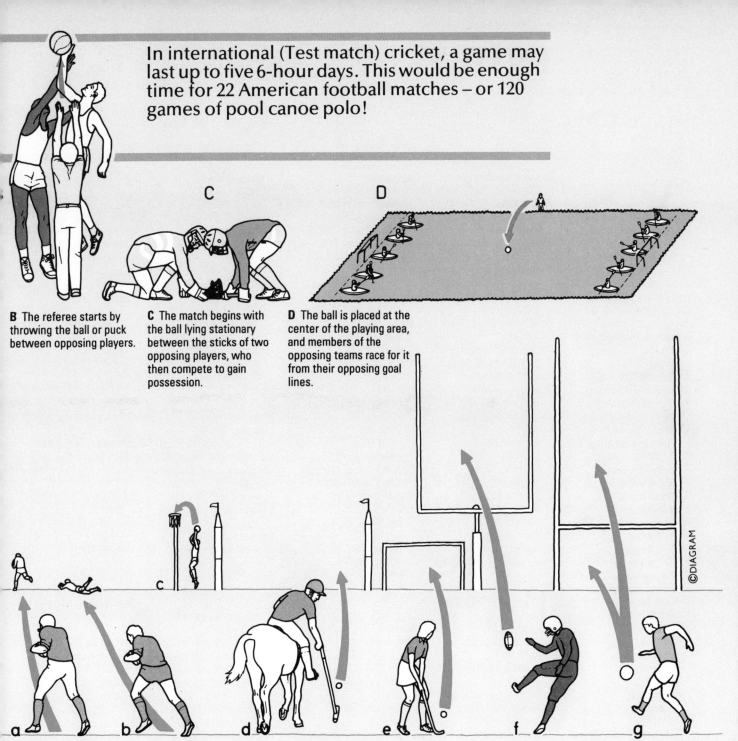

B The referee starts by throwing the ball or puck between opposing players.

C The match begins with the ball lying stationary between the sticks of two opposing players, who then compete to gain possession.

D The ball is placed at the center of the playing area, and members of the opposing teams race for it from their opposing goal lines.

Ways of scoring *above*
In most team games you score at your opponents' goal line in one or more ways. The most common procedures are listed here and illustrated *above*. (The table *right* indicates which procedure is used in each game.)
a Ball carried over the opponents' goal line.
b Ball touched down beyond the opponents' goal line.
c Ball into the opponents' basket.
d Ball between the opponents' goalposts.

e Ball between the opponents' goalposts and beneath the crossbar.
f Ball between the opponents' goalposts and above the crossbar.
g Ball between the opponents' goalposts and either under or over the crossbar (for different numbers of points scored).

Handball games			Football games			Stick-and-ball games		
Starting	Scoring		Starting	Scoring		Starting	Scoring	
B	c	Basketball	A	a+f	American football	A	e	Ball roller hockey
D	*	Canoe polo (pool)	B	d	Australian football	A	e	Bandy
A	e	Canoe polo (o/water)	A	a+f	Canadian football	D	e	Cycle polo
A	*	Guts	B	g	Gaelic football	B	g	Camogie
A	c	Korfball	A	b+f	Rugby league	C	e	Field hockey
A	c	Netball	A	b+f	Rugby union	B	g	Hurling
B	c	Pato	A	e	Soccer	B	e	Ice hockey
A	*	Tchouk-ball	A	g	Speedball	C	e	Lacrosse
A	e	Team handball	A	b	Touchball	B	d	Polo
A	*	Ultimate frisbee				B	e	Puck roller hockey
A	*	Volleyball				B	e	Shinty
D	e	Water polo				D	*	Underwater hockey

*other scoring procedure

INDEX

A

Aconcagua, Mount 128
Acrobatics, sports, see
    Sports acrobatics
Acropolis Rally 41
Aerials, skiing 104, 107
Aerobatics 118-119
Ages of athletes 16-17
Aikido 136-137, 139-141
Air speed records 76-77
Air sports, display events
    116-120
    racing 72-73
Airgun shooting 142-147
Airplanes 72-73
    altitude records 131
    speed records 76-77
Alaskan Iditarod Trail
    sled-dog race 54-55, 79
All American Futurity
    horse race 55
Alleys, bowling 155
Alpine skiing 46-47
    longest race 79
    physical demands 18,
    20-21
    record speed 75
    (in comparison 146)
Altitude records 128, 131
American football 167
    ball 182
    clothing 178
    duration 184
    goals 174
    physical demands 18-19,
    21
    pitch 172
    scoring 185
    starting 185
    team 177
    (in comparisons 122, 136,
    143, 185)
America's Cup 66-67
Animals, altitude records
    128, 131
    depth record 130
    equestrian events
    122-125
    jumping 86-87, 89
    racing 54-57
    running speeds 28-29,
    34, 74-75
    (in comparisons 90, 140,
    152)
Annapurna, Mount 128-129
Antro di Corchia 129
Ararat, Mount 128
Archery 142-147
    physical demands 20
Arches, roque 150-151

Arena, equestrian sports
    122-123
Arm lengths of athletes 17
Armstand dive 111
Arrow 144-145
Artistic (Olympic)
    gymnastics 95-96, 98-100
Ascot Gold Cup horse race
    55
Association croquet
    150-151
Association football, see
    Soccer
Asymmetric bars, artistic
    gymnastics 96
    exercises 98
Athletes, physical
    characteristics 12-17
Australian football 166
    ball 182
    duration 184
    goal 174
    physical demands 19
    pitch 172
    scoring 185
    starting 185
    team 176-177
Autocross 44
Autograss 44-45
Automobile T-bone dive 87

B

Backstroke 58
Backward dives 111
Badminton 158
    court size 159
    net 159
    physical demands 20
    racket 163
    shuttlecock 162
    (in comparison 182)
Balance beam, artistic
    gymnastics 96
    exercises 98
Balance routines, sports
    acrobatics 97, 101
Ball, modern rhythmic
    gymnastics 97
    exercises 100
Ball roller hockey 169
    ball 182
    duration 184
    goal 175
    pitch 172
    scoring 185
    starting 185
    stick 181
    team 177
Ballet skiing 104, 106-107

Ballooning 116-117
    altitude records 131
    endurance records 126
Balls, alley games 155
    billiard games 156-157
    bowls games 152
    croquet 150-151
    golf 148
    net games 162
    team games 182-183
    wall games 162
Bandy 169
    ball 182-183
    clothing 178
    duration 184
    goal 175
    rink 172
    scoring 185
    starting 185
    stick 181
    team 177
Banger racing 44
Barefoot water skiing 95,
    104, 106-107, 121
Barrel jumping 87
Baseball 170
    ball 182
    bat 181
    clothing 178-179
    infield 170, 172
    physical demands 18-20
    team 177
    (in comparisons 61, 153,
    155)
Baseball throwing 85
Bases 170, 175
Basketball 164
    ball 182-183
    clothing 178
    court 172
    duration 184
    net 175
    physical characteristics
    of players 12, 14-15,
    17
    physical demands 18-19,
    21
    scoring 185
    starting 185
    team 177
    (in comparisons 61, 83,
    136)
Baskets 164, 175, 185
Bats, team ball games
    180-181
    also see Paddles
Bathyscaphe 130
Bench press 90-91
Bermuda yacht race 69
Biathlon, winter, see
    Winter biathlon
Bicycle polo, see Cycle
    polo

Bigbore rifles 142-147
Billiards 156-157
    physical demands 20
Birds, diving record 130
    flying speeds 76
    (in comparisons 60, 140,
    162)
BMX 30-31, 35
Boardsailing 66-69
    freestyle 112
    record attempt 127
    record speed 69, 77
Boats, rowing 60-63
Bobsleigh racing 50-51
    physical demands 20
    record speed 75
Body fat 16
Body shapes 12-13
Body surfing 114
Bodyboards 114
Bolt, crossbow 144-145, 147
Boomerang throwing 85
Borghese, Prince Scipione
    41
Borota, Jean 17
Boston Marathon rowing
    race 63
Boules 152-153
    physical demands 20
Bowen, Andy 141
Bowl riding, skateboard 115
Bowling, alley games
    154-155
    run-scoring games
    170-171
    terrain games 152-153
Bowls games 152-153
    physical demands 20
Box lacrosse 169
Boxing 136, 138-141
    physical characteristics
    of boxers 12, 14-17
    physical demands 18-19,
    21
    (in comparison 182)
Brands Hatch motorcycling
    circuit 39
Breasley, Scobie 16
Breaststroke 58-59
    physical characteristics
    of breaststroke
    swimmers 17
Bricks (in comparisons 91,
    132, 140)
Broomball 180
Buenos Aires Grand Prix
    circuit 43
Bullet 144-147
Burke, Jack 141
Burton, Beryl 30
Butterfly stroke 58
Buzkashi 165, 176

C

Caber tossing 92-93
Caliber 144
Calorie consumption 20-21
Caman 180-181
Camel racing 55, 57
Camog 181
Camogie 168
    ball 182
    camog 181
    duration 184
    goal 174
    pitch 172
    scoring 185
    starting 185
    team 177
Can-Am series motor races
    41
Canadian canoes 64-65
    physical characteristics
    of Canadian canoeists
    17
Canadian football 167
    ball 182
    duration 184
    goal 174
    pitch 172
    scoring 185
    starting 185
    team 177
Canoe polo, open water
    165
    ball 182
    clothing 178
    duration 184
    goal 174
    playing area 172
    scoring 185
    starting 185
    team 177
Canoe polo, pool 165
    ball 182-183
    clothing 178
    duration 184
    goal 175
    playing area 172
    scoring 185
    starting 185
    team 177
    (in comparison 185)
Canoe sailing 66-67, 69
Canoeing 64-65
    endurance records 126
    longest race 79
    physical characteristics
    of canoeists 12-17
    physical demands 19-20
    speed record 77
Canopy display events 118
Carnera, Primo 15
Carom billiards 156-157

Cars, ramp jump record 87
    record speeds 75
    types 40-41, 44-45
    (in comparisons 40, 42,
        53, 65, 71, 73, 146,
        148, 160)
Cartridge 144-145, 147
Casting, see Tournament
    casting
Catamarans 67, 69
Catchers 179
Caving 128-129
Center-fire pistols 142,
    144, 146-147
Central Park, New York 32
Cesta 161, 163
Champion Hurdle Challenge
    Cup horse race 55
Chariot racing 55
Cheese, skittles 155
Chimborazo, Mount 128
Chionis 87
Circuits, air racing 73
    cycle racing 30-31
    motorcycling 36, 39
    motor racing 40, 42-45
    powerboat racing 71
    soaring 72-73
    also see Courses, Tracks
Clay pigeon shooting
    142-147
Clean and jerk 90
Clifton Suspension Bridge
    111
Clothing, team ball games
    178-179
Clubs, golf 148-149
Clubs, modern rhythmic
    gymnastics 97
    exercises 100
Colosseum 136
Courses, aerial slalom
    events 120
    air racing 73
    canoeing 64-65
    equestrian events 123
    motor racing 45
    motorcycling 36
    running 26-27
    skiing 46-47, 106-107
    soaring 72-73
    water skiing 106, 121
    winter vehicle racing
        50-51
    yacht racing 68-69
Court handball 160-161
    ball 162
    glove 163
Court (real) tennis 158-159
    ball 162
    racket 163

Courts, croquet 150-151
    handball games 164-165,
        172
    net games 158-159
    wall games 160-161
Cox, rowing 60-62
Craig, Ralph 17
Cresta Run 50, 75
Crews, canoeing 64
    ice yachting 52
    land yachting 52
    rowing 60-63
    winter vehicle racing 50
    yachting 67
    (in comparison 61)
Cricket 170-171
    balls 182
    bat 181
    clothing 178-179
    physical demands 19-20
    pitch 170-172
    team 177
    wicket 175
    (in comparisons 83, 185)
Cricket ball throwing 85
Criterium 30-31
Croquet 150-151
    physical demands 20
Cross-country aerial
    events, air racing 72-73
    hang gliding 116-117
    hot-air ballooning
        116-117
Cross-country phase,
    equestrian three-day
    event 123-125
Cross-country running
    26-27
    in modern pentathlon 133
    physical demands 19, 21
Cross-country skiing, see
    Nordic skiing
Crossbow II 69
Crossbow archery 143-145,
    147
Crown green bowls
    152-153
Cue 156-157
Cue ball 156-157
Curling 152-153
Cycle polo 169
    ball 182-183
    duration 184
    goal 175
    mallet 181
    playing area 172
    scoring 185
    starting 185
    team 177
Cycle polo, indoor 169

Cycle racing 30-35
    longest races 79
    physical characteristics
        of cyclists 12, 14-16
    physical demands 18-21
    record speeds 34-35, 74
    (in comparisons 37, 57)
Cycleball 166
Cycles 34-35
Cyclocross 30-31, 33, 35

D

Daedalus 131
Dakyu 169
Daytona motorcycling
    circuit 39
Dead lift 90-91
Decathlon 132
    physical characteristics
        of decathletes 12,
        14-16
    physical demands 18-19,
        21
Decline in abilities with
    age 16
Degree of difficulty 94
    diving 111
    freestyle skiing 104
    synchronized swimming
        108
Depth records 130
Derby horse race 16, 55-56
Derby, show jumping 123
Destruction Derby 44
Devizes-Westminster
    canoeing race 65
Diamond, baseball 170, 172
Dijon-Prenois Grand Prix
    circuit 43
Dirt-track motorcycle
    racing 37-38
Discus throwing 82-84
    in decathlon and Greek
        pentathlon 132
Display events 94-95
Diving, depth records 130
Diving, pool 95, 110-111
    physical characteristics
        of divers 12-17
    physical demands 20
Dog-sleds, see Sled-dog
    racing
Dover-Cap Gris Nez swim
    79
Downhill skateboarding
    48-49
Downhill skiing 46
    longest race 79
    (in comparison 146)
Drag boat racing 71

Drag racing, cars 45, 75
    motorcycle 37-39
    (in comparison 71)
Dressage 122-123, 125
Driving, carriage 122-123,
    125
Duckpin bowling 155
Dundrod motorcycling
    circuit 39
Dune buggies 45
Duration events, hang
    gliding 116-117
Durations, combat sports
    141
    team games 184
    also see Time limits
Dwyle flunking 171

E

Earthball 165
East African Safari Rally
    41, 79
Ectomorphy 12-13
Eiffel Tower 46
Eisschiessen 152-153
Eisstock 152
Elbrus, Mount 128-129
Elfstedentocht skating
    race 79
Empire State Building 129-
    130, 173
Endomorphy 12-13
Enduros 36, 38
Engine capacities, air
    racing 72
    motor racing 41, 44-45
    motorcycling 38
English billiards 156-157
Epée 137-139
Equestrian events 122-125
    ages of riders 16
    in modern pentathlon
        133
    physical demands 19-21
    also see Horse racing
Eton Wall Game 167
Everest, Mount 128-129
    (in comparison 131)

F

Fastnet yacht race 69
Fédération Aeronautique
    Internationale (FAI) 72
Fédération Internationale
    de l'Automobile (FIA) 40,
    42, 44-45

Fencing 136-139, 141
    modern pentathlon 133
    physical demands 18-20
Field archery 143, 145
    also see Archery
Field hockey 168
    ball 182
    clothing 179
    duration 184
    goal 175
    physical demands 19, 21
    pitch 172
    scoring 185
    starting 185
    stick 180
    team 177
Fielding 170
Figure skating 94, 102-103
Figures, synchronized
    swimming 108-109
Finn yacht 67
Fish, high jumping record
    89
    swimming speeds 59, 77
    (in comparison 61)
Fishing, physical demands
    20
Fivepin bowling 155
Flat green bowls 152-153
Flat-track motorcycle
    racing 37-39
Flatland skateboarding
    112-113
Flatwater canoeing 64-65
Floor areas, gymnastics
    96-97
    (in comparison 109)
Floor exercises, gymnastics
    100-101
Flying, air racing 72-73
    altitude records 131
    display events 116-120
    endurance records 126
    record speeds 76-77
Flying Dutchman yacht 67
Foil 137-139
Football, see
    American football,
    Australian football,
    Canadian footbal,
    Gaelic football,
    Soccer
Formula air racing 72-73
Formula motor racing 40-43
    (in comparison 73)
Formula TT 36, 38
Forward dives 111
Francorchamps
    motorcycling circuit 39
Free-fall parachuting 118
Freestyle skateboarding
    112-113, 115

Freestyle skiing 95, 104-107
Freestyle swimming 58-59
 physical characteristics of freestyle swimmers 17
 (in comparison 63)
Freestyle wrestling 136, 139-141
Frisbee games 165
 physical demands 20
 also see Guts, Ultimate Frisbee
Frisbee throwing records 85
Frog jumping 87
Fronton 161

G

Gaelic football 166
 ball 182
 duration 184
 goal 174
 pitch 172
 scoring 185
 starting 185
 team 177
Geldloch cave 129
Giant slalom, skiing 46-47
Giro d'Italia cycle race 32-33
Gladiatorial fights 139
Gliders, see Sailplanes
Glides, skating 102
Gliding, see Soaring
Gloves, boxing 138
 court games 163
 team games 178-179
Goalkeepers 178-179
Golden Globe yacht race 69
Golden Slipper Stakes horse race 55
Golf 148-149
 physical demands 18, 20
 (in comparisons 48, 60, 145)
Gouffre Berger 129
Gouffre Jean Bernard 129
Grand National horse race 55
Grand Prix des Nations cycle race 33
Grand Prix motor racing 40-43
Grass skiing 46-47
Grass track motorcycle racing 37-39
Greco-Roman wrestling 136, 139-141
Greek pentathlon 132

Greens, bowls games 152-153
Greyhound Cesarewitch 55
Greyhound Derby (UK) 55
Greyhound Derby (USA) 55
Greyhounds, racing 54-55, 57
 long jumping record 87
 record speeds 74
Grotta di Padriciano 129
Grotta di Trebiciano 129
Gum-boot throwing 85
Guts 165
 Frisbee 183
 goal lines 174
 playing area 172
 scoring 185
 starting 185
 teams 177
Gymnastics 96-101
 physical characteristics of gymnasts 12-17
 physical demands 19, 21
 (in comparison 109)

H

Hakozaki 164
Hambletonian trotting race 55
Hammer throwing 82-84
 physical demands 20
 also see Scots hammer
Handball, physical demands 18-19, 21
Handicapping, air racing 72-73
 yacht racing 68
Hang gliding 116-117
 altitude records 131
 endurance record 126
 pylon event 120
Harness horse racing 55, 57
 physical demands 20
Harvard step test 19
Heart-lung system 18-19
Heart size 18
Hecht vault 98
Height gain events, hang gliding 116-117
Heights, altitude records 128, 131
 of athletes 14-15
 (in comparisons 97, 145)
Helicopter flying 116-117
 record speed 76
 slalom 120
Henie, Sonja 17
Henley Regatta 63
Henley, Sarah 111

High jump 88-89
 in decathlon and pentathlon 132-133
 physical characteristics of jumpers 12-16
 physical demands 19, 21 (in comparison 159)
Highboard diving 110-111
Highland Games 85, 92-93
Highland Games weight 85
Hill climb, cycling 30, 33
 motor racing 45
Himalayas 128-129
Hip widths of athletes 17
Hockenheim Grand Prix circuit 43
Hockey, see Field hockey, Ice hockey, Indoor hockey, Roller hockey
Holani 168
Hoop, modern rhythmic gymnastics 97
 exercises 100
Hoops, croquet 150-151
Horizontal bar, artistic gymnastics 96
 exercises 98
Horse high jump 89, 124
Horse long jump 87
Horse racing 54-57
 longest race 79
 physical demands 20 (in comparison 69)
Horse riding, see Equestrian events
Horseshoe pitching 152-153
 physical demands 20 (in comparison 182)
Hot rods 44
Human cannonball 147
Hurdle racing, horse 55
Hurdling, track athletics 24-28
 in decathlon and pentathlon 132
 physical demands 21 (in comparison 123)
Hurley 181
Hurling 168
 ball 182
 duration 184
 goal 174
 hurley 181
 pitch 172
 scoring 185
 starting 185
 team 177
Hydroplanes 70-71
 record speeds 77

I

Icarus 131
Ice dancing 95, 102-103
Ice hockey 169
 clothing 178-179
 duration 184
 goal 175
 physical demands 18-19, 21
 pitch 172
 puck 183
 scoring 185
 starting 185
 stick 180
 team 177
 (in comparisons 49, 136, 143)
Ice motorcycle racing 37-39
Ice skating, barrel jumping 87
 figure skating 102
 ice dancing 103
 physical demands 18, 20
 races 48-49
 speed record 74
Ice yachting 52-53
 record speed 75
Indian kickball 79
Indianapolis 500 motor race 41-42
Indianapolis motor racing circuit 42
Indoor cycle polo 169
Indoor hockey 169
Inferno skiing race 79
Inning 170-171
Irons, golf 148-149
Isle of Man TT motorcycle race 36, 39

J

Jacks, terrain games 152
Jai alai 161
 ball 162
 cesta 163
 court size 160
 physical demands 21
Jalopy racing 44
Járama Grand Prix circuit 43
Javelin throwing 82-84
 in decathlon and Greek pentathlon 132
 physical demands 20 (in comparisons 61, 144, 182)
Jeu provencal 152
Jockeys (in comparisons 15-16, 61)

Jousting 139
Judo 136-137, 139-141
 physical characteristics of competitors 14
 physical demands 19, 21
Jumping, see High jump, Long jump, Ramp jumping, Show jumping
Jumps, BMX 30
 equestrian events 124, 133
 figure skating 102
 freestyle skiing 104, 107
 gymnastics 98, 100-101

K

Karate 136, 138-141
 physical demands 19-20
Kart racing 45
Kayaks 64-65
 physical characteristics of kayak canoeists 17
Kendo 136-139, 141
Kentucky Derby horse race 55-56
Kermesse 30-31
Kick-off, team games 184
Kilimanjaro, Mount 128
King George VI and Queen Elizabeth Stakes horse race 56
Kneeboard surfing 114
Knox Johnston, Robin 69
Korfball 164
 ball 182
 basket 175
 duration 184
 playing areas 172
 scoring 185
 starting 185
 teams 177
Kyalami Grand Prix circuit 43

L

Lacrosse, men 168
 ball 182
 clothing 178
 crosse 180
 duration 184
 goal 175
 physical demands 18-19, 21
 pitch 172
 scoring 185
 starting 185
 team 177

Lacrosse, women 168
  ball 182
  crosse 180
  duration 184
  goal 175
  physical demands 18-19,
    21
  pitch 172-173
  scoring 185
  starting 185
  team 177
Land speed records 74-75
  (in comparisons 53, 146)
Land yachting 52-53
  record speed 74
Landsailing 112
Lawn croquet 150-151
Lawn mower Grand Prix,
  British 45
Lawn tennis, see Tennis
Le Mans motor racing
  circuit 42
Le Mans 24-hour motor
  race 40-42, 79
Leg lengths of athletes 17
Liège 24-hour motorcycle
  race 39, 79
Liffey Descent canoeing
  race 65
Lifts, skating 102
Lindberg, Charles 161
Little Brown Jug pacing
  race 55
Loch Lomond swimming
  race 79
Locke, John 86
London-Holyhead cycle
  race 79
London-Monte Carlo
  powerboat race 79
London-Sydney car rally
  41, 79
Long Beach Grand Prix
  circuit 43
Long-distance running 24,
  26-29
  physical characteristics
    of runners 12, 14-17
Long jump 86-87
  in decathlon, pentathlon,
    and Greek pentathlon
    132
  physical characteristics
    of jumers 12-16
  physical demands 19-20
  (in comparison 60)
Long-track motorcycle
  racing 37-39
Luge toboggan 50-51
  record speed 75

M

Macocha cave 129
Madison Square Garden
  136, 147
Malibu surfing 114
Mallet, croquet 151
  cycle polo 181
  polo 180
Marathon events 78-79
  canoeing 65
  carriage driving 123, 125
Marathon, running 26-28
  physical characteristics
    of runners 15
  physical demands 18, 21
Maryland Hunt Cup horse
  race 55
Medley races, swimming
  58
Melbourne Cup horse race
  55
Mesomorphy 12-13
Metropolitan Museum,
  New York 32
Mexican 1000 motor race
  79
Middle-distance running
  24, 26-28
  physical characteristics
    of runners 13-17
Midget car racing 45
Milan-San Remo cycle race
  33
Mixed pairs high diving 111
Modern pentathlon 133
  physical characteristics
    of participants 12,
    14-16
Modern rhythmic
  gymnastics 95, 97, 100
Moguls, skiing 104,
  106-107
Mont Blanc 128
Monte Carlo Grand Prix
  circuit 42-43
Monte Carlo Rally 41
Montreal Grand Prix
  circuit 43
Monza circuit,
  motor racing 43
  motorcycling 39
Motocross 37-39
Motor-paced cycling 31, 34
  speed record 75
  (in comparisons 37, 43)
Motor racing 40-45
  longest races 79
  physical demands 20
  record speeds 75
  (in comparisons 71, 73)

Motorcycling 36-39
  jumping 87
  longest race 79
  physical demands 20
  record speed 75
  (in comparison 71)
Mountaineering 128-129
  physical demands 21
Muscular demands 19
Muzzle velocity 146-147

N

Nanda Devi, Mount 128
Nations Cup, show jumping
  123, 125
Navigation and
  observation events,
  aerial 116-117
Netball 164
  ball 182
  basket 175
  clothing 178
  court 172
  duration 184
  scoring 185
  starting 185
  team 177
Ninin dori, aikido 139, 141
Ninepin bowling 155
Nordic skiing 46-47
  in winter biathlon 133
  physical characteristics
    of skiers 16
  physical demands 18-19,
    21
Nürburgring motorcycling
  circuit 39

O

Oaks horse race 56
Oar, rowing 61-62
Object ball 156-157
Observation trials,
  motorcycling 36
Obstacle equestrian
  events 122-125
Ocean racing 68-69
Octopush, see Underwater
  hockey
Off-road motor racing 45
  longest race 79
Offshore powerboat racing
  70-71
Offshore yacht racing 66,
  68-69

Olympic Games, ages of
  medallists 17
  cycling 32-33, 35
  physical characteristics
    of athletes 12-17
  rowing 63
  skate racing 48-49
  swimming 58-59
  throwing events 82-84
  weightlifting 90-91
  wrestling 141
  yacht classes 66-67
Olympic Games, ancient
  Greek 83, 132, 144
Olympic gymnastics, see
  Artistic gymnastics
Olympic trap shooting 142,
  147
One Thousand Guineas
  horse race 56
Osterreichring Grand Prix
  circuit 43
Ostrich racing 55, 57
  running speed 74
Owens, Jesse 29
Oxford and Cambridge
  Boat Race 63
Oxygen usage 18-19

P

Paced cycling, see
  Motor-paced cycling
Pacing races 55, 57
Paddle games 158-161
Paddle tennis 158
  ball 162
  court size 159
  paddle 163
Paddleball 160-161
  ball 162
  paddles 163
  physical demands 20
Paddles 158-160, 163
Pairs skating 102-103
Pala 163
Paletta 163
Par, golf 148
Parachuting, see Sport
  parachuting
Parallel bars, artistic
  gymnastics 96
  exercises 99
Parallel races, skiing
  46-47
Parascending 116-117
  slalom 120
Paris-Tours cycle race 33

Pato 164
  ball 183
  basket 175
  duration 184
  playing area 172
  scoring 185
  starting 185
  team 177
Peak and fell races 26-27
Pellet, airgun 144-146
Pelota 161
  pala 163
  paletta 163
  racqueta 163
Pentathlon 132
  physical characteristics
    of pentathletes 13-17
  physical demands 21
Pentathlon, modern, see
  Modern pentathlon
Perez, Pascual 15
Physical rating of sports
  18-21
Pierre St Martin cave 129
Pietermaritzburg-Durban
  canoeing race 65
Pigeon racing 54-55, 57
  record speed 57, 76
Pike position 95
  diving 110
  synchronized swimming
    109
  trampolining 99
Pin, alley games 154-155
Pistol shooting 142-147
Pitch, run-scoring games
  170-172
  team games 172-173
Pitching 170-171
Pivots, modern rhythmic
  gymnastics 100
Platform tennis 158
  ball 162
  court size 159
  paddle 163
Plunging 110
Pocket billiards, see Pool
Points cycle races 31, 33
Pole vault 88-89
  in decathlon 132
  physical demands 19-20
Poles, skiing 107
Polo 169
  ball 182
  clothing 178
  duration 184
  goal 174
  mallet 180
  physical demands 20
  playing area 172
  scoring 185
  starting 185
  team 176-177
  (in comparison 61)

Polo crosse 169
Pommel horse, artistic
    gymnastics 96
    exercises 99
Pool (pocket billiards)
    156-157
    physical demands 20
Pools, canoe polo 165
    diving 110
    swimming 58-59
    synchronized swimming
        109
    underwater hockey
        172, 175
    water polo 172
Popocatépetl, Mount 128
Powerboat racing 70-71
    longest race 79
    physical demands 20
    record speeds 77
Powerlifting 90-91
Practical shooting 142, 145
Precision flying events
    116-117
Precision landing events,
    aerial 116-117
Prix de l'Arc de Triomphe
    horse race 56
Processional rowing races
    62-63
Publius Ostorius 139
Puck roller hockey 169
    duration 184
    goal 175
    playing area 172
    puck 183
    scoring 185
    starting 185
    stick 180
    team 177
Puissance events 124
Pursuit races, cycle
    racing 31, 33, 35
    skating 48
Pusher, underwater
    hockey 181
Putter 148-149
Pylon, air racing 73
Pylon event, aerial 116,
    120

Q

QE2 58

R

RAC Rally 41
Race walking 24, 26-28
    longest races 79
    physical characteristics
        of walkers 12, 14-16
Racehorses 55
    average weight 15
    speeds 56-57, 74
Racket, net games
    158-159, 163
    wall games 160, 163
Racqueta 163
Racquetball 160
    ball 162
    physical demands 19
    racket 163
Rallies, air 73
    motor racing 40-41, 79
    motorcycling 36
Rallycross 45
Ramp jumping 86-87
Randori kyoghi, aikido
    139, 141
Rapid-fire pistol 142-147
Real tennis, see Court
    tennis
Regatta rowing races 62-63
Relative work, parachuting
    118
Ribbon, modern rhythmic
    gymnastics 97
    exercises 100
Richards, Sir Gordon 16
Rifle shooting 142-147
Rings, artistic gymnastics
    96
    exercises 99
Ringvaart Regatta 63, 79
Rinks, crown green
    bowling 152
    skating 103
    (in comparison 107)
Rio de Janiero Grand Prix
    circuit 43
Road races, cycling 30-33,
    35
    motor racing 40-43
    motorcycling 36, 38-39
Rocket car, record speeds
    75
    (in comparison 146)
Rodeo 122
Roller-cycling 33
Roller derby 48
    physical demands 20
Roller hockey, see Ball
    roller hockey, Puck
    roller hockey

Roller skating, endurance
    record 126
    figure skating 102
    ice dancing 103
    physical demands 18, 20
    races 48-49
    speed record 74
Rope, modern rhythmic
    gymnastics 97
    exercises 100
Roque 150-151
Round Britain yacht race
    69
Rounders 170-171
    ball 182
    bat 181
    pitch 170-172
    team 177
Routines, synchronized
    swimming 108
Rowing 60-63
    longest race 79
    physical characteristics
        of rowers 12, 14-17
    physical demands 18-19,
        21
    speed records 63, 77
Rugby fives 161
    ball 162
    court size 160
Rugby league 167
    ball 182
    duration 184
    goal 174
    physical demands 19, 21
    pitch 172
    scoring 185
    starting 185
    team 177
Rugby union 167
    ball 182
    duration 184
    goal 174
    physical demands 19, 21
    pitch 172
    scoring 185
    starting 185
    team 177
Running 24-29
    in decathlon and
        pentathlon 132
    endurance records 126
    longest races 79
    physical characteristics
        of runners 12-17
    physical demands 18-19,
        21
    speed records 28-29, 74
    (in comparisons 49, 57,
        59, 63, 123, 125)
Running game target event
    142-143, 145, 147

Saber 137-139
Sail areas, land and ice
    yachting 52-53
    yacht racing 67
Sailboards, see
    Boardsailing
Sailing, see Yacht racing
Sailing, land, see
    Landsailing, Land
    yachting
Sailplanes 72-73
St Andrews' Old Course
    149
    (in comparison 48)
St Leger horse race 56
St Paul's Cathedral 47
Sandboarding 115
Sambo wrestling 136-137,
    139-141
Scots hammer 85
Scrambling, see
    Motocross
Scuba diving, depth
    records 130
    physical demands 20
Sculling 60-62
Sella Descent canoeing
    race 65
Sepak takraw 167
Shadow skating 102
Shell, rowing 61, 63
Shinai, kendo 138
Shinty 168
    ball 182
    caman 180-181
    duration 184
    goal 174-175
    pitch 172
    scoring 185
    starting 185
    team 177
Shooting 142-147
    in winter biathlon 133
    in modern pentathlon
        133
    age of competitors 16
    physical demands 19
Short-track racing, ice
    skating 48-49
    motor racing 44-45
    motorcycle racing 37-39
Shot put 82-84
    in decathlon and
        pentathlon 132
    physical demands 20
Shotgun shooting 142-147
Shoulder widths of
    athletes 17
Show jumping 122-125
Shuttlecock 158, 162
Sidecar combinations 36-38

Silverstone Grand Prix
    circuit 42-43
Skate sailing 52-53
Skateboarding, bowl
    freestyle 115
    endurance record 126
    flatland freestyle
        112-113
    jumping 87, 113
    racing 48-49
    speed record 74-75
    (in comparison 34)
Skating, see Ice skating,
    Roller skating
Skeet shooting 142,
    146-147
Skeleton toboggan 50-51
    record speed 75
Ski-jump 87
Skibob 50-51
    record speed 75
Skiing, see Alpine skiing,
    Freestyle skiing, Grass
    skiing, Nordic skiing,
    Water skiing
Skittles 154-155
Sky diving, speed records
    76
    also see Sport
        parachuting
Slalom, boardsailing 68
    canoeing 64-65
    hang gliding 116, 120
    helicopter 116, 120
    motor racing 45
    parascending 116, 120
    skateboarding 49
    skiing 46-47
    water skiing 121
Sled-dog racing 54-57
    endurance record 126
    longest race 79
Smallbore pistol 142-147
Smallbore rifle 142-147
Smirnoff Sailplane Derby
    79
Snail racing 54, 57
Snatch 90
Snooker 156-157
    physical demands 20
Snowboarding 115
Soaring 72-73
    altitude records 131
    endurance records 126
    longest race 79
    speed record 76
Soccer 166
    ball 182
    clothing 178-179
    duration 184
    goal 174
    physical demands 18-19,
        21
    pitch 172

scoring 185
starting 185
team 177
(in comparisons 84-87, 183)
Softball 170-171
ball 182
bases 175
bat 181
physical demands 20
pitch 170-172
team 177
Soling yacht 67
(in comparison 61)
Somatotypes 12-13
Somersaults 95
diving 110-111
freestyle skiing 104
gymnastics 98-101
synchronized swimming 109
Speed skating 48-49
longest race 79
speed record 74
Speedball 166
ball 182
duration 184
goal 174
physical demands 19
pitch 172
scoring 185
starting 185
team 177
Speeds, see appropriate sport
Speedway, cycle 31, 33
motorcycle 37-39
Spelunking 128-129
Spins 95
freestyle skiing 104
skating 102
synchronized swimming 109
Spirals, skating 102
Spirit of Australia 77
Sport parachuting 116-118
free-fall altitude records 131
sky diving speed records 76
Sports acrobatics 94-95, 97, 101
Sportsboats 70-71
Springboard diving 110-111
Sprinting 24-29
in decathlon, pentathlon, and Greek pentathlon 132
physical characteristics of sprinters 12-17
physical demands 18-19, 21
Sprints, cycle 31-33, 35
motorcycle 37-39

Squash 160
balls 162
physical demands 18-19, 21
racket 163
Squat 90-91
Stage races, cycling 30, 33, 79
Star yacht 67
Starting, team games 184-185
Starting blocks 24
Starting positions, motor racing 40
track athletics 24, 27
Steel strandpulling 92-93
Steeplechase, horse racing 55
three-day event 123-125
track athletics 24, 26-28
Step sequences 95
artistic gymnastics 100
freestyle skiing 104
modern rhythmic gymnastics 100
skating 102-103
Sticks, team games 180-181
Stock car racing 44
Stock rods 44
Stones, terrain games 152
Straight position, diving 110
Strasbourg-Paris walking race 79
Substitutes, team games 176-177
Sumo wrestling 136-137, 139-141
(in comparison 40)
Surf canoeing, distance record 126
Surfing 114
endurance record 126
physical demands 20
Swahn, Oscar 16
Swimming 58-59
endurance records 126
longest races 79
in modern pentathlon 133
physical characteristics of swimmers 12-17
physical demands 18-19, 21
speed records 77
(in comparison 63)
Sydney-Hobart yacht race 69
Synchronized swimming 94, 108-109

T

T-bone dive 87
Table tennis 159
ball 162
paddle (bat) 163
physical demands 20
(in comparison 17)
Tables, billiard games 156-157
table tennis 159
Tanto randori, aikido 139, 141
Targa Florio motor race 79
Target and precision landing events, aerial 116-117
Target archery 143, 145
also see Archery
Target areas, combat sports 138-139
Target, target sports 144-145
Tariff value 94, 111
Tchouk-ball 165
ball 182
duration 184
goal 175
playing areas 172
scoring 185
starting 185
teams 177
Team handball 165
balls 182
clothing 178
court 172
duration 184
goal 175
scoring 175
starting 185
team 177
Tempo routines, sports acrobatics 101
Tennis 158
ball 162
court size 159
physical demands 18-19, 21
rackets 163
(in comparisons 58, 61, 67, 138, 150, 159, 182)
Tenpin bowling 154-155
physical demands 20
(in comparisons 35, 83)
Texas Water Safari canoeing race 65, 79
Three-day event 122-125
physical demands 20
Throw-off, team games 184
Throwing events 82-85
physical demands 19-20

Time limits, dressage 125
freestyle skiing 107
gymnastics 98, 101
synchronized swimming 108
water skiing trick events 107
Time trials, cycling 30, 33, 35
motorcycling 36
Toboggans 50-51
Tornado yacht 67, 69
Tossing the caber 92-93
Touchball 166
ball 182
durations 184
end zones 174
physical demands 20
pitch 172
scoring 185
starting 185
team 177
Touchdown 166-167, 185
Tour de France cycle race 30, 32-33, 79
physical characteristics of participants 18
physical demands 21
Tour of Britain cycle race 33
Tour of Flanders cycle race 33
Tour of Italy, air rally 73
cycle race 33
Tour of Lombardy cycle race 33
Tour of Spain cycle race 33
Tournament casting, accuracy event 143-145
distance event 85
physical demands 20
Tower Bridge, London 111
Track cycle racing 30-31, 33, 35
Tracks, cycling 30-31
motor racing 44-45
motorcycling 37, 39
running 26-27
skating 48-49
(in comparisons 31, 54-55)
Trampoline 97
exercises 99
Trampolining 95, 97, 99
physical demands 21
Trans-Am series motor races 41
Transatlantic yacht race 69
Transcontinental running race 79
Transpacific yacht race 69

Trials, motorcycling 36
Tricks, boardsailing 112
skateboarding 113, 115
water skiing 104, 106-107
Trimaran 69
Triple jump 87
(in comparison 60)
Trireme 63
Trisul, Mount 128
Trotting races 55, 57
Trou du Glaz 129
Try, rugby 167
TT road racing 36, 39
TT steeplechase 37-39
Tuck position 95
diving 110
synchronized swimming 109
trampolining 99
Tug of war 92-93
physical demands 19-20
Tumbleturn 104
Tumbling, sports acrobatics 97, 101
Tumbling track, sports acrobatics 97
Twists 95
diving 111
sports acrobatics 101
synchronized swimming 109
trampolining 99
Two Thousand Guineas horse race 56

U

Ultimate Frisbee 165
duration 184
end zones 174
Frisbee 183
playing area 172
scoring 185
starting 185
team 177
Underwater hockey (octopush) 169
duration 184
goal 175
playing area 172
puck 183
pusher 181
scoring 185
starting 185
team 177
Unicycle 33-34

V

Van Drenthe Assen
  motorcycling circuit 39
Vaulting horses, artistic
  gymnastics 96
  exercises 98
  (in comparison 99)
Volleyball 165
  ball 182
  clothing 178
  court 172
  net 175
  physical demands 18-20
  scoring 185
  starting 185
  team 177
Vuelta a Espagna cycle
  race 33

W

Wake turns 104
Walking, endurance record
  126
  also see Race walking
Washington D.C.
  International horse
  race 56
Water polo 165
  ball 182
  clothing 178
  duration 184
  goal 175
  physical characteristics
    of players 12, 14-17
  physical demands 19, 21
  playing area 172
  scoring 185
  starting 185
  team 177
Water skiing, endurance
  record 126
  physical demands 19-20
  racing 70-71
  record jump 87
  record speed 77
  slalom 121
  tricks 104, 106-107
  (in comparison 47)
Water speed records 77
  (in comparison 146)
Water turns 104
Watkins Glen Grand Prix
  circuit 43
Weapons, combat sports
  138-139
Wedge, golf 148-149

Weight classes, boxing 140
  judo 140
  steel strandpulling 93
  tug of war 93
  weightlifting 91
  wrestling 140
Weight throwing 82-85
  physical characteristics
    of throwers 12-17
Weightlifting 90-91
  physical characteristics
    of lifters 12, 16-17
  physical demands 18-20
Weights, see appropriate
  sport
Whitbread Round the
  World Yacht Race 69, 79
Wicketkeepers 178-179
Wickets 171, 175
  (in comparison 181)
Wildwater canoeing 64-65
Wimbledon 17
  (in comparisons 61, 67)
Winter biathlon 133
Woods, golf 148-149
World Championship Derby
  sled-dog race 55
World Championship motor
  racing 40-43
Wrestling 136, 139-141
  in Greek pentathlon 132
  physical characteristics
    of wrestlers 12, 16-17
  physical demands 18-19,
    21
Wright brothers 72

Y

Yacht racing 66-69
  longest race 79
  physical demands 19-20
  record speeds 77
Yachting, land and ice,
  see Land yachting, Ice
  yachting
Yachts, types of 66-67,
  69
Yamashita vault 98

Z

Zacchini, Emanuel 147
Zandvoort Grand Prix
  circuit 43
Zolder Grand Prix circuit
  43